# Non-traditional Security

## State, Society and Democracy in South Asia

# Non-traditional Security

## State, Society and Democracy in South Asia

Edited by
**Lok Raj Baral**

ADROIT

*Published by*
ADROIT PUBLISHERS
4675/21, Ganpati Bhawan, Ansari Road,
Daryaganj, New Delhi-110 002
Phones : 011-23266030, 23263506

*Published in association with*
Nepal Centre for Contemporary Studies (NCCS)

*Distributors*
AKHIL BOOK DISTRIBUTORS
e-mail: akhilbooks@yahoo.com
akhilbooks@hotmail.com



ISBN : 81-87392-76-2

*Printed in India on behalf of M/s Adroit Publishers by*
Arpit Printographers E-mail : arpitprinto@yahoo.com

NCCS is grateful to the Ford Foundation for supporting this project

# Preface

This book is the product of a regional seminar on "Non-Traditional Security: State, Society and Democracy in South Asia" organized by Nepal Centre for Contemporary Studies (NCCS). It has tried to reconceptualize security from a democratic perspective because democracy is being interpreted as an overall empowerment of people. Democracy is also a way of life providing psychological, economic, social, political, environmental and military security and hence the role of the state is also focussed upon in this light. Democracy in developing countries like Nepal is inclusive and people-centric.

The present volume would add a new meaning and definition of non-traditional security in South Asia. The title of the book "Non-Traditional Security: State, Society and Democracy" has therefore become wide in scope. Some leading scholars of South Asia have contributed to the book, making it more representative in character. The Ford Foundation deserves credit for its continuous support for the activities of NCCS. The regional seminar was one of such events, among many others, of NCCS. The authors of the volume deserve thanks for their enthusiastic response to the seminar as well as to the book. Members of NCCS, particularly Krihsna P. Khanal, Krishna Hachhethu, Hari Sharma, Prem Raj Goutam, Til Bikram Nembang, Sarita Giri, Pushpa Bhushal and Chandra Bhadra. D.K. Sharma of Adroit Publishers and his colleague, Sudhir Vatsa have worked hard for the production of the book. I thank them for taking much care for quality production. Iswor Kharel of NCCS deserves special appreciation for his seriousness and prompt action on any matter concerning the Centre.

# Contents

# List of Contributors

**B. Ramesh Babu**, is a former professor and Head of Political Science Department, University of Mumbai, India. An expert in International Affairs, he has many books and articles to his credit.

**Wasbir Hussain** is associate fellow, Institute for Conflict Management, New Delhi and Consulting Editor, *The Sentinel*, Guwahati, India.

**Sridhar K. Khatri** is Executive Director, South Asia Centre for Policy Studies. A former professor at Tribhuvan University, he was also Executive Director of Regional Centre for Strategic Studies, Colombo.

**Dhruba Kumar** is associated with Centre for Nepal & Asian Studies (CNAS), Tribhuvan University, Kathmandu, Nepal. Author of books and articles on security and other related areas he was also a visiting fellow in many universities.

**S.D. Muni** was a professor and Chairman at South Asian Division, Jawaharlal Nehru University, New Delhi. Author of many books and articles, Professor Muni was also the ambassador of India to Laos.

**Jehan Perera** is Director of National Peace Council, Colombo.

**Indrajit Rai** is a security expert.

**Hasan-Askari Rizvi** was Professor and Chairman, Department of Political Science at the University of the Punjab, Lahore, Pakistan. A security expert, he has written many books and articles on military and security.

# 1

# Introduction
## Democracy and Freedom as Key Elements to Non-Traditional Security

***Lok Raj Baral***

### Introduction

Writing an introduction to a book on *Non-Traditional Security: State, Society and Democracy* is indeed a daunting task. Its reasons can be many, but are not beyond identification. First, South Asian political and military elites are not yet capable of grappling with the issue of non-traditional security based on a holistic approach. Barry Buzan in his classic book *People, States and Fear: the National Security Problem in International Relations* has stated that "the national security problem cannot be understood without reference to factors at all three levels of analysis", i.e. individuals, states and the international system[1]. According to Buzan, "The concept of security binds together individuals, states and the international system so closely that it demands to be treated in a holistic perspective"[2]. Based primarily on the military aspect of security, which is the core of traditional security doctrine, traditional security relies heavily on force and state-centric strategy, though the traditional security in recent times has also undergone a change by combining some elements of non-traditional security such as human security, individual security, economic security, political security, environment security or what we call "comprehensive" security.

Nevertheless, traditional security is generally understood as a "military force" that was basically used against averting threats stemming from foreign powers. Thus, territorial security, security of national sovereignty, and independence were the bottom lines of traditional security. As Ayoob writes: "To begin with, as it has been traditionally used in international relations literature, the term security is based upon two major assumptions: one, that most threats to a state's security arise from outside its borders and, two, that these threats are primarily, if not exclusively, military in nature and usually require a military response if the security of the target state is to be preserved."[3]

There has been a tendency to measure the hierarchy of a state on the basis of military force whether or not that force has the potential of defending the country at the time of internal catastrophic changes or during political upheavals that occasionally erupt in the developing world. The agenda of non-traditional security is now increasingly becoming more complex and intertwined with the 'new security dilemma' being faced by these countries. Ayoob's 'primacy of domestic' or 'primacy of political' factors have made the "Third World countries" more conscious of defining and redesigning the new security paradigms as these countries cannot survive alone by laying too much focus on the military aspect of security. Internal 'frailties' and vulnerabilities precipitated by a variety of factors and causes make the states weak and whatever military might it develops turns out to be irrelevant to coping with national disasters.

Most of these states have a tendency to anchor their national security position in the so-called "nationalism" which is normally used or misused for insuring regimes whose legitimacy is too fragile to be sustainable. In Nepal, for instance, King Gyanendra's coup of 1 February 2005, which drove the King to take back all powers as well as to depart from the established constitutional process, is being justified in the name of safeguarding the country and the people against 'terrorism' perpetrated by the Communist Party of Nepal (Maoist). Since the King has already dismantled the established parliamentary system, he is facing both national and international condemnations for taking such a retrogressive step against democracy and human freedoms. His regime is now much more vulnerable to domestic conditions and international pressures. The royal regime's anchor is the military, and international terrorism, against which he tries to gather international support. A Chinese philosopher, Lao-Tzu (sixth century B.C.) has however emphasized that military force is not the 'Tao' or "way" for human beings to follow.

The "realist" school of security also alludes to power and defence capability as the source of security. The other school is idealist that subsumes security under peace and other values concerning democracy and freedoms. In one of his recent articles, Henry Kissinger has argued that neither of them alone fulfils the need for security today and hence the need for working in tandem. So America's idealism that embraces freedom, democracy, etc. alone would not be adequate if the realist dimension is missing. So both should have a complementary role. "It is the fusion of strategy and values, the meaning of the practical and the ideal—and not an overemphasis on one at the expense of the other— that holds the key to Lebanon's future"[4].

It is also close to the "neo-realist-school of security" that puts high premium on the role of the state. According to this school, security of the state constitutes the security of citizens and those within it. Violence and other threats emanating from different sources should be averted by state.

The second school sees non-traditional sources of security/insecurity that still make the state as the pivotal actor. However, in South Asia, as Sridhar Khatri has observed, there has been a slight recognition of factors concerning non-traditional security through the instrumentality of South Asian Association of Regional Cooperation (SAARC). "The best example of this is the SAARC convention on terrorism, which was signed in 1987 and has been ratified by all the member states"[5].

The third school is the extended version of non-traditional security and its focus is on "human security" agenda. The United Nations Development Report, 1994 has paid much attention to the basic needs of human beings such as food, health, education, migration, environmental degradation, population growth, drug trafficking, and international terrorism[6]. Human security lays emphasis on the individual as the unit or the referent point of security, while comprehensive security is also covered by both the 'neo-realist' and non-traditional security. Human security's main focus is on human development, cooperative role of the state for enhancing human development, good governance, and such similar elements that promote human beings. It is pervasive from cradle to grave, as human development is a very comprehensive area. The basic needs or welfare approaches embraced by some governments are some of the baselines for promoting human development. Now democracy and freedom are increasingly becoming integral parts of human development. Precisely it can be said that human security challenges its coercive role of the state—its coercive mechanism, its emphasis on absolute doctrine of sovereignty, its inhuman treatment meted out to the people in the name of preservation of territorial integrity, national independence and sovereignty. If the people are empowered in every sense—social, economic, political, and psychological or mental, then only human security can be achieved [7].

The literary meaning of non-traditional security itself is elastic. Yet, it is more encompassing and inclusive than 'traditional security' that focuses on the absoluteness of state. Coercive power of the state that demands compliance is the core of this school.

The Nepal Centre for Contemporary Studies (NCCS) has taken democracy (inclusive democracy), freedom and social justice as the key elements of non-traditional security in view of the emergent threats emanating from the failures of nation-state building processes in South Asia. For, many regional countries have neither the stateness with its full traditional vigour and ethos, nor have they been able to hog the human security policy for empowering the general people. On the contrary, in spite of being weak in every sense, they rely excessively on the force of the state as the instrument of keeping order. Some South Asian states, for example, have tried to slog through making advances in some areas while encountering failures in others.

However, countries like India and Sri Lanka persevere to continue democratic polity despite their penchant for using the instruments of traditional security. Bangladesh is also grappling with the overwhelming impact of Islamization that in turn gives rise to social and political conflicts. Clash of religions and increasing trends of sectarian violence are likely to give grounds for domestic and regional conflicts. Reports of the Bangladeshi territory being used as a safe haven by the 'terrorist groups' of India and its fall-out on impairing Indo–Bangladesh relations have poured in inrecent times. States and peoples thus feel the pinch of insecurity. The traditional threats of foreign invasion are replaced by other threats of varied nature and dimensions. And their remedies lay not in military response or in other instruments of coercion but in addressing these social, political, economic and other problems. Poverty alleviation, reduction in social disparity gap, empowerment of poor and deprived sections of society plus a host of other factors need to be taken as priority areas. These areas generally remain neglected due to the entrenched socio–economic and political reasons and institutions and help create structural violence. And "states seem more often to be the problem than the solution"[8].

The non-traditional security that encapsulates both comprehensive and human security cannot be set aside with the people becoming more educated and conscious of their actual positions in the society and state. The project of security has therefore become multidisciplinary in nature. "There has been for some time a questioning of the primacy of the state-led military element in the conceptualization of security. This has led to the widening of security agenda by claiming a security status for a range of issues beyond the purely military dimension"[9].

The present security discourse is thus concerned with non-traditional security with a large canvas of human security and development. The three identified thematic components focus on state, society and democracy because of a new paradigmatic change in making them interrelated. Moreover, empowerment of all people living within a state is one of the core areas of today's governance, despite the continued struggle between the traditional ethoses of the state with all sorts of authoritarian tantrums. As Ken Booth states, "Security and emancipation are two sides of the same coin. Emanicipation, not power or order produces true security. Emancipation, theoretically, is security".[10]

In Nepal, the reconstruction of the state is a precondition for efficient democratic governance in view of the rigid nature of the Nepali state. Other South Asian countries might have similar built-in problems that stand in the way of creating an equalitarian society and polity. Nepal's case is relatively complex in view of the traditional monarchy and its hold on the military. Thus, neither is radical transformation possible nor is the political force capable of stabilizing democratic processes in the country. Pakistan is another example where non-traditional security, which lays emphasis on human development and empowerment, is paramount. The state identified with the militarized and securitized state rules the roost. Nepal is also now passing through the "reverse wave" of democratization showing no trace of a new roadmap for the country.

The trajectories of Nepali democracy have created direct and indirect impacts on the situation of human security. Trends of militarization continue as if the state-centric approach to security is now in full swing allowing the state to divert meagre resources for beefing up the military security alone. Although this is a general South Asian trend, Nepal's case is particularly noteworthy in view of the triangular conflictual relations amongst the King, the Maoists and political parties. Political parties are sore at the King's move to reverse the democratic process by invoking the monarchical doctrine that the latter (monarchy) is the saviour of the country. In Pakistan, a similar situation exists prompting the Army General-turned politician for supporting other dictators as the saviours of the nation. They are one in saying that autocracy paves the way for democracy as the authoritarian instrument would first create conditions for peace and then only can democracy be stabilized. Nevertheless, they forget that peace is also a comprehensive concept, which is disturbed not only by dreaded terrorists but also by the vaulting ambition of monocrats—King, General and others. Even the so-called democrats seem to have provided ladders to such predators who are anxious to find alibis for taking over power. "The crisis of governance emanating from systemic breakdown" as was evident in Nepal has also given rise to much alarming and pervasive crises. "Thus, the crisis of legitimacy (both rational-legal and performance)" overwhelms the system, making the people skeptical about the democratic order itself[11].

Democracy and human freedoms have become the mantras of today's security discourse thus finding faults with bad governance if it fails to honour such freedoms that enhance the processes of empowerment of all sections of people irrespective of caste, class, creed, region, gender and so on. It can also be called human governance because of much importance attached to freedom from wants and freedom from fear. The four freedoms enunciated by Eleanor Roosevelt during the course of declaration of human rights by the United Nations have now been vindicated in human rights movements across the world. The United Nations has come out more vociferously in recent years for what it calls "humanitarian intervention" if the need arises for insuring human freedoms[12]. Much earlier in the late 1990s, the UN Secretary General, Kofi Annan, justified the intervention saying: "The [UN] Charter protects the sovereignty of peoples. It was never meant as a license for governments to trample on human rights and human dignity. Sovereignty implies responsibility, not just power". He further said, "We will not and we cannot accept a situation where people are brutalized behind national boundaries".[13] It is also a safeguard against the rising tendency of governments to be more aggressive against freedom and democracy.

It is now evident that the conventional doctrine of non-interference in other countries' internal affairs has significant dilution, the latest case being Nepal where democracy and human freedoms are flagrantly violated by the action of the King. Democratic vibrancy and resilience has now been turned into sycophancy and eulogies for the King and his action. However, democratic values internalized by the people of Nepal are not compromised with the political parties and members of civil society resisting the King's action. The international community at large, particularly the democratic countries and the UN, has also taken exception to the royal coup of February 01, 2005 urging the King to restore democracy and freedom in the country. The three governments—the United States, the United Kingdom (the European Union included) and India—have formed a coalition to coordinate their strategies for restoring democracy. While the UK and India did stop the arms supply to the royal regime, the US continues to put its defence supplies under constant review.

What is more surprising to the royal regime is that the West European countries, the US and India have categorically stated that they welcome the seven-party coalition formed against the King's rule thus provoking the royal government to lodge a mild protest against them. Other countries and international agencies have also come out against the royal regime urging the King to restore democracy sooner than later. The Non-Governmental Organizations of Nepal had strongly lobbied at the 61st session of the United Nations Human Rights Commission for a "special Rapporteur" to monitor the human rights situation. Consequently, the Nepali authorities, by way of avoiding sanctions under Item 9 accepted the Rapporteur despite the existence of a National Human Rights Commission in Nepal[14]. It was interesting to observe how in Geneva the NGOs supported by international groups had been able to hold a parallel session of human rights focusing on Nepal's deteriorating human rights situation following the imposition of state of emergency by the King. Later, by way of responding to the open support of three governments for the seven-party oppositional coalition formed for the restoration of democracy, the foreign ministry called the Indian and British ambassadors, surprisingly excluding the American, to the foreign office in order to caution (to make *sachet*) them against the alleged interference in internal affairs of Nepal. It seemed that the Nepali government lacked the courage to lodge a strong protest.

No other countries of South Asia have undergone such trial and tribulation as Nepal. The military coup in Pakistan was put under sanction following General Pervez Musharraf's coup of 1999 that toppled the elected government headed by Nawaz Sharif. However, after some time, most governments opposing the coup made peace with the General restoring business as usual. Other countries involved in insurgencies of different kinds—separatists, Maoists, and independents—are under criticism when the international human rights groups find the overindulgence of security forces in committing human rights' violation.

There has also been a lurking fear that the supply of weapons to what Ayoob calls "quasi-states to failed states" would jeopardize democracy and freedom as such states may try to be secure only with military power. In South Asia, the trends of militarization are fast developing in established democracies like India and Sri Lanka as well as in countries whose vulnerabilities are on the increase. Countries like India and Sri Lanka have all the ills of misgovernance, but democratic polities have endured due to the continued civilian control over the armies. No military coups have ever been attempted, nor are the elected elites savoury for upsetting the established democratic institutions. In sharp contrast to them, the Praetorian guards rule Pakistan and the traditional monarch in Nepal whose mainstay of power is the army.

The struggle between an emphasis on non-traditional security that embraces all aspects of human and comprehensive security and the state-centric and ruler-centric approaches to security is under way. Yet, the recent developments in South Asia have demonstrated that the penchant for militarization at the cost of human freedoms, democracy and other basic needs such as food, shelter, clothes, health, environment, freedom from fear, etc. are on the rise. Nepal has increased its military from 50,000 to 90,000 within a period of ten years along with the rise of armed police force and civil police. And the excuse is the Maoist insurgency waged for making Nepal a republican state. More than 15,000 people have already lost their lives (more than 80 per cent killed by the Army) and the rest by the Maoists. A virtual reign of terror prevails in Nepal due to atrocities committed by both the Maoists and the security force. The Amnesty International Report 2005 put Nepal in the second rank for its gross rights violation. "There is a growing culture of impunity and disregard for the rule of law among the forces who have systematically obstructed the courts and the national Human Rights Commission of Nepal". The Report further said that the security forces continued to kill unarmed civilians, often claiming that they had died in an "encounter" with the Maoists, or while trying to escape from custody. The killing spree is also found from the side of the Maoists as if the wars claimed to have been waged by state and the Maoists defy any rationality. The Maoists state that they want to end the exploitative feudal state. How would the gun alone bring about a sustainable change if democratic culture that demands tolerance and freedoms was denied? What is the mission of security forces except the vaguely articulated "peace" to be brought about by force?

Other countries of the region as well as the US, specifically for its human rights' violation in Iraq and Afghanistan, are not spared by Amnesty, though in other respect of human development including the freedoms guaranteed to its citizens, is beyond comparison. From the viewpoint of human development, South Asia is composed of both low and medium-level countries with the ranks set by the United Nations Development Project (UNDP). According to the UNDP, Pakistan has been ranked 142, Nepal 140, Bangladesh 138, Bhutan 134, India 127, Sri Lanka 96, and the Maldives 84 with a human development index among 177 countries in the reverse order.[15] Education and gender indicators are not also satisfactory except in the Maldives and Sri Lanka. Yet, the magnitude of the problems and other dimensions vary in view of the size of population and territories of countries like India, Pakistan and Bangladesh. Nevertheless, the stability of institutions and regularity of elections seem to matter much.

The foregoing narrative tries to stress on freedoms and democracy as key variables for relating them to human security. Lok Raj Baral has described it under the rubrics of "democratic security/insecurity". So democratic institutions and governance and inviolability of freedoms are sine qua non for security. Although the state enters in various levels and nature, its core elements—sovereignty, territory, government and population—become integral elements of democracy and human freedoms. Freedoms in the present parlance embrace those basic needs that can hardly be denied by any legitimate government. Democratic security thus makes people central to the state, not to the rulers. The first Prime Minister of independent India, Jawaharlal Nehru, said that he was the "first servant of India". Even the concept of democracy is approached anew in recent years making the people the arbiter of destiny. In Nepal, the word democracy is translated as *loktantra* because the word *praja* gives a separate identity to the citizens of a country. The subject (praja) in political terms is deprived of the essence of democracy, i.e. the right to oppose or contest if they like to do vis-à-vis the state. The subject political culture is not democratic as the people are to show their obedience to the traditional ruler—the King, whose legitimacy of power is not derived from people but from tradition and other criteria of ascription.

When the core issue of legitimacy of power still remains unsettled encouraging the traditional monarchy to be assertive and active, the scope of conflict is widened with the three forces at loggerheads—the King, the political parties and the Maoists. The two—political parties and the Maoists—are now apparently moving closer to each other because of the usurping of power by the King. The Maoists have supported the seven-party alliance formed against the royal move on moral grounds. One of the demands of the seven-party alliance is a constituent assembly, a core demand of the Maoists. In the past, no governments had ever dared embrace this demand obviously in view of the sensitivity of the Palace. Now this issue has been able to enter into the agenda of the seven-party alliance.

How could non-traditional security be enhanced when democracy itself is endangered? The other core issues of nationality and oppressed and suppressed people also give rise to conflict and they continue to be unresolved. Since 2002, the reverse wave of democratization began in Nepal. It has widened the scope of conflict and state's vulnerabilities.

The impact of globalization on non-traditional security in South Asia is very strong. The post-Cold War situation is dominated by a unipolar world with the United States becoming the only superpower. Its impact on international politics is felt today with most former communist countries turning into liberal democracies. Ramesh Babu has aptly narrated such a phenomenon when he lists eight points that provide succour to the US to be a unitary power. Ideological polarization that embraced the liberal system across the world along with the adoption of market economy or liberalization policies by most of the states prompted Francis Fukuyama to declare "The End of History and the Last Man". It was considered a triumph of democracy.

Even the US has realized the need for the United Nations despite its failures to fulfill its mission of establishing peace and international security. Similarly, international law is well vindicated even at a time when the member countries are engaged in conflict. A "World without international law is simply beyond the realm of imagination", writes Babu. Revolutionary changes made possible by IT and media have changed the world as well. Now people in South Asia are well disposed to electronic means, making us realize that idea and information cannot be captive in the present world. Nevertheless, the authoritarian governments try to block the channel of information by snapping telephones, mobile and Internet services in the name of curbing terrorism. It happened in Nepal following the imposition of state of emergency by the King on 1 February 2005, disrupting the flow of information. However, such a decision met with strong resistance from within and outside the country.

Similarly, international terrorism, environmental and ecological problems, and expanding and extending influence of Western culture are taken as the elements of globalization. Now for the developing countries, the movements of labour force across the international borders and economic opportunities being made available have also contributed to economic emancipation. Nevertheless, there are various risk factors because of the export of raw man/woman force to the Gulf countries, Korea, Malaysia and some other countries. Reports of exploitation of workers even costing lives pour in. Yet, many South Asian countries have been much benefited by job opportunities found outside their countries. Nepal's reduction of poverty from 42 per cent to 30 per cent has been attributed to remittances sent by the Nepali labourers from abroad.

Wasbir Hussain's paper gives a security perspective from the North-east India where cross-border migration and human trafficking had been taken as a perennial threat to the security of India. The changing demographic complexion in that part of the country due to the "unabated cross-border migration of people" has caused jitters as well as generated conflict between the local people and the migrants coming from across the Indo–Bangladesh border (former East Pakistan). Hussain states that "the influx of Bengalis from the plains of erstwhile East Pakistan, now Bangladesh, has reduced Tripura 's tribal population to a minority". And Hussain's opening remark, "if America is a salad bowl of cultures, South Asia is no melting pot" can aptly summarize the crux of the problem. Neither have the people been able to be in the melting pot, nor can they maintain their separate identity as in the salad bowl. It is more intriguing that cultural dimension is less evident in the strained relations between the migrants and the local people despite commonality of religion and culture of both. Economic factors and changing demographic picture therefore seem to have enhanced the feeling of insecurity.

Tensions among the various refugee groups constitute a threat to security for the host country. The Assam, Tripura, Bodoland, and other movements are directed against "foreigners" and against peoples coming from other states of India. The interested parties have used the refugees and migrants for domestic politics too as such refugees and migrants are often used as vote banks. According to Hussain, "the migration of people from Bangladesh has raised threat perceptions among Indian security agencies which feel that the migrants could be easily used by Islamist fundamentalist forces as also by the Pakistani Inter Services Intelligence (ISI)... ". Whether or not migrants or refugees can become spies or insurgents, they can create difficulties for a host country in numerous ways including the conflicts to be generated by food scarcity, health, lack of education, lack of shelter, etc. which are the core areas of human security/insecurity.

Giving due emphasis on capacity building to deal with a variety of problems related to human security, Sridhar Khatri has tried to encapsulate some of the ingredients of human security with a theoretical background. Security approaches have undergone a sea change in the post-Cold War era because countries increasingly engaged in domestic crises precipitated by bad governance, crisis of legitimacy, perennial political uncertainty, trends of religiosity and economic and security dilemmas. In this context, Khatri maintains that "an important 'new' security agenda for South Asia is still the old agenda closer to the neo-realist model of India and its neighbours learning to take into India's growing economic power and de facto existence of the two nuclear powers in the region". As a growing power, India has to face some challenges because of its centrality in South Asia—how it is going to deal with its "small" neighbours and with what strategies are the likely problems to be encountered by India. Khatri suggests that a proactive role for defining its new role in South Asia for "achieving regional stability without inflaming the insecurity of the smaller neighbours would be relevant.

Dealing with intra-state conflicts is another security agenda in South Asia. It is a more complicated scenario because of heterogeneity of groups involved in conflicts. Ideological, religious, sectarian, ethnic and separatist groups are all active in the region and what would be remedies for them is difficult here to assume. However, some political and ideological conflicts such as the Maoist insurgency in Nepal can be addressed if the involved parties adopt a more flexible approach. Sridhar has listed some characteristics of conflicts in South Asia as the following:

- Largest number of armed groups
- Longest duration of conflict
- Rising number of fatalities in terrorist-related violence.

Coming close on the heels of these features are the trends of violence and the trinity of militancy, militarism and militarization narrated by Dhruba Kumar in his paper exclusively devoted to Nepal. "Militarization is the use of the military to solve political problems. It implies the growing dominance of the military over civilian institutions, with a simultaneous decline in democratic institutions and the freedoms and rights of citizen. Militarism is commonly understood as the array of customs, actions and thought associated with a armies and wars yet 'transcending true military purpose' "[16]. Precisely speaking, militarization is a process of developing military structures and culture that subsume democratic political culture. So militarization and democratization are incompatible phenomena. That is why the military solution to political problems is inconceivable. One analyst has aptly summarized King Gyanendra's direct rule of 100 days saying that whatever promises were made by the King to end the Maoist insurgency as well as to make a dramatic change for making peace proved to be false. He writes: "The most staggering outcome of the last hundred days, however, has been the loss of legitimacy of the two regimes wielding guns"—the royal regime that came with a big bang by dismantling democratic institutions, and the Maoists who were hell-bent on establishing a new republic by force. "The latest developments show that they have realized that there is no victory for them down the road they are taking".[17]

It reminds us that the trends of militancy and counter offensive measures mounted by both the state security forces and the insurgents have dumped the non-military approach to ending violence. The demand for sophisticated weapons and technological innovations have not armed the state but they have contributed a lot to empowering the insurgents. Thus, on both sides, militarization that claims both manpower and resources is on the rise as if both the combatants—the state and the insurgents—are playing a zero-sum game. It is a course dangerously played for mutual destruction. Stating that "militancy, militarism and militarization" has state and non-state facets with the non-state side being called as rebellion, insurgency and revolution that aim at change. And the state arms itself for beefing up its capacity to counteract such rebellion as has been going on in Nepal since 1996. When militarism occurs, the state turns into a garrison state seeing no other options but to equip itself with more weapons and military-dominated strategies. Dhruba Kumar says, "Nepal is a microcosm of militancy and militarism" as both the RNA and the Maoists have become dreadful forces in the eyes of the people. In this context, Jayadeva Uyangoda argues, "The idea of security immediately evinces an exemplarily docile and subservient behaviour from citizens, communities and social institutions. That behavour, a one-way commitment to political obligation, demands an unwavering loyalty to the state, its sovereignty, its territorial integrity, its stability—in short, to its security".[18]

Incompatibility between state and human security is articulated by S.D. Muni who is of the opinion that even the Westphalian state has accepted people as one of the four elements of the state, hence there is no point in taking human security as a separate concept. Without the protection of the state, the protection of its people is inconceivable.

However, when the question of state-centric approach arises by rationalizing the military and its ramifications as the key to security, ignoring other components, especially people, it naturally prompts analysts to put emphasis on people as the agenda of security. It can therefore be said that there are no qualms between human security and state security, though the coercive nature of the state gets high premium due to intermingling of regime interest and larger people interest. The regime that is generally personified in the name of state security tends to become irrational resulting in juxtaposed positions of state and people or citizens. When the state plays an inimical role by augmenting its firepower against the rights of people, then the issue of human or individual security becomes prominent. Thus, examined dispassionately, laying emphasis on human dimension of security is not wrong. At a time when governments, both elected and nominated, are confronting the multitude of crises originated mainly from domestic sources, democracy and human rights are being redefined and contextualized in order to make democracy more egalitarian and people-centric.

Moreover, it seems that the issue of human security is also the issue of making democracy effective and popular by adopting the concept and practice of inclusive democracy. Muni shares the view with others that South Asia's track record of human security is rather disappointing due to the problems of governance and rampant corruption. The problem of establishing democratic credibility has become a stupendous task in some countries.

Jehan Perera is exclusively devoted to Sri Lanka's internal crisis. Despite its twenty-two-years ethnic conflict, Sri Lanka has been able to retain its democratic institutions. Yet, its ongoing ethnic conflict and the separatist war have given rise to the country's "intractable and destructive problem". It is not only the Liberation Tigers of Tamil Eelam (LTTE), the Sinhalese-dominated JVP have also separately launched insurrections for opposite reasons. The Sri Lankan peace process got severe jolts time and again but it is still holding on following some kinds of quid pro quo reached by the government and the LTTE.

To Indra Jit Rai, poverty alleviation, education and health services and similar other basic needs constitute human security. Drawing heavily from a variety of sources, particularly the UN Human Development Report, Rai indicates a major shift in security concepts from territorial to people's security, and from armaments to security through human development. Taking Nepal as a case study, Rai suggests six important actions for poverty alleviation. They are: empowerment of individuals and communities, gender equality, pro-poor growth, management of globalization, active state, and special actions for special situations. The author stresses that the higher the level of human security, the greater would be the chance of stability of polity.

One of the main causes of the origin of the Maoist insurgency in the Western hills is the entrenched feudalism and abject poverty. The oppressed and suppressed people could thus easily be lured by the Maoist slogan for ending such a plight of the people. The following elements need to be properly addressed to enhance human dignity.

- Dignity of the individual;
- Adherence to universalistic norms;
- Elevation of individual achievement over privilege or disprivileges of birth;
- Accountability in public life.[19]

It has been accepted that the traditional security exclusively dependent on military and other state agencies alone cannot address the burgeoning issues of governance. As it has been said, "the inadequacy, however, of a military approach to national security in South Asia is becoming clearer for at least four reasons that derive from the seminal changes that have occurred in the international security regime".

First, "the locus of conflict has shifted from the external to the internal sphere", with non-military and non-traditional threats to security acquiring greater salience. It has both national and international dimensions with non-traditional security becoming much dominant than other domains.[20]

The non-traditional security is now in the backseat because of the failures of South Asian governments to diversify their resources and strategies to human development. The rise of military budget and the continued orientation of power elites to rely more on traditional security or the coercive power of the state have amply proved it. Yet, at the public level, human security is assuming significance as crises faced by the South Asian countries are related more to the domestic situation and crisis of governance than anything else. In a modern society, the following features concerning human dignity can be mentioned. First, the legitimacy of a regime is a must for insuring both human and state security. If rulers stick to the traditional game by personifying their regime, they are always exposed to threats and instability. The royal coup of 1 February 2005 in Nepal has highlighted this point because the King does not find any new roadmap but to harp on his commitment to multiparty democracy. Thus, he is under pressure from both the parliamentary parties who want to restore parliament first and then reach the agenda of constituent assembly, and the Maoists who want a republican democracy. The King on his side is not likely to retract his step by obliging the parties and the Maoists unless he is forced to do so by the movement.

Second, a military solution would not be adequate to resolve political crises as is evident in Nepal and Sri Lanka. In Nepal, it seems that there would be greater polarization of forces including the Maoist against the royal regime. Even if the King commands the loyalty of the army, he is not likely to solve the Maoist problem by force alone. Progressive socio-political agendas advanced by both the political parties and the Maoists need to be addressed by him. Ironically, it will be a dangerous course for his own position and even existence.

Finally, the reconstruction of some states of South Asia is assuming significance today. Nepal's political or security crisis is much attributed to its feudal structure and unchanged nature of the state and the continued domination of traditional institution and culture. It has been realized by a wide section of Nepali intelligentsia that there is only a thin possibility of monarchy and democracy going together. Political forces want to establish constitutional monarchy with the King as titular head or a republican democracy but the King defies such a role. He wants to be both active and dominant in politics without any limitations on his power. Some royalists argue that in a Hindu monarchical state, the King's powers are unlimited and whatever ordinances or decrees he declares are beyond the purview of any other organ of the state. Such arguments are nevertheless repugnant to political parties including the Maoists who want to establish a democratic order based on social justice and popular sovereignty. Unless the issue of monarchy vs. people remains unresolved, security continues to be an elusive issue.

## NOTES

1. Barry Buzan, *People, State and Fear* (New Delhi: Transasia publishers, 1987) Indian edn, p. 245.
2. Ibid.
3. Mohammed Ayoob, *The Third World Security Predicament: State Making, Regional Conflict, and the International System* (Boulder, Colorado: Lynne, Rienner, 1995), p. 5.
4. See Henry A. Kissinger, "Realists Versus Idealists", *The Kathmandu Post*, 15 May 2005.

5. See Shridhar K Khatri, "What is the Security agenda for South Asia?", Paper included in this book.
6. Human Development Report 1994 (UNDP: Oxford University Press,1994). See also Sridhar, Ibid.
7. Kanti Bajpai has precisely identified four instruments/means of security. They are: human development and human governance, not force, are preferred instruments; State's cooperative role both at the national and international levels; soft power, rather than military power, should be the criterion for ensuring security; and collaboration between state and other non-governmental organizations, and international agencies is a must for human security. See Kanti Bajpai, "Beyond Comprehensive Security: Human Security" in Delhi Policy Group, *Comprehensive Security: Perspectives from India's Regions*, seminar Proceedings August 2001 (New Delhi: Delhi Policy Group, 2002), pp. 1–27. As mentioned in Khatri, ibid.
8. David P. Barash, Charles P. Webel, *Peace and Conflict Studies* (Thousand Oaks: Sage, 2002), p. 205
9. V.R. Raghavan, *Economic and Socio-Political Dimensions of Security in South Asia: Seminar Proceedings*, Kathmandu, May 2002 (New Delhi: Delhi Policy Group, 2002), p. xi–xii.
10. Ken Booth, "Security and Emancipation", *Review of International Studies*, 17.4.1991, p. 319.
11. In greater detail, see Lok Raj Baral, *Nepal: The Problem of Governance* (New Delhi: Konark, 1993); Baral, "Expanding Domain of Security in the New Millenium: A View from Nepal" in Rajesh M. Basrur, (ed.), *Security in the New Millenium: Views from South Asia* (Delhi: India Research Press, 2001), pp. 45–81.
12. For more details about UN intervention, see Thomas M. Franck, *Recourse to Force: State Action Against Threats and Attacks* (Cambridge: Cambridge University Press, 2002) pp.135–73.
13. See Kofi Annan, *The Question of Intervention* (New York: United Nations, 1999), pp. 6, 13, 20.
14. See *The Kathmandu Post*, 24 March 2005.
15. *Regional Poverty Profile 2004* (Kathmandu: SAARC Secretariat, 2004), pp. 63–72.
16. Anuradha M. Chenoy, *Militarism & Women in South Asia* (New Delhi: Kali for Women, 2002), pp. 4–5.
17. See Ameet Dhakal, "Wonderful 100 Days", *The Kathmandu Post*, 3 June 2005.
18. See Jayadeva Uyangoda, "Security's Insecurity: South Asia's States, Societies and Citizens in the Age of Globalization" in Rajesh Basrur, (ed.), *Security in the New Millenium: Views From South Asia* (New Delhi: India Research Press, 2001), p. 117.

19. Dipankar Gupta, *Mistaken Modernity: India Between Worlds* as mentioned in P.R. Chari, (ed.), *Security and Governance in South Asia* (Delhi: Manohar, 2001), p.161.
20. P.R. Chari, ibid, pp. 162–63.

# 2

## What is the 'New' Security Agenda for South Asia?*

***Sridhar K. Khatri***

The question as to what might be the 'new' security agenda for South Asia is an interesting one, but not as easy to answer. It is easy to deal with this issue from a national perspective by reflecting the national sentiments and priority of individual countries, or even from the point of view of a major power with some degree of interest in South Asia. But to look at the security agenda from a regional perspective is rather difficult since the region as a whole hardly represents a cohesive group, unlike the European Union, which has begun to consider a common foreign and defence policy. Even the EU's recent experience over the American-led war in Iraq shows that a common stand within Europe may not be possible. In South Asia, when one considers the asymmetry in size and capabilities of the countries in the region and the history of suspicion and animosity of the past half century among the neighbouring countries, it is difficult to talk about a common security agenda for the region without falling into the trap of either prioritizing the security concerns of some countries or ignoring the sensitivities of others. Moreover, even when one views the commonality of the region—in terms of similar history, ethnic, linguistic, cultural and religious background—these paradoxically have resulted in mutual dissensions, tensions and conflicts.

To talk about a 'new' security agenda for South Asia is even more difficult, since it assumes that there was an old one. It is true that there

---

* Paper presented at a conference organized by NCCS on *Non-Traditional Security: State, Democracy and Society*, on 16-17 November 2004.

were some debates and discussion on how the security situation might look for South Asia after the end of the Cold War. But before the ideas could crystallize, the terrorist attack on New York and Washington DC on 11 September 2001, reshaped the global security agenda that made South Asia one of the focal points of global security concern with military action by the international community against the Al Qaeda and Taliban in Afghanistan. What is however true is that over the years there have been ongoing discussions on what constitutes the key security issues in the region and how it might be examined.

## II

The debate in the broad sense is between three schools of thought. First, there is the neo-realist school that considers the state as the provider of security, with the logical conclusion suggesting that if the state is secure, then those who live within it are also secure. It perceives that the principal threat to its national interests is violence and coercion by other states and justifies the retaliatory use of force—or threat of its use—to bring about what is largely considered to be a military balance. Cooperation may at best be limited to some form of alliance formation, or within a loose regional/international structure where the state supremacy is secure. This is the model advocated by states in South Asia, with the military—bureaucracy complex championing the cause and the message being strongly articulated by political leaders, often at their behest.

Second, there is the school which sees security threat to states from other states in decline and recognizes the rise of non-traditional threats that can often lead to "economic stagnation, political instability, and, sometimes, state collapse". These threats can come from a number of areas, including terrorism, organized crime, drug trafficking, ethnic conflict and a combination of rapid population growth, environmental decline, and poverty.[1] Proponents of this school question the state-centric model of security, though still recognizing military strategy and balance of power politics as an inevitable part of this process. Where this school differs from the traditional model is how the whole security question should be examined. They pose a number of key questions to challenge the traditional conceptualization of security: *security for whom*, *security from what threats* and *security by what means*? Some of them go as far as to advocate that security of citizens within a state may in fact be incompatible with a nation's security,[2] noting that in some cases the state has been the greatest perpetrator of violence on its citizens.

In South Asia, non-traditional security issues are being examined to some degree at the intergovernmental level through various bodies, but have not made headway as states seem hardly prepared to make the needed commitment after perfunctorily recognizing the security implications. The best example of this is the SAARC convention on terrorism, which was signed in 1987 and has been ratified by all the member states. During the previous Summit in Islamabad in January 2004, governments went as far as to add protocol to control the financing of terrorist activities in the region (as already required by Security Council resolution 1372), but did not commit themselves to passing national enabling legislations within a set timeframe which would make the convention operational. After 17 years, the convention still remains a paper document that has little impact on developments in the region.

The other case is that of the South Asia Growth Quadrangle (SAGQ), which was designed to overcome the political limitations of SAARC and to exploit the potential of a contiguous economic zone in South Asia.[3] After initial objection that this would factionalize the regional initiative by other SAARC members who would be outside the purview of this arrangement, a compromise was reached. Initially, the four SAGQ participating countries (India, Nepal, Bhutan and Bangladesh) were not even sure if cooperation in the energy sectors should be included in the scheme. The idea of moving ahead with the energy sector finally received a push through the intervention of a third party, when President Clinton proposed during his visit to the region in March 2000 to support the South Asia Regional Initiative (SARI) on energy, though one hears that getting the full participation and support of some of the countries participating in the scheme members has been difficult.

It may be useful to keep in mind that security concepts can transform hardcore military matters to broader non-traditional security issues. When the idea of a South Asian Regional Initiative was first introduced by an American expert on the region, it was presented as a "grand strategy" to accommodate the national interests of individual countries by allowing the United States—with possible co-sponsorship by Japan, Russia, Germany and the UK—to overcome the Indo–Pakistani conflict. The central idea was to get the region to move in the direction of greater cooperation by, among other things, reducing arms spending and denuclearization.[4] Subsequently, when the idea was implemented, cooperation in the energy sector became the primary focus, with the South Asia Regional Initiative Women's and Children's Equity being added in 2003.[5]

The point to note is that the emphasis on non-traditional security discourse in South Asia is not limited to intellectuals and academics in the region, but is increasingly recognized by governments who continue to either explore or participate in a vast array of institutional arrangements. Moreover, these schemes are not confined to South Asia *per se*, but in some cases are cross-regional. They include such arrangements as BIMSTEC (Bay of Bengal Initiative for Multi-Sectoral Technical and Economic Cooperation)[6], IOR-ARC (Indian Ocean Rim Association for Region Cooperation) and the Track II Kunming Initiative that includes China. The agendas considered by some of these groups include economic cooperation, but also expand to common security issues that range from environmental security, population movements to the need to responding to terrorism.[7] The drawback in the inter-governmental dialogue has been that it has hardly gone beyond the perfunctory planning and debates.

The third school of thought, which is close to the non-traditional school, is concerned with the notion of "human security", which focuses on the condition of daily life of the people—food, shelter, employment, health, public safety and human rights. The 1994 UNDP Human Development Report included in its definition of "human security" such issues as unchecked population growth, disparities in economic opportunities, migration pressures, environmental degradation, drug trafficking, and international terrorism.[8] This is the theme echoed by Secretary General Kofi Annan in his Millennium Report when he underscored the quest for freedom from fear, freedom from want and the need to secure a sustainable future.

What distinguishes human security from the notion of comprehensive security covered under the neo-realist or non-traditional security ideas is the primary *referent of security as the individual.* "Human security does not ignore state security, but treats it as no more than a co-equal to individual security." Two *values* are of paramount concern in its conception: the bodily safety of the individual; and his or her personal freedom. This includes the *basic freedom* of the individual in relation to one's most intimate life choices (e.g. marriage, personal law, sexual orientation, employment), and *civic freedom* to the liberty to organize for cultural, social, economic, and political purposes. *Security threats* are taken in broader terms, which include not only other states and non-state actors of various kinds, but structural sources at various levels—from the family upwards to the global economy. There are four basic *Security Instruments/Means* inherent in the concept:

- Human development and humane governance are preferred instruments of security, rather than the use of force.
- States must cooperate and collaborate with others to deal with human security threats, but they must also reach out to international organization, non-governmental organization and the civil society to be effective.
- Soft power, rather than military power, should be used as an instrument of persuasion by disseminating information and idea on the imperative of international cooperation on human security.
- States, regional and international organizations, and NGOs should collaborate to develop norms of conduct in various areas of human security.[9]

The human security approach is increasingly gaining currency in South Asia due to two factors. The first has to do with the shifting emphasis on security studies from inter-state to intra-state issues. A compelling reason for the paradigm shift was the recognition that inter-state wars alone do not account for the insecurity that nations face today. In the 13-year post-Cold War period from 1990 and 2002, there were 58 different major armed conflicts in the 46 different locations throughout the world, out of which all but three were internal conflicts.[10] The intra-state conflicts, along with the tendency of states to inflict violence on its own citizens, accounted for the largest number of deaths. According to one estimate, some 151 million persons were killed by government in addition to the death toll from war and civil war (which is said to account for another 39 million). A majority of deaths was perpetrated by governments on their own citizens, with the totalitarian states responsible for 84 per cent of these deaths and authoritarian states for most of the rest.[11] The situation was no different for South Asia, which is known as having one of the largest numbers of armed groups in the world, with the longest duration of conflicts, and an ever rising number of fatalities in terrorist-related violence.

The second reason has to do with the democratization process of the 1990s throughout the world and in South Asia, which Huntington has identified as the "third wave". As with the rest of the world, this led to greater acceptance of a liberal model of a post-Cold War world which sought a stronger international society with more rules to stabilize the evolving international system. With the expansion of democracy in South Asia, this period saw the proliferation of NGOs taking an advocacy role with greater emphasis on openness, human intervention and economic security.

There is a number of areas where civil society has taken on a key role on security issues in South Asia. One important area is the peace process, where its role in the various parts of the region has not always been even. More than in any other part of the region, the civil society in Sri Lanka has played a watchdog role, at times even advocating structural changes to make the peace process effective. During the recent Tokyo Conference on Reconstruction and Development of Sri Lanka, a representative from the civil society criticized the Sri Lanka government and donor communities for having insufficient consultation with civil society groups in preparing major programmes, which was essentially "economic centric" and technical in nature and lacked a political vision of the future of Sri Lanka. While noting that the peace process was too donor-driven and failed to utilize local expertise and institutional memory, it also recommended creating a more effective human rights monitoring mechanism that would be multi-layered, involving community level, national and international participation.[12] Such views get serious hearing in Sri Lanka as much of the donor programmes are integrated with civil society activities. Additionally, over the years the government has also begun to recognize the role of such groups from the rehabilitation issue in developing the roadmap for the peace process.

In Bangladesh, although a peace accord has been signed on the Chittagong Hill Tract, a recent study suggests that it may be flawed as it only focuses on physical reconstruction and fails to make structural changes needed to transform the situation. The study points out that if civil society had been involved in the negotiations, it might have been possible to address of the important issues neglected by the accord, like justice, reconciliation, and moral and social reconstruction.[13] However, the study also seems to indicate that civil society participation on such high value issues as peace process are not without difficulties because the Hill people view its activities with suspicion. This is either because the activities of NGOs are seen as being insensitive to the local needs replicating the programmes of the plains, or their programmes include Bengali settlers.[14]

In Nepal's case, with no established civil society groups versed with the conflict resolution process,[15] the field has been left wide open to political personalities and human rights activists who have taken the lead role in facilitating the peace talks. So far, this has been a process of the blind leading the blind as the government and the Maoists appear to be operating without any clear-cut objectives, and the "facilitators" educating themselves by learning by doing at each step of the way.

Another area where the civil society is engaged in South Asia is issues affecting women and children. Although in the past this took the shape of a band-aid approach designed to bring relief to victims of conflicts, in recent times activities of groups such as Women in Security Conflict Management and Peace (WISCOMP) in India and Nagarik Awaaz in Nepal, have attempted to shape the way people look at conflict. For example, WISCOMP's work in Kashmir has broad structural objectives which include:

- communicating the voices of women in Kashmir valley to a broader platform;
- evaluating the prerequisites and obstacles to peace and exploring a common vocabulary of peace; and
- generating awareness on activities of groups working to bring about a qualitative change in the lives of women of the valley.[16]

Working at the grassroots level, the Naga Mothers Association has been able to not only introduce a more holistic approach to peace and security by including issues of social justice into the debate, but to form a peace team to confront the violent political situation and build capacity for non-violent conflict resolution.[17]

Similarly, the proliferation of small arms and light weapons (SALW) is an issue in which regional NGOs have been involved. Since the 2001 UN Conference on Small Arms, there has been no coordinated regional response for implementing the Programme of Action in South Asia. In early 2003, NGOs and individuals in South Asia met in Colombo to develop a future strategy on SALW, which included the establishment of the Asia Small Arms Network (SASA-Net) to coordinate civil society work across the region.[18] Such a reformist approach is likely to have an incremental effect on state policy given the threat posed to each states by the availability of small arms and light weapons in South Asia.

However, the civil society in South Asia has yet to work together as a cohesive group towards a common goal on security matters. On the one hand, it continues to face an identity crisis in terms of its role in society as well as the ethics of its engagement (to whom are they accountable?). On the other, South Asian civil society is faced with a credibility problem, especially as the state often has the tendency to view it as likely agents for promoting agendas of donor countries/ institutions, while the public sees it as an easy money-making institution. Unlike in Western Europe, it is still not possible to think of civil society and governments in South Asia working in partnership on security matters, with a few exceptions.[19]

## III

After having examined how security approaches have changed over the years in South Asia, we are still left with the main question: "What is the 'new' Security Agenda for South Asia?"

Although it might sound paradoxical at this stage, an important 'new' security agenda for South Asia is still the old agenda closer to the neo-realist model of India and its neighbours learning to live with each other at the beginning of the new millennium. The new approach has to take into account India's growing economic power and de facto existence of the two nuclear powers in the region. The lessons of the Brasstacks Crisis in 1987, the 1990 Crisis and the Kargil Crisis in 1999 suggest that the danger of nuclear confrontation between these two neighbours, with unimaginable consequences for the region, is all too real. SAARC's experience in the past half decade has shown that dialogue and understanding between India and Pakistan is essential if the rest of South Asia is not to be held hostage again to the rivalry between the two countries. There is also the danger that without adequate progress on the Indo–Pakistani front, there might not be a forward movement on the non-traditional security issues as well. One of the positive signs after the start of the "composite dialogue"[20] recently between the two countries has been the indication by India that on the sticky energy issue it would be willing to import gas by pipelines through Pakistani territory under international guarantee.

As the pre-eminent power in the region, India is faced with a Catch-22 situation in dealing with its smaller neighbours: if it takes major initiatives, it is most likely to be seen as exercising its hegemony in the region; and if it does not come up with ideas, it is seen as defaulting on its responsibilities. A former Indian Foreign Secretary once described India's 'pivotal role in South Asia' as its 'special responsibility' in promoting cooperation and "giving impetus to the movement in view of the asymmetry prevailing in the region, with India being the main factor for this asymmetry". He suggested that in order to turn this asymmetry into opportunities, particularly in dealing with the smaller countries in the region, it would be important to take a long-term view as what is perceived as a negative-sum game in the short run could be a positive-sum game in the medium and long term. The example he provides is the link between economic condition in Bangladesh and migration of Bangladeshis to India. If India can help by opening up its market and encourage a larger flow of investment, one of the pull factors of migrants to India could be eliminated.[21]

At the beginning of the new century, a greater challenge for India is how to manage its growing political, economic and military power in dealing with its smaller neighbours in the region. With coalition politics becoming the norm in India, the debate on foreign policy has become more open than ever before. As one analyst recently put it, India today needs to decide how it is going to use its influence to achieve its regional objectives. The author points out that the choice is either to follow the "increasingly invisible" role followed by the National Democratic Alliance government headed by Mr. A.B. Vaypayee, which allowed India to play a secondary role to the US in Nepal and to Norway, the European Union and Japan in Sri Lanka, or opt for greater Indian visibility that would make the country more than a spectator to the developments in Nepal and Sri Lanka, respectively.[22] The trick for any government in New Delhi, however, is to define for itself a proactive role for achieving regional stability without inflaming the insecurity of the smaller neighbours, while at the same time strengthening its strategic relationship with the major powers in the world.

The second important security agenda in South Asia is learning to deal with intra-state conflicts. There are three significant features of intra-state conflicts in South Asia.

- *One of the largest numbers of armed groups*—South Asia has one of the largest numbers of 'non-state armed groups' in any region in the world. Out of the 18 identified by the *Military Balance 2002–2003* of the International Institute of Strategic Studies, 3 are in Bangladesh, 8 in India, 5 in India/Pakistan, and one each in Nepal and Sri Lanka. Most of the armed groups are transnational in character, which often leads to accusations of cross-border terrorism.

- *Longest duration of conflicts*—Comparatively speaking, studies show that conflicts in South Asia have lasted longer than in any other region of the world. Of the eight armed conflicts in the region, only one (East Pakistan) ended in the same calendar year, and another (Baluch) lasted 4 years (1973–77). Only the Khalistan conflict (1984–92) belongs to a group where conflicts lasted more than 5 years but less than 10 years. Five armed conflicts (the Chittagong Hill Tract, Mizo, Naga, Eelam, Assam) continued for over 10 years, out of which the Naga qualifies as one of the longest armed conflict in the world having lasted 45 years. Scholars suggest that 63 per cent of the armed conflicts in South Asia belong to the category of protracted conflicts, which is three times higher than the global average.
- *Rising number of fatalities in terrorist-related violence*—A report issued by the State Department, entitled *Patterns of Global Terrorism—2000*, suggests that Asia accounts for 75 per cent of all terrorism casualties worldwide. The list of countries in this arc of terrorism includes Afghanistan, Pakistan, Uzbekistan, Tajikistan, Chinese-ruled Xinjiang and Tibet, India, Nepal, Sri Lanka, Bangladesh, and Burma. In South Asia alone, the annual number of fatalities in terrorist-related violence surpasses the death toll in the Middle East, which is often seen as the traditional place of terrorism.

A major fallout in the region after 9/11 and the American "war on terrorism" has been the distortion of our understanding of the nature of conflicts in South Asia by automatically incorporating them under the label of terrorism. Many, if not all, of the intra-state conflicts pre-date 9/11, while some have been in existence for over half a century. A recent report identifies at least 54 groups that are proscribed under various terrorism laws in South Asian countries. They include 32 in India, 1 in Nepal, 11 in Pakistan, 1 in Sri Lanka (currently de-proscribed) and 9 in Bangladesh.[23] As there is no commonly accepted definition of what constitutes 'terrorism', it is an open question if any act of rebellion or insurgency qualifies as a terrorist act if only governments label it at such.[24]

A better way of understanding conflicts in South Asia may be to look at the nature of insurgency, including its operational and tactical objectives. Since insurgencies are not sudden events and take place over a period of time, it might be more useful to look at its various stages. They include the initial *passive stage,* which is the most difficult and protracted period during which insurgents establish an infrastructure, actively recruit, focus on gaining popular support, and demonstrate that they can challenge the authority of the government. During the next phase of the *active stage* the insurgents extend political control and increase military action in armed resistance against government forces. Such groups may use guerrilla warfare strategy to frustrate the authority of the government and intimidation methods through acts of terrorism to intimidate the masses and the established authorities to damage the government's credibility. And finally, after gaining sufficient military strength and popular support, in the *counter-offensive state* the insurgents rely on its ability to launch conventional military attacks, while continuing to rely on guerrilla action to defeat the government's military forces.[25]

Most conflicts in South Asia have been tackled in one form or the other through military means, rather than through concerted efforts to solve the root cause of the problems that would entail substantial structural changes at the political, economic and social levels. Even in the case of the Chittagong Hill Tracts in Bangladesh, where agreements were reached a few years ago, some people contend that such a shaky agreement may not lead to the resolution of the conflict, but only take the conflict to the next stage. In Sri Lanka there is currently a "no war, no peace" situation with negotiations on hold, and the LTTE showing fissures within its ranks and unable to persuade the new UFPA-led government to initiate talks based on LTTE's demand for an Interim Self-Governing Authority.

One expert on India believes that the fight against various kinds of insurgencies in India (ethnic, separatist, cross-border, etc) has led to the 'militarization of Indian imagination'. In the name of combating terrorism, many legal provisions have been passed, which '[harm] the cause of democracy by increasing the impunity and immunity of the state.' Both the state and the terrorists have also constrained debate and dissent in a democratic society. And a 'cult of action' has been promoted, representing the view of politics as managerial and technical, where everything can be set right by decisive action and without patience, good sense and moderation.

The logic behind the 'cult of action' has been extended to calling attention of countries, which allegedly harbour terrorist groups operating against India. Pakistan has been called upon by India to take measures against groups operating from the Pakistani side of Kashmir. New Delhi has repeatedly asked Bangladesh and Nepal to control the activities of allegedly Pakistani intelligence-supported groups acting against India from their country. And more recently, in December 2003, India provided support to the government of Bhutan in taking military action against the Indian ULFA rebels who had been using the small Buddhist kingdom as a sanctuary.

Although there are intermittent peace talks going on at different times between South Asian states and insurgents (Kashmir, Sri Lankan Government and LTTE, Maoists and the Nepalese government), the overall trend has been to seek some kind of military result on the ground. Nepal continues to rely on a military solution to the Maoist conflict with the American and Indian military support, while Pakistan has recently shifted its stance from being a reluctant partner in the global war on terrorism to a "non-NATO ally' of the United States because of its intricate involvement in the campaign against Al Qaeda in South Wasristan.

The capacity of governments and civil society to deal with conflict resolution methods is limited in South Asia. Despite the size of the country and number of insurgencies experienced by India, conflict resolution discipline or experts hardly exist in India. Only Sri Lanka has made some headway due to the two-decade-old conflict in the country. Moreover, there is no sharing of experiences among security experts in dealing with insurgencies in the region. Capacity building in managing conflicts is essential if South Asia is to deal with the growing intra-state conflicts in the region.

And third, with such little work being done on non-traditional security issues in South Asia, the field is wide open to any type of work that can be undertaken. When RCSS first undertook projects on non-traditional security issues, it identified three major issues of importance. They included the following: *Governance in Plural Societies and Security; Environment and Security;* and *Globalization and Security*. The exercise on the three themes proved to be very useful in understanding how a broad range of issues might figure in developing an understanding of non-traditional security issues in South Asia. *Governance and capacity building of institutions* stood out as crucial elements around which non-traditional security issues tend to evolve. Very often violation of principles of transparency, accountability and representation has led to aberrations in the political system of South Asian countries, resulting in disregard for people's aspirations and their marginalization from the mainstream of national politics. The consequence of misgovernance has been high, leading to violence by the affected groups against the state and counter-reprisal by the states against the people.[26]

However, the prospect of inter-state violence over environmental issues was found to be rather slim in this exercise, even though environmental differences can add to existing tensions and apprehensions, and thus perpetuate the general sense of insecurity that pervade inter-state relations in the region.[27] The work on *globalization and non-traditional security issues* emerged with a mixed impression. As globalization may not be totally neutral and asymmetrical, it is considered important to strengthen the capacity of South Asian nations to deal with likely threats and be prepared to derive benefits from this process.[28] ***The common message from the work on the three themes is that the challenge to the well being of individuals is internal, not external.***

The preliminary exercise done by RCSS on non-traditional security issues in South Asia suggests that more in-depth work needs to be undertaken in the area of capacity-building of institutions and democratic structures to deal with the security threat posed to individuals in each of the countries of the region. In particular, this calls for a need to look more closely at the democratization process in the region and its implications for governance and the newer challenges posed to state security. Greater emphasis needs to be placed on the gender perspective when dealing with conflicts, along with how development paradigms can address the concerns of the ethnic and minority groups who are often marginalized by the inefficient and corrupt *political* system of the countries in the region. There is a need to create awareness in the region about conflict-prevention mechanisms, and help build capacity of governments and NGOs in this area.

## IV

A common theme that emerges when one looks at the security issues in South Asia is the need for capacity building to deal with some of the problems that are common to the region. First, there is a need to understand the root causes of conflict through a multi-level analysis by examining the different types of causes for armed conflicts. They include the *background causes* that may be result of exclusion of some groups from power; the *mobilization strategy* that motivates people to rebel against the authority; the *triggers* that lead to the onset of armed conflicts; and the *catalysts* that account for the intensity and duration of the conflict.

Second, there is also a need to explore the possibility of creating institutional mechanisms that can be involved in designing a conflict-transformation process for peace building through quiet dialogue among policy makers, academics and civil society. The present structure of SAARC and its working methods leave issues related to peace and conflict beyond the scope of the organization. A Regional Forum, similar to the ASEAN model, where a basket of security issues could be discussed collectively could eventually lead to the creation of an inter-governmental conflict-prevention mechanism for South Asia, which could be absorbed by SAARC after it matures fully. This approach goes beyond the Track II process, which has been common in South Asia in the past two decades and has produced limited results.

## REFERENCES

1. Jessica T. Mathews, "Power Shift," *Foreign Affairs,* January/February 1997, p. 51.
2. Barry Buzan, *People, State and Fear: An agenda for International Security Studies in the post-Cold War Era*, 2nd edn. (Hemel Hempstead: Sheatsheaf, 1991), p. 238.
3. Forrest E. Cookson and A. I. M. Shahsul Alam, (eds.), *Towards Greater Sub-regional Economic Coopertion: Limitation, Obstacles, and Benefits* (Dhaka: The University Press Limited, 2002).
4. See Stephen Philip Cohen, "SARI: A Peace process for South Asia", in www.acdis.uiuc.edu/Research/S&P/1994-WiSp/S&P_VIII-2/sari.html
5. "South Asia Regional Initiative (SARI) Women's and Children's Equity", in www.usaid.gov.in/UsaidInIndia/Act_SARIEquity.htm
6. Formerly known as Bangladesh, India, Myanmar, Sri Lanka, Thailand—Economic Cooperation.
7. See Dennis Rumley and Sanjay Chaturvedi, (eds.), *Geopolitical Orientations, Reginalism and Security in the India Ocean* (New Delhi: South Asian Publishers, 2004).
8. *Human Development Report 1994* (Oxford: Oxford University Press/UNDP, 1994).
9. Kanti Bajpai, "Beyond Comprehensive Security: Human Security," in Delhi Policy Group, *Comprehensive Security: Perspectives from India's Regions: Seminar Proceedings August 2001* (New Delhi: Delhi Policy Group, 2002), pp. 1–27.
10. Mikael Eriksson, Margareta Sollenberg and Peter Wallensteen, "Patterns of major armed conflict, 1990-2002," in *SIPRI Yearbook 2003: Armaments, Disarmament and International Security* (Oxford University Press, 2003), pp. 109–111.
11. Rudoph J. Rummel, "Power, Genocide and Mass Murder," *Journal of Peace Research,* No. 31 (February 1994), p. 2.

12. Paikiasothy Saravanamuttu, "Civil Society Presentation," paper presented at the *Tokyo Conference on Reconstruction and Development of Sri Lanika* by the Executive Director of the Centre for Policy Alternatives, June 9–10, 2003.
13. Amena Moshin, *The Chittagong Hill Tracts, Bangladesh: On the Difficult Road to Peace* (Boulder, Co.: Lynne Rienner Publishers, 2003), p. 117.
14. *Ibid.*, pp. 76–76.
15. For background on civil society group in Nepal, see: Dev Raj Dahal, *Civil Society in Nepal: Opening the Ground for Questions* (Kathmandu: Centre for Development and Governance, 2001); and Krishna B. Bhattachan, et al. (eds.), *NGO, Civil Society and Government in Nepal* (Kathmandu: CDOSA and FES, 2001).
16. Sumona DasGupta, *Breaking the Silence: Women and Kashmir* (New Delhi: WISCOM); and Mugdha Rai and Niloufer Afridi-Qazi, *Women Reporting Conflict* (New Delhi: WISCOM, 1999).
17. Paula Bannerjee, *Across the Experiences: Naga Women and Sri Lanka* (New Delhi: WISCOM, 2003).
18. International Action Network on Small Arms (IANSA), *Implementing The Programme of Action 2003: Action by States and Civil Society*, pp. 113–117.
19. For the strength and limitations of civil society in conflict prevention field, see "The South Asian Action Agenda" which was endorsed by a regional conference on *The Role of Civil in the Prevention of Armed Conflict in South Asia*, organized by RCSS in Kathmandu from 11–13 September 2004, on www.rcss.org.
20. The issues covered in the "composite dialogue" include: Jammu and Kashmir; peace, security and CBMs; Siachen glacier; Wullar Barrage/ Tulbul Navigation Project; economic and commercial cooperation; terrorism and drugs; and promotion of friendly exchanges in various fields.
21. Muchkund Dubey, "South Asian Cooperation: A Vision of Shared Destiny," *India's Pivotal Role in South Asia: Optimizing Benefits and Minimizing Apprehensions* (New Delhi: CASAC, 2000), pp. 1–10.
22. D. Raman, "Greater Indian Visibility in its Neighborhood," Paper No. 1159, November 8, 2004, in www.saag.org/papers12/paper1159.html.
23. P. V. Ramana, "RCSS Data Chapter on Profiles of 'Terrorist' Groups in South Asia." This is part of the RCSS project on "Understanding and Responding to 'Terrorism' in South" that is currently being completed by the Centre.
24. A consensus nevertheless exists in the international community that even in the absence of a clear-cut definition there are common elements which constitute terrorism. They are:
    - use of indiscriminate act of violence against ordinary civilians, against their life, their property, and their well-being;

- means to attain political goals which could not be attained by ordinary lawful means;
- violence perpetrated against ordinary people who have not direct influence upon or connection with the intended results of those acts;
- means of instilling fear among the people that would further their cause; and action and behaviour intended to humiliate fellow human beings.

See Hans-Peter Gasser, "Acts of terror, 'terrorism' and international humanitarian law," *International Review of the Red Cross*, Vol. 84, No. 847 (September 2002), pp. 552–553. Adam Roberts proposes a similar definition. According to him, terrorism is "the use of violence, often against people not directly involved in a conflict, by groups operating clandestinely, which generally claim to have high political or religious purposes, and believe that creating a climate of terror will assist attainment of their objectives. Terrorism of this kind almost always appears to be non-governmental, but in particular cases movements engaging in terrorism may have a degree of clandestine support from governments." See Adam Roberts, "Defining Terrorism: Focusing on the Targets," International Institute of Strategic Studies, *Strategic Comments*, Vol. 7 (November 2001), No. 9.

25. Eric N. Nyberg, "Insurgency: The Unsolved Mystery," www.globalsecurity.org./military/library/report/1991/NEN.htm. See also Sir Robert Thompson, *Defeating Communist Insurgency: Experiences from Malay and Vietnam* (London: Chatto and Windus, 1966); Ashok Krishna, "Insurgency in the Contemporary World: Some Theoretical Aspects: Part I," *Strategic Analysis*, Vol. XIX, No. 9 (December 1996), pp. 1291–1308; and Ashok Krishna, "Insurgency in the Contemporary World: Some Theoretical Aspects: Part II," *Strategic Analysis*, Vol. XX, No. 9 (December 1997), pp. 1317–1340.
26. P.R. Chari, (ed.), *Security and Governance in South Asia* (New Delhi: Manohar, 2001).
27. Adil Najam, (ed.), *Environment, Development and Human Security* (Lanham, Md.: University Press of America, 2003).
28. Abdur Rob Khan, (ed.), *Globalization and Non-Traditional Security in South Asia* (Dhaka: Academic Press and Publisher Ltd., 2001).

# 3

# Human Security in South Asia*

***S.D. Muni***

**Introduction:**

Any attempt to distinguish between State and Human security is conceptually incompatible. The Westphalian State was conceived with four basic components, namely, the territory, people, government and sovereignty. The security of the state therefore means the security of all these components individually and collectively, including the security of the people, including from the threats of environmental degradation, natural calamities and spread of epidemics. The State is obliged to protect their people from floods, droughts, health hazards like plague and the like, and it generally does its best to brave these threats. If the security of any of the essential and basic components of the state is affected, the security of the whole of the state is affected too. In fact security of each component is linked to the other. For instance, even protection of land is protection of people, for habitation, economic sustenance or movement. Therefore, the underlying assumption that runs through the efforts to contrast state security from human security or comprehensive security is about the nature and character of the state, where the state is not seen or expected to be inclusive or representative enough of all its components, primarily, the human beings. In this respect, there seems to be a clear divide between the established and evolving states, and between the developed and the

* This is the revised version of IDSS Occasional paper entitled "Comprehensive Security: The South Asian Case", published by IDSS, Singapore, in 2002.

developing states. The bias is in favour of the established and the developed state and against the evolving and underdeveloped state. The assumption is that while the former state meets its human security obligation, the latter does not or cannot do so. Seeing the developed State as providing comprehensive security, it was argued that

> in the developed states, the State was seen as major source of security and threat: the military strength of the state protected its people against outside threats; its police force protected them internally; and its social security programmes protected them against ill health, unemployment and extreme hardship.[1]

Notwithstanding the conceptual coherence of the State with regard to its essential components, the experience of the past several decades suggests that in practice, both the developed as well as new and evolving states have pursued their security with far too greater emphasis on the defence of their territories, sovereignties and governments. In doing so, greater reliance has been put upon military and defence-related activities. People, their rights and their needs, their lives and their progress have often been partially or completely neglected. Peoples' security has been taken for granted since it is inherent in the conceptual creation of the state. Due to the dominant thrust of the Cold War-related conflicts and arms races, territorial and political aspects of security constituted the principal concern of security policies and security studies. People got divided along ideologies and military blocs. For the protection of these concerned territories, political systems and the allies of the military blocs, people were called upon, even forced to sacrifice their lives and liberties. With the end of the Cold War and gradual escalation in internal conflicts, the State is even seen as pitted against its own people. Large numbers of innocent people are being killed in ethnic and ideologically extremist internal wars. Both the State as well as the rebellious forces extensively resort to terror as an instrument in these wars. This has reinforced the efforts to look at the security of people as not being identical with that of the State. Let us briefly recall the conceptual shift that has taken place in the discourse on state and human security.

### The Conceptual Shift:

The inadequacy of state-centric military security started coming into focus as the Cold War patterns of conflict gave rise to newer concerns and their costs started becoming unaffordable in terms of human suffering and development. Early signs of this shift were discernible in the call for The UN General Assembly Special Sessions on "Disarmament and Development" and the publication of reports by international commissions headed by Willy Brandt and Olaf Palme.[2] This led to scholarly questioning of the traditional security framework with a plea that such a framework for studying security needed to be revised and enlarged to include conflicts and concerns other than those of inter-state wars.[3] Barry Buzan's study drew attention to the fact that the state, while being recognised as a security provider, was also a source of fear and insecurity for its own people.[4] Ayoob even argued that the state in the Third World pitted against its own people as a source of threat and insecurity, in the process of evolving and consolidating itself.[5] There was also the beginning of conceptualisation of comprehensive security by this time and the incorporation of the new concept into policy programmes. Japan took the lead in this respect and the debate was carried forward into Southeast Asia, which is the principal area of Japan's aid, investment and foreign policy commitments in the developing world.[6] Japan subsequently enlarged upon the concept of "human security" by emphasizing its dual aspects of "freedom from fear and freedom from want".[7] Now Japan's foreign policy documents specifically highlight the country's role in supporting 'human security' efforts all over the world through economic assistance. A Japanese government supported independent Commission on Human Security, co-Chaired by Amartya Sen and Sadako Ogata submitted its report in May 2003, detailing the concepts and approaches to 'Human Security'.

The UNDP Development Report in 1994 sharply focussed attention on nine areas of human security that ranged from food and health security to personal, community and political security. Contrasting state security with human security, the report said:

> For too long the concept of security has been shaped by the potential for conflict between states. For too long, security has been equated with threats to a country's borders. For too long nations have sought arms to protect their security. For most people today, a feeling of insecurity arises more from worries about daily life than from the dread of a cataclysmic world event. Job security, income security, health security, environmental security, security from crime, these are the emerging concerns of human security all over the world.[8]

Europe (particularly the Scandinavian countries and Germany) and international financial institutions like the World Bank and the IMF, also subsequently joined in attaching components of comprehensive security in their respective programmes of developmental assistance. This has also led a number of Western Foundations to encourage, through liberal funding, such studies that went beyond the traditional notion of security and emphasized human and environmental aspects of security as well. In such studies, the focus has particularly been on the developing countries. Special programmes have been designed to generate and analyse data and critically scrutinize various dimensions of human and comprehensive security. Canada is the latest proponent of human security with the emphasis on making this as the principal concern of its foreign policy. The Canadian approach to "human security" seeks to integrate its developmental domain with the military security domain. Thus while accepting economic, environmental and political rights aspects of human security, it also focuses on issues like landmines and humanitarian intervention. Based on the lessons of Kosovo, Canada has been arguing in the UN Security Council "to extend the peacekeeping mandate to include protection of civilians in conflicts".[9] The Japanese established an independent Commission on Human Security has defined the concept in broadest terms, covering almost everything. Its definition of Human Security says:

> To protect the vital core of all human lives in ways that enhance human freedoms and human fulfilment. Human Security means protecting fundamental freedoms—freedoms that are the essence of life. It means protecting people from critical (severe) and pervasive (widespread) threats and situations. It means using processes that build on people's strengths and aspirations. It means creating political, social, environmental, economic, military and cultural systems that together give people the building blocks of survival, livelihood and dignity.[10]

The shift from the traditional concept of security, which emphasized military and political aspects of state security, to comprehensive and human security, which takes into its ambit the economic, developmental, humanitarian and environmental aspects of security, has gained a definite momentum with the end of the Cold War.

The attempts to widen the security agenda were driven by two important strategic developments. One was the decline in the possibility of global wars, at least among major powers. A greater sense of security emerged among the countries of Western Europe, North America and Japan, and in this group, the former Soviet Union also started to be included "once Gorbachev assumed power (there) and embraced an explicit demilitarisation of the Cold War".[11] The second development was the spread of internal ethnic and political conflicts, especially in the developing world. In a way, these conflicts were the results of nuclear deterrence and proxy wars encouraged by the Cold War adversaries. But there was also growing awareness among people all over the world about their expectations and rights vis-à-vis the state. The identity movements that were a reaction to being ignored and ill-treated by the respective states, started getting better organised with the spread of information and awareness as also with the explosion of rising aspirations. Many of these movements became violent and destructive. The Stockholm International Peace Research Institute (SIPRI) began to track the spread of these internal conflicts while American security documents began identifying them as a growing security menace for the world. It was necessary to take into account the causes and consequences of these internal conflicts which led security analysts and researchers to the problems of governance, economic and political discrimination, suppression of cultures and violations of human rights by the states in the process of fighting internal conflicts. Governance, economics, humanitarianism and the environment thus started becoming a part of the agenda of Security Studies.[12]

In the broadening of the security framework, the phenomenon of globalisation has made a significant contribution. Globalisation as a process has increased "human mobility and interaction" tremendously. As a consequence, it has: (a) weakened the boundaries and salience of the state and sovereignty; (b) "ignited identity as a source of conflict" and enhanced sub-state groups and their operations; (c) "anointed the concept of non-physical security" by introducing concerns for the protection of information, technological assets, financial flows, etc., and; (d) diversified threats.[13] The traditional concept of security is not resilient enough to address and to deal with these new dimensions. The thrust of globalisation also includes the expansion of markets and the movement of goods and services. For this, peace and order in the world are preconditions that can be better ensured by de-emphasizing military-related matters. The introduction of social and ecological standards for manufacturing processes and the use of green technologies under globalisation have reinforced the relevance of human and environmental dimensions in security assessment.

The objective conditions created during and after the Cold War for compelling a review and a re-conceptualisation of security cannot be ignored. The events of 9/11 and their aftermath in terms of the global war against terrorism have further sharpened the concern for human security. However, the way in which the traditional concept of security is redefined as human and comprehensive security also deserves closer scrutiny. The broadened definition of security has both conceptual and analytical problems. To begin with, there is considerable incoherence in the various dimensions of broadened definition that include issues ranging from security of trade transactions, information flows, gender equality, child abuse, and good governance to ecological degradation and sustainable development.

> Security as traditionally defined is relatively simple. As more levels of analysis and issues are brought in, the attempt to broaden security becomes increasingly complicated. By specifying referent objects other than the state, security can easily encompass a wide range of things. It is possible to argue that the security of many actors is intimately linked and that it is not profitable to study any given type of actor in isolation but rather as part of a whole. An easy mistake to make is to regard all threats to human well being as threats to security. By taking such a route, it is possible to become hopelessly confused as anything and everything 'bad' becomes a 'security concern'.[14]

Some of those who strongly advocate a widening of the security concept, such as Barry Buzan, acknowledge, "Progressive widening endangers the intellectual coherence of security, putting so much into it that its essential meaning becomes void". Buzan confesses: "I am a widener, but have been sceptical about the prospects for coherent conceptualisation of security in economic and environmental security."[15] Adding to the conceptual incoherence and confusion, the Commission on Human Security says:"any concept of human security must be dynamic. And that is why we refrain from proposing an itemized list of what makes up human security".[16]

Besides the overall incoherence of the newly added dimensions of security, some of the concepts within these dimensions have also become politicised due to frequent usage by leaders and power brokers in their strategies of domestic and international support mobilisation. For example, the concepts of "sustainable development", "good governance", "democracy", "human rights" (individual or collective, political and individual freedom or right to basic needs), etc., may be mentioned in this respect. These concepts are attractive and have acquired a special place in the political lexicon of ruling elites both in the developed as well as developing countries. They also figure prominently in various multilateral resolutions and documents. But about their exact meaning, there is considerable divergence from one leader to another and from one country to another. Their precise contents are also so subjective that their analytical (empirical) and policy relevance have lost meaning.[17] At times, on policy and analytical levels, there are also conflict and incompatibility between one concept and the other of the broadened security framework; such as between "economic growth", "equal distribution of wealth" and "sustainable development".

**Ideological and Strategic Underpinnings:**

Besides its conceptual incoherence, the broadened framework of human and comprehensive security also seems to suffer from a strategic bias. It is unmistakably directed towards the developing countries. Since the developed Western world has ensured welfare, prosperity and social stability for its citizens, it is the state in the Third World that is held responsible for failing to provide required human security to its people. The Third World states are accordingly pressurized to follow the comprehensive security agenda. While the developed states continue to consolidate their military security, the developing states are asked to concentrate on human and ecological security by diverting resources from defence expenditures. For instance, the US has justified its military build-up to fight on two and a half fronts in different parts of the world simultaneously. It can also carry out innovative expansion in nuclear and missile defence, like the development of National and/or Theatre Missile Defence (NMD/TMD). Even under the newly evolved non-proliferation régime of NPT, and CTBT, the recognised nuclear weapon powers have privileges that are denied to others. The message inherent in the calls to the developing countries for lowering defence expenditures, adherence to non-proliferation regime and implementation of comprehensive security agenda is that the developing states should remain confined to their respective territories and peoples, leaving the management of global security to the major powers. And in pursuing such management, intervention may be justified in the name of "humanitarian" causes. We have noted above the Canadian argument for the justification of humanitarian intervention in the interest of human security. This will also restrain any move on the part of any of the ambitious or "rogue" developing states that would disturb the prevailing global power hierarchy and nuclear order.

The expanded security agenda is the result of globalisation and "capitalist expansion".[18] We have noted above the involvement of the capitalist world and associated institutions like the IMF and the World Bank. Taking note of the ideological linkages between capitalism and human security a Pakistani security analyst commented, "discourses about 'human security' play a key role in mystifying the consequences of capitalist expansion as well as in creation of new markets in capital poor countries". She further adds:

> Despite the link between foreign policy and development issues, in the context of human security, donors usually ascribe mal-development to the selfish policies of particular governments, rather than to international structures. Hence when human security issues are promoted, it is with unstated idea that governments have failed and that at issue is governance rather than the binds in which governments find themselves upon taking over.[19]

In this respect, the imposition of social and environmental conditionalities on trade flows and the linking of non-proliferation and arms reduction policies and sanctions with economic aid and technology transfers also need to be recalled. One, however, does not need to stretch the argument of capitalist expansion as the world at large has come to accept this as the only road to development and prosperity, at least in the absence of any other viable alternative.

The question of the imperatives of globalisation for expanded security agenda needs to be looked at carefully. The globalisation imperative clearly underlines the global nature of human security and environmental protection. Then why should the burden of implementing the wider security agenda be put only on the weak and vulnerable states in the developing world? For balanced economic development in the poorer countries, favourable terms of trade, and conditions for smooth flow of capital and technology need to be ensured by the international community. This is not much in evidence even where state transactions are involved.[20] Similarly, with regard to internal identity, ethnic and ideological conflicts, there are globalised networks of support and sustenance in the areas of arms, finances and political backing. While the affected state in the developing world is held responsible for mal-governance, very little is offered by the international community to share the global part of the burden. This is equally true in the field of preserving global ecological balance. In fact, there is hardly any emphasis on the global component of efforts in ensuring the enlarged framework of security. Nobel Laureate Oscar Arias is not off the mark when he says:

> Disparities in the global order create tensions and conflicts that transcend borders. The global neighbourhood offers no sanctuaries. No shelters are available to insulate people from disease, poverty, nuclear holocaust

> or environmental catastrophe. These problems and threats are not individual crises; they are all elements of the great crisis confronting the global neighbourhood. It is a crisis that demands global solutions and global unity. Without these solutions, human security will not be possible.[21]

The protest against globalisation is growing in the developed world. The examples of this protest, i.e., against the G-8 summit held in Genoa (Italy) in July 2001, and at the Mumbai World Social Congress held in early 2004 may be mentioned here. It may be hoped that as such protests gain strength and momentum, the parameters and implications of globalisation on human concerns will start correcting the anti-developing state biases underlying a widened notion of security.

One may like to raise the question here that while the globalised and great power, now single super power-dominated world order impinges so heavily on the Third World State, which is even otherwise inherently weak and has poor resources, it would be unfair to blame that state in the name of failure on the part of human security, at least in terms of developmental dimension. The question is also pertinent here because "human security" failure has come on the global agenda for action and can be seen as providing legitimacy for military intervention. The reflections of this agenda in "humanitarian intervention" as envisaged under the rubric of "responsibility to protect" are clearly evident. We have argued elsewhere that the assessment of a situation, whether it is ripe for humanitarian intervention or not, and how to carry out that intervention lies almost entirely with the dominant powers in the world order.[22] The case of Iraq is the living example and no one is asking the question if Iraq's human security situation has improved or worsened after the US unilateral war. The dimension of the role of world order and external powers in protecting "human security" has been claimed and highlighted, but in violating and vitiating this "human security" is not even being hinted at in the delineation of the concept of "human security".

In view of the conceptual difficulties and inherent bias of human and comprehensive security, it may be advisable to keep in mind two suggestions when operationalising the expanded framework of security. Ayoob offered one when he diagnosed state formation process as the root of insecurity in the Third World. He said:

> I am aware of the link between the political realm and other societal realms, ranging from the economic to the ecological. However, I have adopted the position that issues such as economic deprivation and environmental degradation do not automatically become part of the

> security calculus of Third World states; they do so only when they gain enough prominence to be able to produce political outcomes that can threaten the survival or effectiveness of the states and regimes.[23]

Under the second suggestion, emphasis may continue to be laid on the traditional approach to security while paying due attention to the areas of economic, societal and ecological development separately, for the overall stability and order in a given country or region. Pettiford's conclusion in this respect after a study of Central American security problems is worth keeping in mind here.

> The traditional concept of security does not show itself amenable to stretching. Stretching causes the concept to lose meaning without offering any compensating advantage. Thus rather than redefine security, as traditionally understood, it might be enough to recognise its limitations in terms of when and where it should be applied, and to investigate its linkages to other areas of International Relations. Traditional security could then continue to exist alongside more serious considerations of problems of more serious interest to Third World states, such as environmental problems and survival within the world economy, using non-realist tools of analysis.[24]

The point he is underlining is not the neglect of questions and concerns related to human security, but why they should necessarily be brought, for policy or analytical purposes, under the ambit of security. Such arguments have also been made in relation to the security situation in Asia.[25] If the state is seen as neglecting the human developmental and security aspects, the state should be reprimanded for that and be asked to correct its behaviour. Enlargement of the scope of security studies may not be the logical and effective remedy for this.

### South Asian Security—Persisting and Emerging Concerns:

When we look at South Asian security issues, we find that while these issues have not been unconcerned or unaffected by the broadening of the security agenda, traditional concerns of State security and inter-state conflicts continue to be relevant.[26] There are two important factors that contribute to these persisting concerns, namely, the unresolved territorial issues and the nuclearisation of India and Pakistan. The persisting and protracted conflict between India and Pakistan on Kashmir may be seen as both an icon of the territorial (at least from the Pakistani perspective) conflict as also a flashpoint for a possible future nuclear conflict. There are other unresolved smaller territorial tension points between India and its smaller neighbours. The Sino–India border dispute is being negotiated for resolution, but the settlement may still take years, if not decades. There are also internal conflicts generated by ethnic as well as ideological (left) extremism in Sri Lanka (Tamil Eelam) and Nepal (Maoist rebellion) that directly threaten not only the people's security but also the prevailing status and existence of the respective states. Ethnic insurgencies have also been persisting in India's Northeast region and other parts of South Asia.[27]

South Asia is equally deeply engulfed in human security concerns. All the three principal concerns of human security, namely, security of life and freedom from fear, freedom from want and search for quality of life, and security of environment, are present in South Asia. Loss of life in raging insurgencies like the Maoist rebellion in Nepal and the ethnic war in Sri Lanka has been phenomenal. Communal antagonism has played its ugly role in internal violence in South Asian countries like in India's Gujarat state. Terrorism poses a formidable challenge to almost all the South Asian countries and in combating terrorism, human rights to life and freedom have been seriously curtailed. On the economic and developmental fronts South Asia suffers from widespread poverty, in some countries like Nepal, even exceeding 40%, extremely poor health services, inadequate access to education and poor infrastructure to cope with environmental challenges.[28] The instances in South Asia of poor farmers committing suicide and families selling their daughters for prostitution due to poverty are galore. There are also food riots and hunger deaths. And such instances are not confined to any single country.

The state in South Asia is clearly responsible for its failure in the area of human security. All states suffer from lapses in governance on account of lack of transparency, spread of corruption and absence of clearly defined responsibility towards people.[29] However, the character and inherent structure of state in South Asia must be critically examined to explain these failures. The South Asian region has witnessed the rise of sectarian and undemocratic states in the span of the past several decades. It is the sectarian state that is often insensitive and discriminatory towards the rights of minorities. Sometimes the rise of sectarian forces and tendencies, even without the transformation of the character of the State, poses a challenge to the minorities and excluded people. The autocratic state on the other hand spends more on security forces and remains indifferent to the basic rights of freedom of its people. The point that the sectarian and autocratic states in South Asia have generated threats to human security needs no elaboration. This is not to argue that threats to human security do not exist in democratic and plural states, but in such states, there is greater political and social space as also more effective access to state power to seek redressal.

The States in South Asia are also generally weak and vulnerable to fulfill their developmental obligations towards the people. They suffer from serious resource crunch to undertake massive investments needed to enhance the living standards of the people. In the areas where developmental efforts have advanced, the fruits of development are unevenly distributed due to administrative inefficiency, distorted legal and tax regimes and deep-rooted corruption. Instances of corruption breaching the traditional security structures and institutions of the State are also numerous in South Asia.

No one therefore can ignore or overlook the responsibility of the State in the dismal human security situation in South Asia. But it would be misleading to assume that *only* the State is the culprit in this respect. The external dimension of human security in South Asia also needs to be critically evaluated. The role of international financial institutions in South Asia's poverty alleviation and developmental programs has remained controversial. A Pakistani economist underlines that:

> "Regardless of the economic and political imperatives of adopting IMF structural adjustment programs, the macro economic policies associated with such programs adopted in various forms by South Asian countries have, by and large, had an adverse impact on poverty and income distribution".[30]

In the more recent years, adverse implications of globalisation on South Asia's 'human economy' have also been highlighted. The South Asia Human Development Report 2001, clearly brings out that 'globalisation has integrated markets without enhancing the quality of peoples' lives', it has not helped in 'reduction of poverty' and allowed 'income inequalities to grow', and that global economy has emerged without facilitating the evolution of the institutions of 'global governance'.[31] At a different level, globalisation, through flow of arms, money and drugs across the borders, has also led to the intensification of conflicts and enlarging of human deaths and destruction. The role of international economic forces in the areas of human security in South Asia is growing. A new dimension of this can be seen in the emergence of the donors' clubs, particularly in relation to relief, rehabilitation and reconstruction work in conflict and insurgency affected areas in Nepal and Sri Lanka. These donors' clubs have committed impressive amount of resources, like $4.5 bn in Sri Lanka, but disbursement of such committed resources has been made conditional on the pursuance of the principal donors' specific strategic and economic objective in respective conflicts.

The pursuance of external power's strategic objectives has also led to the strengthening of autocratic and undemocratic regimes in South Asia. The cases of the strengthening of General Musharraf in Pakistan in the context of the "global war on terrorism" and the Monarchy-led Royal Nepal Army in Nepal in the name of containing the Maoist rebellion are obvious examples in this respect. In both the cases, the internal conflict situations have been intensified resulting in further deterioration of the Human Security situation in the respective countries.

This discussion leads us to the conclusion that the challenge of 'human security' in South Asia cannot be met only by action at the South Asian level. The external forces play a critical role in vitiating human security situation in the region and unless action is mounted both at the local as well as external aspects of the problem, we will achieve little in ensuring real security.

## REFERENCES


1. Greg Mills, "The 21st Century Security Agenda: The End of 'Defence' as we know it?" *Strategic Analysis*, April 1997, pp. 173–89.
2. Willy Brandt's report was *North-South: A Programme for Survival; Report of the Independent Commission on International Development Issues*, London 1980. The Palme Commission's report was *Common Security: A Programme for Disarmament; The Report of the Independent Commission on Disarmament and Security Issues*, London, 1982.
3. Richard Ullman, "Redefining Security", in *International Security*, Vol. 8, No.1, 1983; Joseph Nye, "The Contribution of Strategic Studies: Future Challenges," *Adelphi Paper 235*, IISS London, 1989; Jessica Mathews, "Redefining Security", in *Foreign Affairs*, Vol. 68, No.2, 1989, pp. 163–77.
4. Barry Buzan, *People, States and Fear* (Hamel Hempstead: Wheatsheaf, 1983).
5. Mohammad Ayoob, *The Third World Security Predicament: State-making, Regional Conflict and International System* (Boulder: Lynne Rienner, 1995).
6. Robert W. Barnett, *Beyond War: Japan's Concept of Comprehensive National Security*, Washington 1984; Alan Rix, "Japan's Comprehensive Security and Australia", in *Australian Outlook*, Vol. 41, No. 2 August 1987; Noordin Sopiee, "Malaysian Doctrine of Comprehensive Security",

in *Journal of Asiatic Studies*, Vol. XXVII, No. 2, 1984; Muthiah Alagappa, "Comprehensive Security Interpretations in ASEAN Countries" in Robert A. Scalapino, Seizaburo Sato, Jusuf Wanandi and Sung-joo Han (eds.) *Asian Security Issues: Regional and Global*, Research Papers and Policy Studies, No. 26, (Berkeley: University of California. 1988)

7. Statement by Yukio Takasu, at the International Conference on "Human Security in a Globalized World", Ulan Bator, 8 May 2000. http://www.cpdsindia.org.
8. There is a growing body of literature on "Human Security". See for instance, "Redefining Security: The Human Dimension" in *Current History*, No. 94, May 1995.
9. See the Canadian Foreign Minister Lloyd Axworthy's interview in *Jane's Defence Weekly*, www.cpdsindia.org. For the official Canadian Foreign Ministry's paper on "Human Security: Safety for People in a Changing World", see http://www.dfait.maecigc.ca/foreignp/HumanSecurity.
10. Commission on Human Security, UN Publications, May 2003, p. 4.
11. Barry Buzan, "Rethinking Security after the Cold War", Cooperation *and Conflict*, Vol. 32, No. 1, 1997, pp. 5–28.
12. John Chipman, "The Future of Strategic Studies: Beyond Grand Strategy", *Survival*, IISS, London, Vol. 34, No. 1, 1992, pp. 109-31; Ronnie Lipschutz (ed.), *On Security*, (Columbia University Press, New York, 1995). On the environmental dimension of security, see Raimo Vayrynen, "Environmental Security and Conflicts: Concepts and Policies", in *International Studies*, (New Delhi: Sage), Vol. 35, No. 1, 1998, pp. 3–21.
13. Victor D. Cha, "Globalization and the Study of International Security", in *Journal of Peace Research* Vol. 37, No. 3, May 2000, pp. 391–403.
14. Lloyd Pettiford, "Changing Conception of Security in the Third World", in *Third World Quarterly*, Vol. 17, No. 2, London, 1996, pp. 289–306.
15. Buzan, "Rethinking Security After the Cold War", op. cit. Also see Giacomo Luciani, "The Economic Content of Security", in *Journal of Public Policy*, Vol. 8, No. 2, 1989, pp. 151-73, and Daniel Deudney, "The Case Against Linking Environmental Degradation and National Security", in *Millennium*, London, 1990, Vol. 19, No. 3, pp. 461–76.
16. Report of the Commission, 2003, p.4, op.cit.
17. Pettiford, "Changing Conception of Security in the Third World", op. cit. n. 11.
18. Edward J. Amadco and Tariq Banuri, "Policy, Governance and the Management of Conflict" in Banuri (ed.), *Economic Liberalisation: No Panacea*, Oxford, 1991.
19. Saba Gul Khattak, "Security Discourse and the State in Pakistan", in *Alternatives*, Vol. 21, No.3, July–September, 1996, pp. 341–62.
20. Heikki Patomaki, "Good Governance of the World Economy", in *Alternatives*, Vol. 24, No. 1, January–March 1999, pp. 119–42.

21. Oscar Arias, "Economic and Disarmament after the Cold War: Human Security: Our Common Responsibility", in *Disarmament*, Vol. 19, No. 3, 1996. (Reproduced in *Strategic Digest*, July 1997.)
22. See my paper presented at the APISA Conference in Goa, 2003. The revised version of this paper will appear in BCIS Journal, Colombo, 2005.
23. Mohammed Ayoob, *The Third World Security Predicament*, op. cit., p. 190.
24. Pettiford, "Changing Conception of Security in the Third World", op. cit., n. 11.
25. Amiav Acharya and Arbind Acharya, "Human Security in Asia: Conceptual Ambiguities and Common Understandings", A paper presented at the International Conference on 'Beyond the Washington Consensus—Governance and the Public Domain in Contrasting Economies: The Cases of India and Canada', Centre For Studies in Rural and Industrial Development. Chandigarh, February 2001.
26. Navnita Chadha Behra has made a strong plea in favour of widening the security agenda in South Asia by underlining the fact that the hiatus between the people and the state in South Asia is growing fast and that the state modelled on the European pattern cannot serve South Asian needs. See her "Discourse on Security: A Contested Terrain" in her book on the subject. Also the proceedings of Wilton Park (U.K.) Conference on "The New Security Agenda in South Asia", 5–8 July, 2004.
27. Some details have been discussed in the author's IDSS paper. Op.cit.
28. South Asia Human Development Reports prepared by Mahbub-ul-Haq Human Development Centre, Islamabad provides strong data on all these counts. South Asia's human security failure has also been brought out in several studies, particularly IPCS New Delhi and RCSS, Colombo.
29. Akmal Hussain, "Poverty, Growth and Governance in South Asia", in V.A. Pai Panandikar (ed.), *Problems of Governance in South Asia*, (New Delhi: Konark Publishers), 2000.
30. Akmal Hussain, op.cit
31. Remarks made by Devaki Jain at the release function of this report in New Delhi in 2002.

# 4

# Human Security: Poverty Alleviation, Education and Health Services (A Nepali perspective)

***Indrajit Rai***

*"We need another profound transition in thinking—from nuclear security to human security."*

It is the primary duty of every government to provide security to the people it governs. National security is a comprehensive term that entails defending the values the people cherish. What do we, the people of Nepal, cherish as our values that need to be defended. The concept of security has for too long been interpreted narrowly as security of territory from external aggression, or as protection of national interests in foreign policy or as global security from the threat of a nuclear holocaust. It has been related more to nation-states than to people. Similarly, security in the region of South Asia is also defined as "national security", which is concerned primarily with security of territory and the regime. It is concerned with upholding or protecting the integrity of the territory of the state both from external aggression and internal dissension.

The developing nations were sensitive to any real or perceived threats to their fragile identities. Forgotten were the legitimate concerns of ordinary people who sought security in their daily lives. For many of them, security symbolized protection from the threat of disease, hunger, unemployment, crime, social conflict, political repression and environment hazards. Therefore, The important view of security is "Human Security", which is based on wider notions of justice and equity. It is concerned primarily with the improvement of the living standards of the people and their ability to enjoy the fundamental freedoms which are essential for their all-round development.

For most people, a feeling of insecurity arises more from worries about daily life than from the dread of a cataclysmic world event. Will they and their families have enough to eat? Will they lose their jobs? Will their streets and neighbourhoods be safe from terrorism? Will they be tortured by a repressive state? Will they become victims of violence because of their gender?

When we talk about Nepal, perception of threat in mind, Nepal has least possibilities of direct external arms attack but there are maximum chances of threats for the people of Nepal. In other words, Nepal is not secure from internal threats— insurgency, poverty, education and health problems. Nepal is an economically weak and poor country and has its own peculiar types of problems in human security. The people of Nepal are not secure at all. More than ten thousand Nepalese have been killed in the Maoist war in Nepal and nobody knows how many people might be killed in the near future. Human security in Nepal is in a very pathetic condition, because innocent people are being crushed between the government's security forces and the rebels' forces. The security forces and Maoists are violating the rules of human rights. Nepalese people are tortured by both, with the result that every day hundreds of people are migrating from Nepal to India and other foreign countries to live in a secure manner and also to get employment. Recently the world witnessed an event, where twelve innocent Nepalese were brutally killed by Iraqi rebels on 31st August 2004. The Government of Nepal could not do anything for those Nepalese.

If we look at the present status in the health sector of Nepal, we find that tremendous efforts are made to reduce infant and child mortality rates. Significant improvement has been made in basic indicators of human development over the last decade. The life expectancy of males at birth has risen from 55 in 1991 to 60.8 in 2001, while for females the increase has been more dramatic, from 53.5 in 1991 to 61 years in 2001. Under-five mortality was 126 in 1996 and reduced to 91 deaths per 1000 births in 2001.

The almost unbridgeable gulf between the vast majorities of the poor and the ruling establishment is the political reality of South Asia. Their national security perspectives are determined and shaped by these internal tensions and the need to keep these vast majorities of unhappy citizens under control. Almost every state of South Asia is internally unstable. This instability is caused by internal conflict and armed struggles that espouse a variety of causes—national self-determination, elimination of class exploitation and discrimination on the basis of caste and ethnicity. The more these states are forced to adopt hard military measures and do away with democratic institutions, the more difficult it will be for them to change their state-centric national security policies, which bring them into a conflict-ridden relationship with their neighbours.

The new dimension of human security is likely to revolutionize society in the 21st century. A consideration of the basic concept of human security must focus on four of its essential characteristics. Human security is a universal concern. It is relevant everywhere, both in rich and poor nations. There are many threats common to all people—such as employment, drugs, crime, pollution, and human rights violations. Their intensity may differ from one part of the world to another, but all these threats to human security are real and growing.

The components of human security are interdependent. When the security of people is endangered anywhere in the world, all nations are likely to get involved. Famine, disease, pollution, drug trafficking, terrorism, ethnic disputes and social disintegration are no longer isolated events, confined within national borders. Their consequences travel the globe. Human security is easier to ensure through early prevention than later intervention. It is less costly to meet these threats upstream than downstream. Human security is people-centred. It is concerned with how people live and breathe in a society, how freely they exercise their choices, how they make available social opportunities— and whether they live in conflict or in peace.

There is a link between human security and human development: progress in one area enhances the chances of progress in the other. But failure in one area also heightens the risk of failure in the other, and history is replete with examples. Failed or limited human development leads to a backlog of human deprivation—poverty, hunger, disease or persisting disparities between ethnic communities or between regions. This backlog in access to power and economic opportunities can lead to violence. The concept of human security stresses that the people should be able to take care of themselves: all people should have the opportunity to meet their most essential needs and to earn their own living. This will set them free and help ensure that they can make full contribution to their own development and that of their communities, their countries and the world. Human security is a critical ingredient of participatory development. Human security is therefore not a defensive concept—that way it is territorial or military security. Instead, human security is an integrative concept. It is embedded in a notion of solidarity among people. It cannot be brought about through force, with armies standing against armies. It can happen only if we agree that development must involve all people.

**International response to new concept:**

Since the end of the Cold War, the international community has experienced rapid globalization accompanied by the economic liberalization and marked progress of information technology. At the same time, this process has significantly deepened the interdependence of the world; having brought substantial benefits to many people on the one hand and widened the gap between the rich and the poor both nationally and internationally on the other.

Today, as many as1.3 billion people are forced to live on less than one dollar a day. The massive and rapid movement of the people, goods, money and information encouraged transitional problems to spread, including the smuggling of persons, arms and drugs as well as infectious disease. To overcome these direct threats to people, the traditional concept of "state security" alone, whose objective is to protect the boundaries and the people of the state, is no longer sufficient. Indeed, the importance of the state security will not and should not shrink at all, but additional responses are necessary to address diverse threats comprehensively, capturing the inter-linkages among them from a human perspective. "Human Security" is to represent such an aspiration.

Human security aims to protect people from critical and pervasive threats to human lives, livelihood and dignity, and thus to enhance human fulfillment. For these objectives, human security tries to integrate and strengthen initiatives that emphasize human-centred perspectives. Each of us is equal in having his/her own potential and should be respected as a human person regardless of nationality, race, gender and other identities. The development and prosperity of mankind have been sustained with the accumulation of creative ambitions of people themselves. Once their survival, livelihood and dignity is threatened individuals and groups of people can hardly realize their potential and capabilities. Even the future of a society as a whole could be at risk.

To respond effectively to the diverse and interconnected challenges in the increasingly interdependent world, states, international institutions and civil society must integrate their efforts, and build and sustain societies that enhance people's capabilities. This is the goal of the concept of human security.

The 1994 "Human Development Report" by the United Nations Development Programme (UNDP) was the first to mention human security publicly in the international community. This report defined human security as providing safety for the people from hunger, disease, oppression, and other chronic threats as well as protecting them from sudden and hurtful disruptions in the patterns of daily life. In the light of the coming 21st century, the report emphasized the perspective of focusing on the life and dignity of individuals in the context of development.

At the UN Millennium Summit in 2000, the UN Secretary General Kofi Annan presented a report with two keywords: "Freedom from fear, freedom from want", stressing the need to tackle the various global threats. Then Prime Minister of Japan, Yoshiro Mori, declared at the summit that Japan would uphold human security as one pillar of Japan's foreign policy, and called for the establishment of an international commission on human security to further and deepen the concept. Following Mori's proposal, Annan announced the establishment of the "Commission on Human Security" when he visited Japan in January 2001. The commission held five meetings and a number of dialogues throughout the world as well as various researches, and compiled a final report in 2003. The content of report was submitted to Prime Minister Koizumi in February 2003, and the final report was submitted to the Secretary-General in May 2003.

The final report stresses the need for comprehensive and integral actions by the international community. Calling for a paradigm shift of "security" from staying on the narrow state security ideas to extending its focus to include people's perspective. The reports defines human security as "to protect the vital core of all human lives in ways that enhance human freedoms and human fulfillment, and calls for a strategy of "protection and empowerment" to secure people's lives, livelihood and dignity. The Commission arrived at policy conclusions in the following ten areas:

1. Protecting people in violent conflict.
2. Protecting people from proliferation of arms.
3. Supporting the security of people on the move.
4. Establishing human security transition funds for post-conflict situations.
5. Encouraging fair trade and markets to benefit the extreme poor.

6. Working to provide minimum living standards everywhere.
7. According higher priority to ensuring universal access to basic health care.
8. Developing an efficient and equitable global system for patent rights.
9. Empowering all people with universal basic education.
10. Clarifying the need for a global human identity while respecting the freedom of individual to have diverse identities and affiliations.

**The components of human security:**

*"The world will never be secure from war if men and women have no security in their homes and in their jobs."*

There have always been two major components of human security: freedom from fear and freedom from want. This was recognized right from the beginning of the United Nations. But later the concept was tilted in favour of the first component rather than the second. It is now time to make a transition from the narrow concept of national security to the all-encompassing concept of human security.

People in rich nations seek security from threat of crime and drug wars in their streets, the spread of deadly diseases like HIV/AIDS, soil degradation, rising levels of pollution, fear of losing their jobs and many other anxieties that emerge as the social fabric disintegrates, whereas people in poor nations demand liberation from the continuing threat from hunger, disease, and poverty while also facing the same problems that threaten industrial countries.

The concept of security must thus change urgently in two basic ways:

- From an exclusive stress on territorial security to a much greater stress on people's security.
- From security through armaments to security through sustainable human development.

The list of threats to human security is long, but there are seven main categories, as follows:

- Economic security
- Food security
- Health security
- Personal security
- Community security

- Environment security
- Political security.

**Economic Security:**

*"Only about a quarter of the world's people may at present be economically secure."*

Economic security requires an assured basic income—usually from productive and remunerative work or in the last resort from some publicly financed safety net. But only about a quarter of the world's people may at present be economically secure in this sense. Many people in the rich nations today feel insecure because jobs are increasingly difficult to find and keep. In the past two decades, the number of jobs in industrial countries has increased at only half the rate of the GDP growth and failed to keep pace with the growth in the labour force. Young people are more likely to be unemployed in advanced countries like the US and UK. Even those with jobs may feel insecure if the work is only temporary.

One of economic insecurity's severest effects is homelessness. Nearly a quarter of a million New Yorkers—more than 3% of the city's population and more than 8% of its black children—have stayed in shelters over the past five years. London has about 400,000 registered homeless people. France has more than 500,000—nearly 1000 in Paris. The situation is much worse in developing countries. In Kolkata, Dhaka and Kathmandu, more than 25% of the people constitute what is sometimes called a "floating population".

The problems are even greater in developing countries, where open registered unemployment is commonly above 10% and total unemployment probably way beyond that. Again, this is a problem especially for young people: for youth in Africa, the open unemployment rate was above 20%. And it is one of the main factors underlying political tensions and ethnic violence in several countries.

In Nepal, 90% people are dependent on agricultural profession. A Nepali's per capita income is $210, which is much less in comparison with other advanced countries like Switzerland ($44320) and the US ($28,740). All villages of Nepal are devoid of young men and women due to Maoists' insurgency and their unlawful daily activities with the result that all young people are gathered in cities and district headquarters. Only small children and old people are staying in villages and lead a worse life with no production of crops. Most of the development budgets are being diverted to defence for the purchase of defence materials. On the other hand, every day Maoists are destroying several physical infrastructures of millions of rupees. In such circumstances, the economic condition of Nepal is vulnerable.

**Food Security:**

*"People go hungry not because food is unavailable but because they cannot afford it."*

The availability of food is a necessary condition of security—but not a sufficient one. People can starve even when enough food is available. The overall availability of food in the world is not a problem. Even in developing countries, per capita food production increased by 18% on an average in the 1980s. And there is enough food to offer everyone in the world around 2500 calories a day—200 calories more than the basic minimum.

But this does not mean that everyone gets enough to eat. The problem often is the poor distribution of food and lack of purchasing power. Some 800 million people around the world go hungry. A point to be noted is that in South Asia, 30% of the babies are born underweight—the highest ratio for any region in the world and a sad indication of inadequate access to food, particularly for women, who eat last in the household. Similarly, Nepal always faces problems in supplying food to its remote hill districts. During Dasai and Tihar festivals shortage of food materials is reported in several parts of the country. The Government of Nepal has given a contract to Skyline Airways for the supply of rice to those districts by fixing transportation charges at the rate of Rs. 44.90 per kilo. Due to bad conditions of aircrafts, food supply is frequently affected.

**Health Security:**

The world population is going to be more than 6.4 billion and its growth rate is more than 1.2 per cent. If the population growth rate continues at this rate, within a few years the whole population of the world is likely to face critical health problems and starvation. In developing countries, the major causes of death are infectious and parasitic diseases, which kill 17 million people annually, including 6.5 million from acute respiratory infections, 4.5 million from diarrhoea and 3.5 million from tuberculosis. Most of these deaths are linked with poor nutrition and unsafe environment—particularly polluted water, which contributes to nearly one billion cases of diarrhoea a year.

In both developing and industrial countries, the threats to health security are usually greater for the poorest people in the rural areas, particularly children. In the developing countries in 1990, safe water was available to 85 per cent of urban people. In industrial countries, poor and racial minorities are more exposed to disease.

The disparities between rich and poor are similar regarding access to health services. In the industrial countries, on an average there is one doctor for every 400 people, but for developing countries there is 1 for nearly 7,000 people (in Sub-Saharan Africa the figure is 1 per 36,000). Disparities in health spending among developing countries are also marked. The Republic of Korea spends $377 per capita annually on health care, but Bangladesh only $7, and Nepal spends about $5 only.

Women in particular are more vulnerable to such diseases. One of the serious hazards faced by them is childbirth: more than three million women die each year from the problems related to childbirth. Ensuring access to safe and affordable family planning, basic support at home during pregnancy and delivery could prevent most of these deaths.

**Personal Security:**

Perhaps no other aspect of human security is so vital for people as security from physical violence. In both rich and poor nations, human life is increasingly threatened by sudden, unpredictable violence. The threats take several forms:

- Threats from the state (physical torture)
- Threats from other states (external war)
- Threats from other groups of people (ethnic tension)
- Threats from individuals or gangs (crime, streets violence)
- Threats directed against women (rape, domestic violence)
- Threats directed against children (child abuse)
- Threats from nature and accidents (natural disaster and road accidents)
- Threats to self (suicide, drug use).

The personal security of the Nepalese people is always under threat.

The Maoist violence has created such a situation that ordinary people in villages find themselves in a cross-fire between the Maoists and the security forces. Reports of violation of human rights and innocent killings of people have become routine affairs. On an average, 23 people are killed every week in the ongoing conflict that has so far claimed over 10,234 lives, and displaced 34,303 people. The whereabouts of 1,097 persons are unknown, while 124 have been released by the state. The whereabouts of 280 individuals abducted by the Maoists are unknown while 27 have been released. Such figures go on increasing each day as the spree of killing, fleeing and other forms of violence continues.

### Community Security:

Most people derive security from their membership in a group—family, community, organization, racial or ethnic group that can provide a cultural identity and a reassuring set of values. Such groups also offer practical support. The extended family system, for example, offers protection to weaker members, and many tribal societies work on the principle that heads of households are entitled enough land to support their families.

Traditional communities, particularly ethnic groups, can also come under much more direct attack from each other. About 40 per cent of the world's states have more than five sizable ethnic populations, one or more of which faces discrimination. In several nations, ethnic tensions are on the rise, often over limited access to opportunities. About half of the world's states have recently experienced some inter-ethnic strife. And this has been especially serious where national conflict was exacerbated by cold war rivalry.

The restructuring of the country on the basis of community by the Maoists fits well into the spirit of community security. As we know, they have declared nine different regional provinces like Kirat, Magarat, Madeshi, etc. This type of division made on ethnic basis will lead the country to communal disharmony and conflict.

### Threats to Human Security:

Some global challenges to human security arise because threats within countries rapidly spill beyond national frontiers. Other threats take a global character because of disparities that encourage millions of people to leave their homes in search of a better life, whether the receiving country wants them or not. Political insecurity and forced circumstances of all kinds can be added to the list of human security. The following causes seem to be prominent for posing threats to human security:

- Disparities in economic opportunities
- Excessive international migration
- Environmental degradation
- Drug production and trafficking
- National and international terrorism.

The World Summit for Social Development offers a fresh opportunity for the international community to shift its emphasis from territorial security to human security. Endorsing the concept of human security is a key challenge for the 21st century. The following areas are covered by the summit:

- To make full contribution to global human security and to bind together in solidarity.
- Request national governments in rich and poor countries to adopt policy measures for human security.
- Recommend further that today's framework of global institutions be revived and redesigned to prepare those institutions fully for doing their part in tackling the urgent challenges of human security.

### Poverty Alleviation

Poverty is perhaps the most basic cause of the escalation of conflict, violence, clash, depression and disorder in a society. Financial weakness of a person or a state is taken to be the major criterion for defining "poor". Eradicating poverty everywhere is more than a moral imperative and a commitment to human solidarity. Almost all countries committed themselves to this goal at the World Summit for Social Development in1995. Although poverty has been dramatically reduced in many parts of the world, a quarter of the world's people remain in abject poverty.

**South Asia is the most affected region in terms of human security. And it has the largest number of people in income poverty: 515 million and South Asia, East Asia and South-East Asia and the Pacific have more than 950 million of the 1.3 billion people who are income-poor. Within these broad groups some people suffer more than others—particularly children,**

**women and the aged. Children are especially vulnerable—hit by malnutrition and illness just when their brains and bodies are forming. Some 160 million** children are moderately or severely malnourished. Some 110 million are out of school.

There are many Least Developed Countries (LDC) in the world. The definition of Least Developed Country is based on economic parameters. According to the World Bank's definition, the criteria of LDC include per capita GDP of $100 or less, 10 per cent or less share of manufacturing in total GDP, literary rate of 20% or less and the majority of people living on $1 or less a day. In order to uplift a nation from its LDC position, the international community has set a target growth rate of 7.2 per cent in annual growth rate of agricultural production.

Poverty is the greatest enemy of all the poor people. However, financial sufficiency alone is not the only means to erase the poverty tag. Lack of income to attain basic necessities like food, shelter, clothes, health, education, etc. are prime causes of poverty but the following assets remain integral: (*a*) social assets: network relations, reciprocal obligations; (*b*) human assets: good health, capacity for basic manual labour; (*c*) natural assets: land, house, shelter, etc. (*d*) financial assets: saving, access to credit, source of income (e) physical assets: access to infrastructure, machines and tools of production.

Nepal has also set its own Agenda 21 in 2002 in cooperation with Organization for Economic Cooperation and Development (OECD) and World Conservation Union (WCU). It has focused on sustainable income generation, improvement of health, control of population growth and management of migration settlement; promotion of forests, ecosystem and biodiversity; increasing the literacy rate; establishments of institutions and developmental infrastructures; maintenance of peace and security and stable internal government system.

**Poverty Profile and Causes of Poverty**:

The PRSP points out that, in terms of income poverty, at the end of 2001/02, 38% of Nepal's population was below the poverty line; only slightly less than the 42% estimated in the 1996 Nepal Living Standards Survey (NLSS). Most of the poor (90%) live in rural areas. Poverty is also more severe and intense in remote rural areas, especially the mid-Far Western hills and mountains. In 1996 the poverty rate was 44% in rural areas, (compared with 23% in urban areas and only 4% in

Kathmandu Valley); and it was high as 53% in the Far-Western Terai region, even higher (56% in the Mountains and higher still (72%) in the Far Western hills and Mountains. The PRSP also shows that poverty in Nepal is not a matter of low income alone.

It is likely that a significant reduction in poverty has taken place after 1996 even against the backdrop of the conflict. A comparison between the 1996 indicators and the Rural Household Survey 2001, if confirmed by the Nepal Living Standards Survey 2003/04, indicates that poverty may have declined significantly in all regions of the country. This reduction could be explained by at least three reasons. First, Nepal's GDP grew at an average rate of 4.8 % (per capita growth of 2.5%) per annum between 1996 and 2001. Second, agriculture, which is the backbone of the rural economy, grew by 3.7% per annum during the same period. Third is the 30% per annum growth of remittances especially in the second half of 1990s. However, fiscal years 2001/02 and 2002/03 were not favourable for poverty reduction due to negative or low growth, in part caused by the intensified conflict.

The PRSP has identified the following key factors contributing to rural poverty:

- *(i)* The past pattern of economic growth and development has been skewed, urban-centric and inequitable. While the rapid growth in manufacturing, trade and services primarily benefited urban areas; rural incomes improved little over the past two decades, as agricultural growth barely exceeded rural population growth.
- *(ii)* The rural poor had little access to basic social and economic services and infrastructure (education, health, drinking water, and roads). This in turn limited their opportunities for income generation and human development.
- *(iii)* Social exclusion of certain caste and ethnic groups, women and those living in remote areas (from resources, income and employment opportunities and human development) due to a variety of reasons (such as lack of voice, political representation and empowerment and remoteness).
- *(iv)* Poor governance including a weak civil administration, misuse of resources and lack of accountability helped to perpetuate the vicious cycle of under development and poverty.

To mitigate these disparities and to reduce the poverty rate from 38% to 30% by the end of the Tenth Plan (2006/07), the PRSP formulated a closely interrelated four-pillar strategy:

*(i)* Achieving high, broad-based and sustainable economic growth. While promoting faster growth in traditional non-agricultural sectors (such as manufacturing, trade and services), the PRSP seeks to accelerate agricultural growth to increase income, employment and food security in rural areas.

*(ii)* Improving the quality and availability of social economic services and infrastructure (primary education, healthcare, drinking water and sanitation, roads and electricity) for rural communities.

*(iii)* Ensuring social economic inclusion of the poor and marginalized groups by designing and implementing programmes under the first two pillars to serve their needs, and by carrying out targeted programmes for them.

*(iv)* Vigorously pursuing good governance to improve service delivery, efficiency, accountability and transparency.

### Efforts of Poverty Alleviation

The overriding objective of development efforts in Nepal is poverty alleviation. In spite of noticeable progress achieved over the past decade, there is still widespread poverty, with 38% of the population living below the poverty line. Segments of the poor are hardcore poor barely eking out a subsistence on a fragile, vulnerable ecosystem; and large areas of the country lack even the most basic infrastructure. There are also wide variations in poverty levels based on rural–urban divide, geography, gender, and ethnic groups and occupational castes.

Poverty in Nepal has persisted for decades, and it is recognized as a deep-seated and complex phenomenon, for which there are no quick and easy solutions. What has changed particularly over the last decade is the socio-political situation in the country. Following the democracy movement of 1990, people's expectations have risen; but the country and government actions, although successful in many areas, have largely failed to fulfill the expectations of poverty alleviation.

Nepal is currently experiencing a complex socio-political situation, which has intensified over the past few years. It has created considerable insecurity in many parts of the country, making it difficult for the government agencies and development partners to carry out development activities in such areas. The situation also pre-empted a significant and rising share of the government's limited financial and administrative resources for maintaining peace and security in the country. The costs so far are in terms of human lives, destruction of property and infrastructure, increased security expenditures. There are many underlying causes for the present situation, some of which are political and ideological in nature.

The evaluation of the Ninth Plan and the poverty situation clearly demonstrates that past development efforts have fallen behind in meeting the expectations of poverty reduction. Poverty is more widespread particularly in rural areas; and that is deeper and more severe among women, ethnic and dalits, and those living in backward areas—Mid and Far Western and mountain areas. Poverty could not be reduced to a desired level due to the failure to achieve high and sustained broad-based economic growth particularly in rural areas; inadequate human development commensurate with heightened desire and need of the people in large part due to less than satisfactory implementation of public actions to effectively provide essential social and economic services and infrastructure to the poor and backward communities and areas; poor accountability, economic malpractices, and poor implementation and monitoring of development programmes.

The Tenth Plan's campaign against poverty reduction is being launched against the backdrop of a fragile economy. After a decade of fairly robust growth, Nepal's real GDP growth became negative (-0.6%) in 2001/02, for the first time in nineteen years. In part, this has been due to: (a) The global recession and the after-effects of September11, 2001 events (b) More importantly, the present Maoist insurgency has been an even bigger destabilizing factor, through increased insecurity, destruction of physical assets/ infrastructures, bandhs (strikes), loss of working hours and loss of business confidence, among others.

Nepal is caught in a vicious cycle of poverty and economic stagnation at present. Poverty is providing a fertile ground for the disorder, which in turn is pushing the economy into a down spiral, undermining its capacity to vigorously pursue the poverty reduction agenda. The Tenth Plan recognizes that, in view of the existing turmoil, ways and means must be found quickly, despite budget constraints, to effectively implement the development agenda aimed at addressing the underlying causes of poverty and regaining public support and confidence, while concurrently pursuing possible approaches to sustain peace and restore law and order. In this context, the Tenth Plan has formulated an appropriate poverty reduction strategy based on four pillars—to promote faster and pro-poor economic growth, equitable access to social and economic infrastructure and resources for the poor and marginalized groups, social inclusion and targeted programmes and improved governance.

**Six Points for Poverty Alleviation:**

After a long international experience it is found that six important actions are necessary to eradicate poverty in the 21st century, which are as follows:

1. *Empower individuals, households and communities* to gain greater control over their life and resources by:
   - Ensuring their access to assets as a protection against vulnerability. Access to credit and other financial services is vital, as is security of tenure, especially for housing and land.
   - Ensuring food security for households and all their members.
   - Ensuring education and health for all, along with access to reproductive health care, family planning and safe water and sanitation.
   - Building social safety nets to prevent people from falling into destitution and to rescue them from disaster.
2. *Strengthen gender equality* to empower women and to release their vast underused energy and creativity. Poverty eradication without gender equality is impossible and a contradiction in terms. Among key priorities are equal access to education and health, to job opportunities and to land and credit and actions to end domestic violence.
3. *Accelerate pro-poor growth* in the 100 or so developing and transition countries whose economies are growing only slowly, stagnating or declining. A minimum target should be 3 per cent annual per capita growth.

Pro-poor growth is not just growth. It means mainstreaming poverty reduction into national policy-making—easy to say, tough to achieve. It is growth that:

- Restores full employment and opportunity expansion as a high priority of economic policy.
- Creates an enabling environment for small-scale agriculture, micro enterprises and the informal sector.

- Restructures public expenditure and taxation to support poverty reduction and social security.
- Reverses environmental degradation and secures a sustainable livelihood, especially on the marginal lands on which about half the world's poorest people depend for their livelihoods.

4. *Improve the management of globalization,* nationally or internationally—to open opportunities, not close them. Needed are better policies, fairer rules and fairer terms for poor and weak countries to enter markets, especially those for agriculture and textile exports. The aim must be to create employment and avoid a "rush to the bottom". But mainstreaming poverty reduction in international action is difficult even when explicitly required in international agreements.
5. *Ensure an active state,* committed to eradicating poverty and providing an enabling environment for broad political participation and partnerships for pro-poor growth. A strategy for poverty eradication must focus not only on what needs to be done, but also on how to ensure that action is taken. This requires such fundamental reforms as promoting political participation by all, ensuring accountability and transparency in government, preventing the criminalization of politics, promoting a free flow of information and freedom of press and ensuring a strong role for community groups and NGOs in policy-making and legislative decision-making. The legitimacy and strength of the state are based on its capacity to mobilize for fighting poverty.
6. *Take actions for special situations* to support progress in the poorest and weakest countries and to prevent reversal:
   - Conflict prevention and resolution and peace-building efforts in war-torn countries combining political initiatives with support for economic and social reconstruction. Even in a crisis, human development is possible.
   - More effective support for sub-Saharan African and other least developed countries, combining faster action on debt relief, higher priority in aid allocation and a sharper focus in aid on poverty reduction and on achieving education and health for all by 2015.

## PRSP's Key Objectives and Strategy

In the meeting of Nepal Development Forum, which was held in February 2002, His Majesty's Government of Nepal (HMGN) was preparing the Tenth Plan, which is also its Poverty Reduction Strategy Paper (PRSP). The PRSP was finalized in April 2003; and the government has been implementing it over the past one and a half years. This report evaluates the progress achieved so far.

The initial condition for the PRSP's implementation was highly unfavourable. The past two years have witnessed heightened social and political instability and an unprecedented fiscal crisis. Nevertheless, considerable progress has been made to date in many areas, which provides a solid foundation for the future; and it could be argued that, from a technical viewpoint, Nepal is now better positioned to make stronger efforts to reduce poverty, with assistance from development partners.

However, whether these recent achievements can even be sustained, let alone translated into significant progress in reducing poverty, will depend on how well and how quickly Nepal can handle the social, political, and economic challenges, which threaten to engulf the nation. As extensively discussed during the pre-consultation meetings, the continuation of the Maoist conflict and the political standoff pose a major risk to the economy. Investment, economic growth, revenue performance and macroeconomic stability are all likely to be adversely affected; and in the absence of peace and elected local bodies, it will be increasingly difficult to carry out development activities in the rural areas to reduce inequalities and social exclusion (which are seen to be some of the prime causes of the conflict) and to improve service delivery to the poor. Thus, while government intends to expand development activities in rural areas as rapidly as possible, it is equally necessary to seek an early resolution to the conflict and political impasse, if Nepal is to achieve any significant progress in reducing rural poverty over the next few years.

## Social Sector Development

PRSP stresses the importance of human resources development for reducing human poverty and improving the quality of life in rural areas. Education, health, rural drinking water and sanitation are particularly important in this regard. In addition, basic infrastructure such as (even low quality) roads, electricity, and telephone communication can help improve the living conditions for the poor in rural areas. Since the list of factors of social development is quite long, the first two important factors are chosen to be explained.

### Education

Education plays a vital role in human security. A person cannot have personal security and avail of his fundamental rights in absence of education. Education is thus the fundamental right of people and essential for the further enhancement of the quality of humanity. Almost all countries of the globe accept this fact and provide free primary education for the population within 5–9 age brackets. Along with free primary education, compulsory education has been a priority in many developing countries. So far as Nepal's position is concerned in this regard, an experiment with compulsory primary education, which was launched in five districts about a few years ago, faced great difficulties. The controversy of free versus cost-based primary education continues even today.

Violence and disruptions related to Maoists' insurgency have dealt a blow to education. It has literally terrorized the "school" environment, which often becomes the first victim to most "bandhs" and agitations. The future of millions of boys and girls continues to be held in ransom to lingering conflict. The goal of achieving the education target (Education for all) by 2015 depends largely on the effective implementation of government policies. EFA budget for the fiscal years 2004–09 is $815 million. Of this, $480 million (59 per cent) is being spent on recurrent expenditures. The education expert expressed concerns over the quality of education. A total of Rs. 15,616 million had been earmarked for education for fiscal years 2002–04, which secures 15.25 per cent of the total government budget.

The major strategy adopted for improving primary education is decentralization of management of schools by handing them over to school management committees at the local level, which is also gathering dust with increased social insecurity and government's inability to reach insurgency-hit schools across the country. On the other side, several primary schools are being run by the private sector. They are investing a lot in the education sector. The government needs to encourage such efforts by putting in place effective mechanisms. Regarding the private sector's involvement in education, the government has to develop a clear regulatory framework making private and public sector's education complementary to each other.

Guided by the objective of "Education for all", the PRSP aims to improve access to, and quality of, primary education. It also seeks to expand literary programmes (to help improve livelihood of deprived groups, women and disadvantaged children), secondary education, and also vocational/technical and higher education, in order to produce technical and skill manpower. Expanding teacher-training programmes, improving syllabus and teaching materials (through adequate funding and private sector involvement) and strengthening school monitoring and supervision system are also parts of the strategy.

Several initiatives have been adopted recently to implement this strategy: On the basis of the Seventh Amendment to the Education Act, 2001, 724 schools were handed over to School Management Committees (SMCs) by March 2004, along with necessary resources, and responsibilities for school management and hiring of teachers, with oversight and technical support from VDCs and district officers. Another 276 schools will be handed over to SMC by the end of 2003/04. The government intends to further expand this programme to cover one-third of primary schools by the end of the Tenth Plan.

The regular budget in education is being channelled through district development committees, enhancing their involvement. To help improve access to and quality of education and increase student retention, community primary schools are also given block grants equivalent to one teacher's salary, (1911 schools had received this grant by March 2004) which can be used for school improvements. To improve teacher attendance and supervision, the recruitment of teachers will be handed over to communities from the next fiscal years. Steps have been taken to improve access of girls and those from "oppressed and backward communities", for example, providing attendance incentives, basic facilities to such students in private/boarding schools, and setting up a Rural Education Development Fund. These will be supplemented by scholarships (including cost of tuition and subsistence) to girls and to those from deprived communities.

Budget allocations for education have been protected, with about 15% of total public expenditures allocated to the sector in both 2002/03 and 2003/04; while the share of primary education within the sector budget has been raised to 55 per cent in 2001/02 to 9 per cent in both 2002/03 and 2003/04. Even more importantly, a system-wide approach to replicate these initiatives is being adopted through the formation of a strategic five-year "education for all 2004–2009" programme with sectoral and project funding from donors.

After one year of the transfer of management of public school to communities, the Ministry of Education and Sports (MoES) will bring out a regulation on 'School Grant Implementation Regulation 2061' within a month for community schools. The directives will sort out the problems of grants given to community schools. So far 1123 public schools have been transferred to community schools. Earlier, the government used to provide Rs. one lakh for the transfer of school management to communities haphazardly. The directives state that the fund should be utilized for the said purpose only.

The regulation states that the government will provide grants of Rs. 11,000, Rs.13,000 and Rs. 21,000 for the administrative expenditure of primary schools, lower secondary schools and secondary schools respectively and Rs.300, Rs.500 and Rs.500 under miscellaneous expenditure for their teachers. The "block grants" include Rs. 53,000, Rs. 66,300 and Rs. 97,500 for primary, lower secondary and secondary school respectively, under the special support programme, Rs. 50,000 for the community schools run by NGOs, Rs.3000 for educational improvement in each primary school and Rs. 100 per primary student for stationery. Earlier, the government used to provide Rs. 24 million for the non current cost per school, while this year, the MoES is providing Rs 60 million focusing on per school and per student, besides the non current budget.

**Health:**

The overeaching goal of the development efforts in Nepal is poverty reduction. Improving the health and longevity of the poor is an end in itself and the fundamental goal of economic development, health is considered as the central feature of development. The linkage of health to poverty reduction and to long-term economic growth is much stronger. The health sector can contribute significantly to poverty reduction by avoiding and controlling the diseases, protecting the life of the people and their income, and by providing healthy human resources for economic development.

Along with education, the health sector is of critical importance for reducing human poverty, improving the quality of living in rural areas and mainstreaming marginalized groups and communities. Although there have been significant improvements in health indicators over the past decade, the health system is not adequately meeting the needs of the rural population, especially those of the most vulnerable groups and distant areas. Progress in this area is also vital for the attainment of Millennium Development Goals, since four of the 18 MDG targets (child mortality, maternal health, HIV/AIDS and malaria and other major diseases) fall within health sector.

Nepal has faced growing popular demands for the extension of health services in rural areas. The key sector-wide objectives include: extending essential health care services to all, with special emphasis on the rural poor, expanding maternal and child health and family planning services particularly for the rural population, and ensuring effective control of communicable diseases (such as malaria, tuberculosis and HIV/AIDS). To achieve these objectives, a range of programmes/activities is being undertaken: construction of 250 new sub-health posts to increase access; local recruitment, adequate staffing and training of health workers; expanding supply of drugs and medicines to improve the quality of services; expanding maternal, child health and immunization programmes; strengthening health planning, supervision and monitoring mechanisms, among others.

Significant changes have been noticed in the coverage of health care services. Vaccination coverage has improved significantly over the last ten years. The percentage of children aged 12–23 months who have been fully immunized by twelve months of age increased from 37.2 in 1991 to 60.1 in 2001. Most of the gain was achieved from 1996 when coverage increased from 43 per cent. Between 1996 and 2001, coverage with all three doses of DPT increased from 51 to 71 per cent of children. The contraceptive prevalence rate also increased to 38.9 per cent in 2001 from 24.1 per cent in 1991. The incidence of malaria decreased from 115 in 1992 to 29 in 1997 per 100,000 populations. The case finding rate of tuberculosis improved considerably from 92.3 in 1995 to 106 per cent per 100,000 population in1998. Cure rate of TB/DOTS reached 95 per cent in 2001. The higher case finding and cure rates of tuberculosis indicate the effectiveness of the programme. The incidence of diarrhoea fell considerably in the last decade to 2.3 per child per year episodes in 2000 from 3.3 in 1990.

Now I would like to explain some national policies and plans of the Health Department of Nepal. The National Health Policy was adopted in 1991(FY 2048BS) to bring about improvements in the health conditions of people of Nepal. The primary objective of the National Health Policy is to extend the primary health care system to the rural population so that they benefit from modern medical facilities and trained care providers. In the year 1997, the government developed a 20-year Second Long Term Health Plan for (1997–2017). The aim of the SLTHP is to guide health sector development for the improvement of the health of those whose health needs are not often met. Its targets are as follows:

- To reduce the infant mortality rate to 34.4 per thousand live births
- To reduce the total fertility rate to 3.05
- To increase life expectancy to 68.7 years
- To reduce the crude death rate to 6 per thousand
- To reduce maternal mortality rate to 250 per hundred thousand live births
- To increase total health expenditures to 1 per cent of total government expenditures.

The first two years of the Tenth Plan added momentum in implementation of a second long health plan, 1998 envisaging self-reliance, gender sensitivity, decentralization, good governance, community participation and partnership with the private sector. Although the average life expectancy of Nepalese today has reached 61.9 years and other health indicators are also showing satisfactory results, as per the Millennium Development Goals (MDGs) and Tenth Plan, the following issues and challenges have been found to achieve the objectives of the Tenth Plan, namely, safe motherhood (maternity health), malnutrition, neonatal health HIV/AIDS and other infectious diseases, etc. advancement of traditional medicine and technology with research, production and distribution are the key issues in the field of traditional medicine.

There are many areas where coordination is necessary to improve the health status of the population. The coordination might be at the community level, at the central/regional level, among HMG/N and External Development Partner (EDP) level. However, for the present, the only major responsibilities that needs to be addressed by HMG/N and the EDP are given below:

- Safe motherhood
- Malnutrition
- Neonatal Health
- Child health

- HIV/AIDS and other infectious diseases
- Strengthening Management.

His Majesty's Government of Nepal can carry out :

- Formation of new health policy and legislation
- Improved service delivery including referral system
- Decentralized management of health institutions
- Improvement of supply system
- Displaced people's health.

HMG/ Nepal along with EDPs can carry out:

- Implementation of essential health care package
- Development of human resources for health
- Essential equipment and instruments
- Essential drugs and other medical supplies
- Capacity building for health financing
- Behaviour change communication
- Establishment of geriatric health services
- Addressing global emergencies
- Production, distribution and use of traditional drugs.

In the final analysis, human security is a child who did not die, a disease that did not spread, a job that was not cut, an ethnic tension that did not explode in violence, a dissident who was not silenced. Human security is not concerned with weapons, it is concerned with human life and dignity. On the other hand, when the international community today is worried about the huge stockpiles of weapons and nuclear bombs in the hands of India and Pakistan and feels that this has made the region one of the most dangerous places in the world, for the poor of the sub-continent it is the iniquitous system of governance that represents the real threat to their lives.

It should be pointed out that there is no contradiction between national security and human security. Human security wants to broaden the horizon and concerns of security. It does not call for dismantling of the defence apparatus nor does it recommend that the borders be abandoned to hostile claims. Human security seeks a balance between investment in defence and welfare. It also seeks changes in the nature of governance and politics so that the people have a better chance to enjoy the fruits of freedom and democracy. It is also necessary to point out that the higher the level of human security, the better is the stability of the polity. In fact, the enlightened self-interest of the ruling elite dictates that they should invest more in human security for reasons of their own survival.

## REFERENCES

1. Human Development Report 1994, the United Nations Development Programme (UNDP).
2. Human Development Report 1997, UNDP.
3. National Planning Commission (NPC), Poverty Reduction Strategy Paper 2002–2007.
4. Annual Report 2059/60, Department Health Services, HMG, Nepal.
5. National Planning Commission, UNICEF and New Era. Nepal Multiple Indicators Surveillance Cycle 1, NPC, Kathmandu, Nepal 1995.
6. Ministry of Health. Public Expenditure Review of the Health Sector 2003.
7. Ministry of Finance. Economic Survey, fiscal year 2002/03.
8. Ministry of Education—A Report, His Majesty's Government of Nepal.
9. Ministry of Health—New Era and ORC Macro. Nepal Demographic and Health Survey 2001. Calverton, Maryland, USA.
10. Ministry of Health. Second Long-Term Health Plan 1997–2017.
11. Health Sector Strategy: An Agenda for Change, Kathmandu-2002.
12. National Planning Commission and UN system–progress report of Million Development Goals, Kathmandu, Nepal 1995.
13. Ministry of Population and Environment. Review of Population Policy in Nepal.
14. Ministry of Health—Nepal health sector programme implementation plan 2003–07.
15. Redefining poverty of Nepal—*The Kathmandu Post*, 12th August 2004.
16. The cost of primary education—*The Kathmandu Post*, 3rd August 2004.
17. Research in education—*The Himalayan Times*, 17th August 2004.
18. Education and WTO—*The Himalayan Times*, 21st July 2004.
19. Educated unemployment challenge—*The Rising Nepal*, 9th May 2004.
20. SAARC standards for educational reform. *The Kathmandu Post*, 21st May 2004.
21. Progress report on Poverty Reduction—an assessment of the Tenth Plan, NPC, Nepal.
22. Poverty Monitoring and Analysis System—Framework Document, NPC, Nepal.
23. Asian Development Project, Appraisal of integrated rural development projects in Nepal (Sagarmatha IRDP) November 1978.
24. Gurung, Sant Bahadur. Rural development approaches in Nepal: some experiences. (Kathmandu: DEVA Publication, June 1998).
25. ISD. A study on the status of human poverty concerns at Sub-level

regional. (Kathmandu: NPC/UNICEF, 1998).

26. CBS (2002), Population Census 2001: National Report, CBS and UNFPA, Kathmandu.
27. ICIMOD (1997), Districts of Nepal: Indicators of development, ICIMOD Kathmandu.
28. Panday, Devendra Raj (1999), Nepal's failed development: Reflections of the mission and maladies, (Kathmandu: Nepal South Asia Center).

# 5

# Globalisation, "Glocalisation" and South Asian Insecurity

**B. Ramesh Babu**

> "Inside every thinking Indian there is a Gandhian and Marxist struggling for supremacy." —*Ramachandra Guha*

Globalisation has been the buzzword on the world scene for nearly two decades. A wide variety of definitions and conceptualizations of the phenomenon is in circulation. While most use the term approvingly, some condemn it as a euphemism for the global capitalist economic integration "imposed by the West on the rest" of the world. Over the past decade the early euphoria over globalization—the end of the sovereign nation state and the imminent emergence of a global community—has lost much of its shine and substance. The reality as always is far more complex and multi-directional than what the early pro-globalisers made it out to be. However, this much is clear that the radical transformation underway since the mid 1980s comprises a paradigm shift in world affairs. How this massive and ongoing change is diagnosed and conceptualized, perceived and projected naturally varies from observer to observer depending upon his/her nationality, ideology and personal predilections. A leading expert on international relations like James N. Rosenau, for example, says that human affairs have become ever more complex and interdependent and policy makers today are confronted with circumstances "much more diffuse, multiple and uncertain" than ever before. He sees a lot of "turbulence" in world politics and a number of "globalizing and localizing" tendencies operating simultaneously. He conceptualizes the process as "fragmegration", a clever coinage for the dual transformation underway, i.e., fragmentation and integration of the State at the same time.[1]

Samuel Huntington sees "a clash of civilizations" in the radical transformation sweeping the globe. Francis Fukuyama anoints liberal democracy as the final form of good governance humans could devise. He foresees its spread all over the world and then, the earth would be blessed with peace and prosperity because liberal democracies do not fight one another! Kenneth Waltz, on the other hand, argues that globalisation is a fad of the 1990s with the "made in America" stamp all across. Thomas Friedman contends that globalisation is a process shaped by markets, not governments. Globalisation means homogenization and the message is clear: "conform or suffer". The underlying driving force is the hidden hand of the free market at work, according to Friedman. Waltz disagrees vigorously and asserts that globalisation is neither inevitable, nor inexorable. He adds, "that America's hidden fist is in full view." What is new in the world today, "is not interdependence of states, but their growing inequality," Waltz points out.[2]

A critical analysis of what globalisation is and what it is not, what are its causes and consequences will necessarily be a prolonged exercise.[3] For our purposes here, globalisation may be defined as the seemingly double-headed phenomenon of supra-national integration and sub-national disintegration transforming the post-Cold War world radically and irrevocably. In reality, these two trends are mutually reinforcing and constitute a single, complex continuum of change. Obviously, the contemporary transformation comes on top of the secular trends of transition away from the state centric international system in the works for a long time. Let us turn our attention to the major constituents of supra-national integration.

## Supra-National Integration

1. National Security. The first and foremost task of all countries is to protect themselves, preserve their territorial integrity and national identity. Ironical as it may seem, as nations became more powerful and acquired more and deadlier weapons, they became more dependent on other countries for their own self-defence and security. During the Cold War era the Big Two indulged in a mad arms race and acquired ever more lethal nuclear arsenals (atom bomb, hydrogen bomb, cobalt bomb, biological and chemical weapons.) In their anxiety to ensure their own "national security", they also built rockets and missiles to deliver their awesome weapons ever more accurately over longer

distances till the whole planet was covered. Both the Super Powers were able to deter the other through Mutual Assured Destruction (MAD! an appropriate acronym). Even after the demise of the Soviet Union and its own emergence as the mightiest nation in human history, the US feels insecure! The nation has embarked on an astronomically expensive global network of anti-missile-missile system operating from outer space, despite its doubtful efficacy. Yet, the US anxiously seeks the cooperation of other nations to ensure its own security.

2. Ideological Polarisation. After the collapse of communism and the demise of the Soviet Union, centrally planned command economy lost its appeal and credibility as a model of development in Asia (and elsewhere). It seems as though capitalism had won by default. While this is not necessarily a logical way of assessing the merits of a system, privatization, liberalization and globalisation have become the new mantras of growth (and development) the world over.[4] Consequently, the long-standing American objective of restructuring major national economies along capitalist lines and integrating them into a global free market under its auspices has regained an extra edge of persuasiveness. Marketisation of economics and globalisation of markets are the new mantras. Most countries all over the world are taking the capitalist path to growth and salvation. Ironically, Russia and the former communist states of Eastern Europe and China are adopting capitalist ways and market mores with a gusto of the proverbial new converts. Consequently the extent of supra-national economic integration effected today is unprecedented in history.

3. The UN and International Organizations. It is fashionable to scoff at the UN and wax eloquent on the inefficacy of the universal international organizations. But, the world has been integrated to such an extent that we cannot do without them. In fact, the UN and the large number of specialized agencies under its banner materially affect our daily lives and welfare of the member states to a degree we do not realise. Even the mightiest nation in human history, the US is realizing that it needs the UN to get out of the bloody mess it got into by invading Iraq against the will of the world body and overwhelming global public opinion!

4. International Law. Violations of international norms and acts of defiance of international law by nation states make news and usually get wide publicity in the media. However, the massive reality on the ground is that most nations comply with most of the rules and regulations of international law most of the time! Otherwise they would be engulfed

in endless quarrels and conflicts on all borders between all states. Water wars would make blood flow instead of rivers; airplanes would collide in mid air; none of us could watch the TV or listen to the radio; trade and commerce would grind to a halt; in short, there would be utter chaos in the world. A world without international law is simply beyond the realm of imagination.

In this context, it is good to refer to the Law of the Sea Treaty, Kyoto Protocol, and International Criminal Court. Each one of them represents a historic advance in the role and reach of international law on the seas (and what lies underneath), global warming and criminal acts against human rights. There is no need to elaborate on their significance to the globalising world of ours.[5]

5. IT and Media. Revolutionary advances in IT and media of communications have made all nations and all people everywhere neighbours of one another, whether they like it or not. When Marshall MacLuhan talked of "the Global village" in the early 1960s, it was an aspiration or at the most a projected destination for the world. Today it is a living reality, nay a virtual reality. This certainly is the most far-reaching form of supra-national integration—a phenomenon hardly imagined possible even two decades ago. Individual nations have lost control over their airwaves and the skies above them virtually completely.

6. Environment and Ecology. International interdependence and supra-national integration are most pronounced in the realm of environment and ecological balance of planet Earth. Human activity and greed, man's scientific, technological prowess and his unwisdom are threatening the future of the planet. The patterns of consumption in the rich countries of "the West" and their hegemonic demonstration effect on "the rest" of the world are so powerful and profound that unless moderated, the "progress" and "advances" of the earthlings will "exhaust" the planet into cosmic oblivion.

7. International Terrorism. The scourge of terrorism is the latest threat that is scaring the world to come together. This is not the place to dilate on the classic quarrel about your terrorists vs. my freedom fighters. The compellingly tragic danger of terrorism illustrates the very high degree of international interdependence and demands an equally great extent of supranational integration to fight it effectively. Suddenly "September 11" dramatized the threat immeasurably and the vulnerability of even the mighty US. Terrorism is now a global menace par excellence.

8. Americanisation of Culture. This certainly is a powerful source of supra-national integration. The United States of America has always

exerted an "imperialism of attraction" over the rest of the world. The revolutionary changes in the IT and media of communications have enhanced the role and reach of the magnetic influence of America's life styles, conceptions of happiness, rights and duties, roles of men and women. Moreover, the very perception of the success of "the Americanization of the World" adds to its appeal and efficacy.[6]

## Sub-National Disintegration

Let us now turn our attention to the major constituents of sub-national disintegration of the State and the emergence of multiple challenges to its primacy from within.

1. Declining National Consensus. Nations are forged out of humiliations suffered in common and victories shared by a people. The struggle for "Home Rule" unites people and promotes the feeling of oneness among them. However, competition and quarrels over "who will rule at home" inevitably divide, subdivide and regroup the people in novel ways. The Nehruvian national consensus and the pervasive sense of shared views on most issues at home and abroad lasted for nearly two decades after India's independence. Non-alignment abroad and "socialist pattern" of society at home were the ruling doctrines for long. But, gradually, the Nehruvian national consensus was eroded. Even secularism has become a contentious issue. Liberalization, privatization and globalisation became the new mantras by the late 1980s. Now, these in turn are being questioned and subjected to modifications and rethinking, especially since the elections of 2004. The important point is that no new national consensus has emerged instead.

2. Democratic Exclusion. While a variety of forces and factors led to the erosion of national consensus, the very philosophy inclusion underlying the self-governing process, ironically, has become a key source of sub-national disintegration. At a time when most other newly independent nations of Asia and Africa were wary of the implications and consequences of liberal democracy's fundamental principle that all citizens are equal before the law, India under the leadership of Nehru took the plunge and adopted universal adult suffrage as the governing principle. Accordingly, the people are supposed to rule themselves, which means that all the people together constitute the decision-making unit. In operational terms this means that the people as a body take a joint decision by consensus or by a majority vote of the representatives.

Since cohesion cannot always be ensured and reciprocal commitment to listen to each other with sincerity and the integrity of the dialogue process cannot be sustained over the long haul, the majority has to prevail and the minority has to yield. Naturally, the defeated sub-groups feel that their voices are not heard and their feelings are not taken into consideration. The sub-group, the caste, community, women, dalits, bahujan, etc. justifiably feel excluded. In the long run, different sub-groups go through this experience of being excluded at different times. There are as many varieties of democratic exclusion as there are sub-groups.[7] Inevitably, in a vast country like India with its teeming millions and multiple identities, the pains of exclusion are numerous, sizeable and recurring. Often excluded sub-groups demand greater autonomy, the right to control their own affairs. Sometimes this feeling of exclusion and injustice leads groups to demand and agitate for their own states. There is no need for me to document that all this and more is happening in India right now. Jammu and Kashmir, Assam and the Northeast, Naxalites and Peoples War Group in several states, and the Khalistan movement of the recent past are proof enough. I think such a process of systemic exclusion and the concomitant demands for "self-rule" by diverse groups are not uncommon in other South Asian states.

3. Unfulfilled Expectations. Once the accursed and exploitative foreign rule is overthrown, it was widely believed in Asia and Africa, that people would rule themselves and all would be well. Everybody would have enough to eat, clothes to wear and a roof over his head. Peace and prosperity, harmony goodwill would descend on the land soon! It must be added though that a certain degree of romanticism is integral to any freedom struggle. But, what followed in India after Independence is disappointing beyond the usual. Even after five decades of self-rule, people of India (and the other countries in South Asia) are among the poorest on earth! A majority of people in rural areas do not have drinking water. Sanitation and public health are woefully inadequate. Starvation deaths and suicides by farmers are daily happenings. India has the distinction of having the largest number of illiterate people in the world. There is no need to statistically substantiate the widespread poverty, destitution and misery stalking the land.

After the stalwarts of the Freedom Struggle disappeared from the scene, the tradition of sacrifice for the country declined and the initial wave of idealism waned. Men of lesser calibre, lesser commitment and far lesser integrity came to the fore. Champions of this or that section or caste, community, religion emerged out of the electoral process.

Political participation of people belonging to all communities, castes, sub-castes, and their mobilization by interested individuals and organizations reinforced one another. Such awakening and mobilization of the lower castes and hitherto marginalized groups is most desirable. In the process Indian polity has become more democratic. But, this has also led to the "black lash" of the upper castes.

Furthermore, the "international demonstration effect" made the less than adequate performance of the successive governments in New Delhi and the States seem worse than the reality on the ground. Thanks to the revolutionary advances in the media, especially the TV, people in India (and other countries in South Asia) vividly see how well people elsewhere in the world live. They are angry and restless because even their modest expectations—the very basic needs of food, livelihood, shelter, sanitation and drinking water—are not met. In their eyes the main culprits are "the rascals in power"!

4. Corruption and criminalisation. Abuse of power, corruption and nepotism, criminalisation of politics; and politicization of crime are playing havoc with public life. They are the key causes behind the non-accountability of governments at all levels across the country. Corruption and bribery, nepotism and fraud are not new to India. But their scale and scope, depth and spread today are literally mind-boggling. As the public outlays on development and welfare, poverty alleviation and upliftment of the poor have grown immensely; the scope and scale of corruption have also increased phenomenally. The coming in of the global MNCs and the FDIs in the wake of liberalization and privatization pushed the scale of corruption to high heavens! The sixty-four crore Bofors scandal of the Rajiv Gandhi era looks like a petty theft compared to the scores of mega scandals that followed. Pervasive corruption is certainly the cancer of contemporary India. Hopefully, the other countries of South Asia do not suffer from this affliction to the same extent.

5. Sub-National Identities. Since the mid 1980s we see an ethnic upsurge all over the world, a renaissance of sub-national identities. The ever mercurial dynamic of "we" and "they" has come to the fore again and narrower and narrower identities and loyalties are on the rise. They are challenging and eroding the all-India or national identity. More and more regions are demanding a state of their own. Chhattisgarh, Uttaranchal and Jharkhand seem to be only the beginning of another wave of redrawing the internal boundaries in our country. Agitation for separate Telangana, Vidharbha, Gorkhaland, Rayala Seema,

and so on are pointers of things to come. In fact, Telangana formation figures in the Common Minimum Programme of the Congress-led UPA Government. Many non-territorial identities like caste, religion, language, socio-cultural congruities are on the rise and are also being mobilized for empowerment, autonomy and freedom. The tribals spread across Andhra Pradesh, Chhattisgadh and Orissa have a longstanding demand for a separate state of Dandakaranya!

## "GLOCALISATION"

Since the 1980s, a variety of new cross-border linkages that transcend or straddle the conventional demarcation of **inter-national** and **intra-national** affairs are emerging. These can be grouped, for analytical convenience, as global to sub-national, national to sub-national, and local to local connections across the oceans. These new linkages are being forged at the governmental and non-governmental levels, and also as a varying mix of the two. The dual transformation (i.e. supra-national integration and sub-national disintegration) discussed earlier and new linkages to be analysed below together are conceptualized here as "glocalisation". The Japanese used the term "global localization" for their strategy of global marketing, i.e. adapting the global outlook to the local marketing conditions all over the world.

1. Global to Sub-National Linkages. In the wake of the global ideological shift rightward since the mid 1980s, the World Bank and the IMF have been promoting "free market capitalism" more vigorously than ever before. They have been pushing "structural adjustment" (i.e., capitalist reconstruction) down the throats of the developing countries in Asia, Africa, and Latin America. In the areas of cutting down subsidies, public sector disinvestment (especially in the power sector), downsizing governments and in good governance, the World Bank has taken initiative in giving "advice and assistance" to a number of countries around the world, including India. Consequently, there is a fairly widespread resentment against the "conditionalities" being imposed at the price of getting loans and grants. There are accusations of secret deals and corruption in high places. The cases of Andhra Pradesh and Maharashtra (i.e., Enron) are noteworthy in this context. The merits of the cases apart, the fact that the global agencies are *in effect* dealing with the sub-national units (i.e., the State governments) directly is indicative of the growing phenomenon of glocalisation. What a householder, farmer, urban/rural consumer pays for a unit of electrical

power is influenced to a great extent (if not determined), by the World Bank officials!

Such "intervention" by outsiders (global agencies or big powers) would have precipitated a national crisis in India (or elsewhere in South Asia) even ten years ago. The fact that a global body's close interaction with a sub-national constituent directly (in effect) and on a continuing basis became acceptable demonstrates the extent of the transformation that had taken place in the global context. Andhra Pradesh and Maharashtra are illustrative of the economic and political issues involved in the reform process sweeping the globe. Such interplay of populist politics and prudent fiscal management is essentially the same in the other states of India (and for that matter in all the developing countries where people elect their governments.)

2. Sub-National Linkages across the globe. Rich and powerful countries always do their best to forge and nurture connections with the diverse segments and opinion leaders in as many countries as possible on a sustained basis. Constraints of resources, skills and range of goals rather than intentions impose limits on the activities of nation states in this regard. For example, it is a long-established tradition of American foreign policy that the US must be ever ready to do business with the "next government in all the countries" world over.[8] To this end the country utilizes its strengths of democracy, freedom, multi-ethnicity and pluralism to the full to gain access to the governmental and civil society leaders in foreign countries. Such "public diplomacy" is legitimate (up to a point) and in the long run fairly effective in influencing the public opinion and popular preferences in other countries. Sub-national units, (States, regions and local governments) all over the world are equally anxious to forge direct links with the people and their counterparts especially in the rich countries of the West. The State Chief Ministers (and heads of governments at lower levels) go on promotional tours to "sell" their states, regions, and cities abroad so as to attract investments and increase trade and commerce by offering incentives and inducements. People of Indian origin living in these countries are specially targeted in this context. Such linkages, obviously, cannot be reciprocally equal in either their extent or significance. What is important for our purposes is their vibrant presence and potential for growth and expansion. In the process the new linkages are transforming the content and the context of global reality irreversibly.[9]

3. Local to local linkages across the Seven Seas. Traditionally the only ties cities across countries used to have were the ornamental ones

called "Sister Cities". Of late more meaningful and significant linkages are being developed and sustained at the local level across countries and continents. NGOs, citizen activist groups, professional associations and even individual mega donors (say Bill Gates) have become active and command ever-growing resources (of men, material and money) in furtherance of their chosen cause or favourite goals abroad.

Much of this activity goes on whether the national or state governments like it or not. Narmada Bachao Andolan led by Medha Patkar, who has become a global icon fighting for the rights of the marginalized and the dispossessed, can be cited as a good example. Her protracted and continuing agitation to protect the human rights and the ancestral property rights of the tribals and other evacuees is an exemplary initiative in defence of "human security" "justice and equality before the law." This is not the place to assess the overall merits of the Narmada High Dam, dilemmas like the rights of several hundred oustees vs. the development of the sate or the environmental hazards involved. What is of relevance for us is the fact that "a local" agitation caught the attention of the world and a complex set of linkages got activated. Consequently, the Japanese Government backed out and prevailed upon the Asian Development Bank to withdraw its financial support. Such "local" agitations often are suppressed and do not gain the global attention they deserve. That the Gujarat Government had gone ahead with the High Dam and is in fact bidding for raising its height is illustrative of an altogether different dimension of governance in India (and elsewhere). The ruling power structures in most countries are usually not responsive to the concerns and anxieties of the poor. This issue will be discussed later in the context of the South Asian insecurity induced by globalisation and glocalisation.

Thousands of NGOs, mostly based in the rich Western nations have inspired the mushrooming of their counterparts in the developing countries all over the world. Such imitation and followership of the West (especially the US) is integral to the "copycat culture" pervasive in most aspects life and work in the Third World countries in general. Whether the issue or concern is the eradication of leprosy or HIV/AIDS, fight against abuse of children or gender discrimination, pollution control or ecology, R&D in non-conventional energies, electoral reform or good governance (you name it), the NGOs and citizen activists, and interest groups are taking the lead. Funds, know-how and experts from the Western and rich nations link up with the "elites" and upper class groups and leaders in the poor countries of Asia and Africa. Any number of examples can be cited from all over South Asia in what is loosely dubbed as "civil society". The relief work done by UNHCR, Red Cross, Oxfam and an Italian Relief agency with respect to the "internal refugees" in Sri Lanka, for example, raised a host of issues of national sovereignty, import of Western values and norms into the relief work, and mutual distrust and tension between the host country and the "foreign" relief agencies.[10] Here again the purpose is not to go into the merits of the case, but to highlight the thriving presence of such local to local linkages across the seven seas and their growing significance at the grassroots level in the host countries. Often governments in the recipient countries are at their wits' end to distinguish between the legitimate and not so legitimate activism of the citizen groups and segments of the civil society promoting their causes abroad. It was alleged that Sangh Pariwar outfits in Gujarat received such "foreign" funds.

4. International Terrorism. This is the newest local to local linkage of lethal significance for the world as a whole. India has been the victim of cross-border terrorism in Punjab, Jammu and Kashmir and the Northeastern states for over two decades. The terrorist groups from outside exploit the local resentments and Government of India's acts of omission and commission. The terrorist outfits also raise much needed funds from sympathetic foreign governments and people of their origin settled in rich countries abroad. Sri Lanka's LTTE is certainly one of the most successful of such organizations in raising funds to sustain its operations for decades. In the case of Islamic fundamentalism, not only funds and weapons, but also trained and motivated recruits come from foreign countries. Furthermore, it is extremely difficult to keep apart international terrorism and armed struggles and organized violent groups operating at home. As recently as in the second week of September 2004, Maoists of Nepal issued posters warning the Government of India that if it interfered in the internal affairs of their country (by giving arms to the King or shoring up the regime militarily) they would spread the armed struggle to India. This coincided with Prime Minister Deuba's State Visit to India seeking New Delhi's help in meeting the challenge of the Maoists! At the same time a contingent of the Nepalese Police arrived in Andhra Pradesh for training in counter insurgency operations even as the Government is embarking on negotiations with the PWG and Janashakti naxalites in the state. On the very day of the Maoist warning, India's Cabinet Panel on the Naxalite issue met in New Delhi. The Chief Minister of Andhra Pradesh, Chhattisgarh, Orissa, Bihar and

Madhya Pradesh were called to Hyderabad for an urgent meeting on 21st September 2004 to be presided over by the Union Home Minister. Ironically the Chief Minister of Uttaranchal, where the Maoist posters were distributed, was not among the invitees to the meeting, which turned out to be "inconclusive", as usual. This complex chain of linkages amply demonstrates that terrorism knows no borders! We have similarly explosive cross connections between Sri Lanka's LTTE and its sympathizers in Tamil Nadu. Illegal migration of thousands of refugees from Bangladesh into the northeastern states of India has escalated into a security problem and a source of tension between Bangladesh and India. The insurgents and radical rebel groups in the northeastern states usually find sanctuaries or safe hideouts in Myanmar and Bangladesh.

International terrorism is undoubtedly the latest scourge against mankind, tranquility at home and world peace at large. Proliferation of terrorism and its ever-growing capacity to hurt and destroy has grossly distorted the contours of traditional jurisdictions of governments everywhere and at all levels (national, state and local). Terrorism has forced national governments to come together to fight the menace. The US under the leadership of President Bush is misusing the menace of international terrorism as a cover to pursue its own agenda of unilateral interventionism, toppling and blackmailing "hostile" regimes and governments and capturing oil and other vital resources abroad.[11] Bush and company seem to have initiated a game plan against Iran along the lines of its "aggression" against Iraq.

The post-Cold War globalisation along capitalist lines, integration of national economies into a global free market under American auspices, "structural adjustment" (not "structural reform") being imposed by the IMF and the World Bank, revamping international trade for the benefit of the rich nations by the WTO, and America's interventionist and aggressive foreign policy are among the chief causes of global insecurity today.[12] It must, however, quickly be added that there are even more powerful and home-grown causes for human insecurity worldwide. The pervasive sense of human insecurity in South Asia pre-dates the contemporary wave of globalisation. The external exploitation certainly exacerbates the situation on the ground. But, the foundations of South Asian insecurity are to be seen in the legacy of widespread hunger, poverty, ill health, illiteracy, injustice and inequity. Destitution, deprivation and, despair define the framework of "non-traditional security" in South Asia.

## South Asian Insecurity

South Asia has been and continues to be one of the poorest, if not the poorest, regions in the world. As per the UN's Human Development Index, India ranks 127 out of 138 countries listed. Some of the other countries of South Asia are a shade better. Centuries of callous neglect by the rulers; the inherent nature of the distorted power structure; an unjust, indefensible caste system, and rigid social stratification have culminated in abject poverty, hunger and deprivation. Resentment, restlessness, anger, frustration and lawlessness stalk the region. Unemployment and under-employment are high and widespread. Protests against old evils, legacies of discrimination and racial prejudice are increasing. We see an upsurge of ethnic and other narrow identities. Newer and newer groups that were hitherto marginalized are waking up and demanding their place in the sun. The Maoist uprising in Nepal; LTTE's prolonged war for dignity, autonomy and cultural/national identity in Sri Lanka; recurrence of military dictatorships in Pakistan; violent and lethal factional fights between the two leading ladies in Bangladesh; endless turmoil in the Maldives; and above all, the deep-seated and widespread resentment; and recurrent eruption of violent protests in several parts of India are indicative of the widespread sense of human insecurity in the whole region. Let us remind ourselves that one-fourth of mankind lives (nay, exists) in the region.

Before I proceed further in analyzing the causes and contours of South Asian insecurity, let me add that my focus hereafter will be on India, because I am acquainted with the predicament of my country and the challenges we are confronted with. Unfortunately, I do not know enough about the non-traditional security problematique in the other countries of South Asia. However, I believe that much of what I say about India is largely applicable to them as well. While each of them has some unique problems and characteristics, the overall situation of poverty, misery and neglect is similar in nature and scope in the region as a whole.

## Farewell to the Welfare State

Globalisation and glocalisation, obviously, are undermining the sovereign nation state from without and also from within. This does not mean that the "State" has become impotent or that its demise is imminent. However, in the wake of the post-Cold War capitalist economic integration, the conception of the nature and the role of the State have undergone and are undergoing radical transformation. While farewell to the State is not in the works (as claimed by some early champions of globalisation), India is going through the political and economic fall out of bidding farewell to the "welfare state"! Business is not the business of the Government, it is asserted. National and State Governments should get out of the business of producing and marketing of goods and services. Governments should confine themselves to governing, maintaining law and order, and providing the basic amenities of food, shelter, sanitation, drinking water, primary education, etc. to the people. It is argued that the State should go back to being a regulator of industry and business and to ensuring a level playing field to all entrepreneurs (domestic and foreign).

Such a shift in the role and reach of the State is easier said than done, especially in India, where the State occupied "the commanding heights" of the economy till recently. Moreover, the task is especially difficult in a self-governing country of continental dimensions and enormous complexities. In the wake of the 2004 elections there is a change of Government in Delhi and some states. The Congress-led UPA Government has succeeded the BJP-led NDA Government. Consequently, a potentially significant shift in the economic reforms area is on the cards. Prominent among the electoral planks of the Congress-led coalition was the promise not to privatize profit-making public sector enterprises, go slow on disinvestment and provide employment to the youth and the needy on a large scale. This was reiterated by the PM in his nationally televised press conference on 4 September 2004. The "left" parties in the UPA coalition are to the left of the left-off-centre electoral posture of the Congress party.

After coming to power, the Congress party and the leftwing partners in the coalition Government have been engaged in a tug of war on the content and thrust of economic reforms. However, it is most unlikely that the reforms actually pursued and implemented would be materially different from their criss-cross and wayward course of the recent past. The marginalisation of the poor and the unskilled, the hungry and the destitute is unlikely to be reversed to a significant degree in the near future. Of course, there will be a lot of populist rhetoric and parading of empty promises like extending reservations to more and more segments of the population that were hitherto left out. Congress had always indulged in such vote bank politics. There is also much loud talk of extending job reservations to the private sector. The UPA or a return of the NDA is not likely to make a radical difference to the poor, the marginalized and the lower strata of the population now, nor in the near future. People in power seldom give it up and entrenched power structures are even more unyielding. Nobody would be happier than I, if I am proved wrong.

## Too Big and Too Small

As the political system unfolds and functions on the ground, the State in India (and the rest of South Asia) is and will remain "too big" and "too small" at the same time. An overwhelming majority of the people perceive the Indian State in that manner. For the vast majority of the poor and the marginalized, the Union Government at New Delhi remains too far away, too alienated and "too big". Whether the left out poor man is in urban slums or rural wilderness, the Government in New Delhi is generally seen as a distant "foreign" agency ruling the roost against his will and interests. The Government is seen as being callously unconcerned about his misery, the drudgery of his daily life, the concerns and anxieties that touch him deeply (such as whether or from where his next meal will come, if his sick child will get medicine in time, and if he will be jobless and so on.) Moreover, those living in the states and regions outside the mainstream like the Northeast, or Jammu and Kashmir, are even more alienated from the Government in New Delhi than the marginalized citizens in the rest of the country. The sense of alienation, mistrust, and resentment of the common man is too palpable to be missed by even a casual observer.

Ironically, the same Government of India is seen to be "too small" vis-à-vis the mighty United States, not-so-mighty West European States, the World Bank, the IMF and, the WTO! There is a genuine and widespread fear whether the Government of India is able to really protect the interests of the country or the people as a whole. The way the governments and the national economies function in South Asia, people have serious doubts about the autonomy of their countries and the commitment of their leaders to the welfare of the nation.

Then there are the perennial problems of corruption and nepotism, lack of transparency and absence of accountability, sheer inertia and inefficiency, a sense of motiveless malignity, which dessicate the legitimacy of the governing institutions and cast doubts over the integrity of the leaders in public life. As a consequence, governmental authority degenerates into power when faced with popular movements seeking redressal of grievances and demanding justice. Absence of equity and fairness inevitably drives people to resort to strikes, *dharnas, rasta rokos* and direct action. Governments see defiance in such popular movements. They are perceived as problems of law and order, and authorities tend to deal with the protesters with "an iron hand". This leads to more resentment and aggravation of popular anger because the authorities not only ignore their just demands arbitrarily, but also treat them as lawbreakers and criminals. Thus starts a vicious spiral of eroding legitimacy falling back on greater force and popular resentment escalating into more violence and more anger. In the process, "authority" degenerates into brute force. There are cries of State violence, allegations of false encounters and so on. At the same time the human rights of the policemen and the soldiers dealing with the restive and sullen crowds are also endangered. In the bargain everyone loses and the basic issues and quarrels become more intractable than before. Decreasing space for "sovereign" action externally and eroding national consensus internally have made the Indian Nation State a site of ever-growing contestation. I would like to think that the situation in the other countries of South Asia is not as bad.

In the process of degeneration in the public life of the nation, patriotism has gone out of fashion. Genuine and passionate all-India identity is lost in the maze of sub-national loyalties and narrower, closer to home and emotionally more potent identities. Caste and sub-caste, religion and region, language and tribe have gained in attachment and bonding. The activation of the narrower and newer badges of belonging are to be welcomed in our self-governing polity because they embody the growing awareness and mobilization among the poor and the hitherto marginalized sections of the vast population. However, expansion of democracy need not be and should not be at the expense of the nation, the motherland. Love for one's country and idealism are needed for rapid economic growth and social justice, especially in the era of capitalist globalisation. The all-India identity must be rekindled, patriotism and idealism must be brought back into the public life of the nation.[13] This can be done. Mahatma Gandhi did it not too long ago. All we need is a few hundred men and women passionately committed to the upliftment of fellow citizens and the honour of the motherland. I have great faith in the idealism of the present and next generation of Indians! Today's youth are better than those of my generation. They are better educated, more goal oriented, less prejudiced. All they need is better guidance and better role models.

## Non-Egalitarian Ethos

Globalisation and Glocalisation have reinforced the non-egalitarian character of the Indian society and the entrenched ethos of hierarchy. The political system in operation since 1947 did not and could not come out of the non-egalitarian ethos of the ancient land and effectively deal with the entrenched caste system and the rigid socio/cultural stratification. The pro-rich and pro-upper middle class tilt of the power structure could not be countered. Consequently, despite considerable growth and significant betterment from the very low levels of socio-economic indicators of the late 1940s, the nation's record of progress in terms of non-traditional human security is rather poor. This is particularly so if we take either the early promise of Free India or the aroused popular expectations of more recent times. India, like so many other developing countries, represents a case of non-fulfilment of the potential and performance below capacity.

## Conclusion

"Human Security" has two major constituents: freedom from fear and freedom from want. The former can be further divided into personal security, community security and political security. The components of the latter are food security, health security, economic security and environmental security. The marginalized and the poor constituting about 40 per cent of the population in India are not free from want. Daily reports of starvation deaths and suicides by farmers, weavers and others substantiate this tragic reality. A sizeable segment of these people is not free from fear either. They could become victims of slumlords, neighbourhood *dadas*, smugglers, drug-pushers and criminal gangs. Dacoits, armed rebel groups and terrorists attack them. The poor masses are also more likely to be ill treated, abused, tortured and killed by the police, the army and the "security forces". The number of people in jails without being charged of any crime is very high for a country boasting of democracy and equality before law. Our record in the number of people dying in custody is equally preposterous. Discrimination against women, exploitation of children and unequal treatment of minorities are pervasive and seemingly beyond remedy.

The picture of "human insecurity" in India (and the state of affairs in general) that I have presented here is overdrawn. It is not an objective and balanced assessment of the ground realities and I am aware of it. The litany of inadequacies and failures overshadow the country's progress and achievements in some areas despite heavy odds. What I have tried to do is to highlight the nature, content and context of non-traditional security problematique in the country. I also hinted that the situation in the other countries in South Asia probably is not much different or measurably better.

It is certainly true that the record of India in some areas is better than several other countries in Asia and Africa. The continuation of democracy is no mean feat. But, that is no consolation to the poor and the dispossessed. The human security situation in India is bad enough and the prospects of improvement do not seem bright. Widespread malnutrition, and starvation deaths (even in rich states like Maharashtra) though our granaries are overflowing, and suicides by 1000 farmers in Andhra Pradesh during the first 100 days of the new Government's coming to power, are indicative of the tragic state of affairs. On 15 July 2004, a group of Manipuri women demonstrated **standing naked** in front of the Headquarters of the Assam Rifles in Imphal. They carried banners saying "Indian Army Rape Us. Indian Army Take Our Flesh." The enraged women were protesting against the rape, detention and murder of Thangjam Manorama Devi by the Assam Rifles on suspicion of terrorist activity. The most unfortunate part of the tragedy is that such instances of "State Violence" are neither rare nor isolated. That was indeed a day of national shame and the dharna by naked women is symptomatic of the deep alienation, pervasive mistrust of and entrenched hostility against the Government in the northeastern states. Of course, it is not fair to blame the security forces in every case. But, on the whole State violence turns the denial of justice for long and the widespread misery for generations into an explosive mix that is ready to burst at the slightest provocation. It was officially acknowledged as recently as 21 September 2004, that varying degrees of Naxalite violence has affected 125 districts across 12 states. There is also the danger of extremism spreading to 24 new districts. In fact, the Naxalites had created "a Compact Revolutionary Zone" running from Andhra Pradesh to Nepal! Internal terrorism provides enormous scope for fishing in the troubled waters by criminal elements, terrorists, hostile governments, covert operations by foreign intelligence agencies and attacks by international terrorists.

For the general run of politicians though, it is business as usual. They take every opportunity to put their hands in the till and rob the community. Not a year passes when the legislators at the centre and the states give themselves enhanced salaries, perks, retirement benefits, discretionary spending funds for "constituency development," foreign travel, etc. These bills are passed in a jiffy! At the slightest pretext they rush to the well of the House, shout at each other, come to blows sometimes and frequently grind the proceedings of the Parliament to a halt. During the first 100 days of the new Government in Delhi, the Parliament was stalled most of the time. The Opposition and the Treasury Benches are equally blameworthy. While the nation is burning (so to say) the two sides are indulged in no holds barred battle over such non-issues as "the patriotism" or otherwise of Veer Savarkar, a controversial leader of yester years. Another big issue is that of "the tainted ministers". The Finance Bill was passed without any discussion whatsoever!

There is no clarity on economic reforms. The Planning Commission creates a needless controversy by inviting "foreign" advisers on its Board. Subsequently all the advisory panels were abolished! Railway Minister and IT Minister talk past each other. The Commerce Minister announces a new foreign trade policy without consulting coalition partners. The "left" parties are publicly blaming the Congress Government for not adhering to the Common Minimum Programme, the pre-electoral agreement among the coalition partners. Instead of governing the country, the new Governments at the centre and states are busy reopening cases against the previous governments. "Populism" of the most irresponsible kind has become the order of the day at the centre as well as in the states. The *tamasha* goes on and the people are disgusted.

Illegal power connections have mushroomed all over Andhra Pradesh and everyone including the Government is against doing anything! The leaders know that "Free power for some means no power to any one". But, that did not prevent the Congress Government from giving free power to farmers in Punjab and then giving it up because, as expected, it didn't work. Even then the Congress party promised free power to farmers in Andhra Pradesh prior to elections. Now, the Congress-led Government in the state finds itself in a mess and is desperately looking for a way out. Despite all this, the Congress-NCP Government in Maharashtra announced free power to farmers on the eve of the elections (to be held on 13th October 2004). This certainly is an example of populism at its worst, the most irresponsible kind of leadership one can find anywhere in the world. Yet, the voters may fall for it! Like their leaders, the people also love to get something for nothing! In the West, they say that a people get a government they deserve. But, in India, the cultural idiom is "As the King, so the People"!

In some sectors like IT, computers, biotechnology, bulk drugs, India has excelled. There are thousands and thousands of Indians who can hold their own with the very best in the world in any number of specializations. There are a few world-class hospitals, centres of learning and research in the country. But, all is lost in the ocean of failure, non-performance, nepotism, corruption, and criminality.

Yet, India is the biggest power in South Asia! She is generally more advanced than her neighbours in science, technology, industrialization, education, and so on. Often, India is described as the dominant country in the region. My quarrel with such a formulation has always been that the dominant country can and should choose not to dominate. Just as at home, India's leadership has failed to lead the region. A more generous, consistent and concerted foreign policy of India towards her immediate neighbours would have led to a South Asia that is less poor, less hungry and less naked, less distrustful of the "Big Brother" and less conflict ridden. I have always pleaded for a more cooperative South Asia in which reciprocity should not be the basis for Indian policies and actions. That calls for "Vision, Mission and Agenda" on the part of India[14] and willing cooperation of her neighbours in the region.

Yet, I am an optimist and always push for the positive in public life. Let me end by quoting an American Baptist preacher, who was a favourite of Rev. Martin Lather King, Jr. His summation about the Blacks in the US, I think, fits my assessment of human security in India. He declared:

> *"We ain't what we wanna be.*
> *We ain't what we gonna be.*
> *But, thank God, we ain't what we was!"*

## REFERENCES

# Dr. Babu is a specialist in international relations and American politics. Formerly he was the Sir Pherozeshah Mehta Professor of Civics and Politics, University of Bombay; Senior Academic Fellow, American Studies Research Centre, Hyderabad; and UGC Emeritus Fellow, University of Hyderabad. Professor Babu is currently Executive Director, Centre for Global Studies, a registered society based in Hyderabad.

1. James N. Rosenau, "New dimensions of security: The interaction of

globalizing and localizing dynamics," *Security Dialogue*, 25 No. 3, (September 1994) 255–81, especially 255–69.

2. Samuel P. Huntington, "The clash of civilizations," *Foreign Affairs*, 72 No. 4 (November–December 1995). Francis Fukuyama, *The End of History*, New York: 1993. Kenneth Waltz, "Globalization and American power," *National Interest*, 59 (Spring 2000) 46–56. Thomas Freidman, *The Lexus and the Olive Tree*, New York, 1999.
3. For an extended discussion of the concept of globalization, see B. Ramesh Babu, *"Glocalisation" and the Indian Nation State: Jurisdictions and Loyalties in Flux* (New Delhi: 2004) Chapter One.
4. B. Ramesh Babu, (ed.), *Changing Global Political/Ideological Context and Afro-Asia* (New Delhi, 1996) Introduction.
5. It is necessary to note that the United States of America is opposed to all of them even though it took a leading part in their formulation.
6. B. Ramesh Babu, "Americanization of the world: Myths and realities," *Freedom First*, 422 (July–September 1944) 23–27.
7. Charles Taylor, "The Dynamics of democratic exclusion," *Journal of Democracy*, 9, No. 4 (October 1998) 14 pages.
8. US Senate, Congress 86, Session 1, Committee on Foreign Relations, *United States Foreign Policy: The Operational Aspects* (Study No.6) (Washington D.C.: Government Printing Office, 1959) 4,5,8 and 9.
9. B. Ramesh Babu, (ed.), *Globalization and the South Asian State* (New Delhi, 1998), especially Chapter One.
10. Nira Wikramasinghe, *Humanitarian Relief Organizations and Challenges to Sovereignty: The Case of Sri Lanka*, RCSS Policy Studies No.1 (Colombo: Regional Centre for Strategic Studies, 1997) 51 pages.
11. According to Bob Djurdjevic, author of the website called *truthinmedia.org*, "the real American NWO (New World Order) is 'perpetual war for perpetual commerce' not 'world peace through world trade,' as the globalist leaders claim".
12. By all accounts the benefits of capitalist globalization have not reached the poor. In fact most analysts assert that in much of Asia and Africa, post-Cold War globalisation has made the poor poorer and the rich richer. For a well-argued view to the contrary see Johan Norberg, *Globalisation and the Poor*, Occasional Paper 1 (Potsdam: The Liberal Institute of the Friedrich Naumann Foundation, 2004) 15 pages.
13. B. Ramesh Babu, "Building a better Bharat for the billion: Revival of all-India identity," in Kausar J. Azam, (ed.), *Ethnicity, Identity and the State in South Asia* (New Delhi: 2001) 320–337.
14. B. Ramesh Babu, "South Asian Union: Vision, Mission, and Agenda," paper presented at an international seminar held in Hyderabad, 8–9 July 2004 (to be published shortly).

## SELECTED REFERENCES

### Books

Broad, Robin, *Global Backlash: Citizen Initiatives for a Just World Economy,* New York: Rowman & Littlefield, 2002.

Debroy, Bibek and Babu, D. Shyam, (eds)., *The Indian Mosaic: Searching for an Identity,* New Delhi: Academic Foundation in association with Rajiv Gandhi Institute for Contemporary Studies, 2004.

Falk, Richard A., *Human Rights Horizons: The Pursuit of Justice in a Globalizing World,* New York: Routledge, 2000.

Ganguly, Rajat, and Macduff, Ian, (eds)., *Ethnic Conflict and Secessionism in South Asia,* New Delhi: Sage Publications, 2004.

George, Robley E., *Socioeconomic Democracy: An Advance Socioeconomic System,* New York, Praeger, 2002.

Ingram, David, *Group Rights: Reconciling Equality and Difference,* Kansas City: Univ. Press of Kansas, 2000.

Knack, Stephen, (ed.), *Democracy, Governance, and Growth,* Ann Arbor: Univ. of Michigan Press, 2003.

Naidu, M.V., (ed.), *Perspectives on Human Security: National Sovereignty and Humanitarian Intervention,* Brandon, Canada: Canadian Peace Research Education Association, 2001.

Palmer, Tan G., *Globalization and Culture: Homogeneity,* Diversity, *Identity, Liberty,* Potsdam: The Liberal Institute of the Friedrich Naumann Foundation, 2003. Occasional paper No.2.

Runge, C. Ford et.al., *Ending Hunger in Our LifeTime: Food Security and Globalization,* Baltimore: Johns Hopkins Univ. Press, 2003.

Singer, Peter, *One World: the ethics of globalization,* New Haven: Yale Univ. Press, 2002.

Tulchin, Josephs., (ed.) (with Amelia Brown), *Democratic Governance and Social Inequality*, New York: Rienner Publishers, 2002.

UNCTAD, *Globalization and Liberalization: Effects of International Economic Relations on Poverty,* New York & Geneva: United Nations, 1996.

World Economic Forum, *Global Governance Initiative: Annual Report, 2004* (20 April 2004) 160 pages, Washington D.C., The Forum, 2004.

### Articles

Anonymous, "Redefining security: The human dimension," *Current History,* 94 No. 592 (May 1995) 229–236.

Ariyaratne, R.A., "Global defiance of globalization?" *Newsletter* of RCSS, 10 No. 2 (April 2004) 5–6.

Axworthy, Lloyd, "Human security and global governance: Putting people first," *Global Governance,* 7 No. 1 (January–March 2001) 19–24.

Babu, B. Ramesh, "A philosophy of globalism: Towards non-hegemonic globalisation," 26 August 2003 – A Lecture delivered at the 7th special SpARC Meeting of the Brahmakumaris, Mt Abu, 26th August 2003.

Babu, B. Ramesh, "Glocalisation and India's foreign policy," in Nalini Kant Jha, (ed.), *South Asian in 21st Century: India, Her Neighbours and the Great Powers* (New Delhi: South Asian Publishers 2003) 46–61.

Babu, B. Ramesh, "Glocalisation and the Indian nation state: A millennial challenge," in Rajen Harshe, (ed.), *Interpreting Globalisation: Perspectives in International Relations* (New Delhi: Rawat Publications, 2004) 168–189.

Barr, Bob, "Protecting national sovereignty in an era of International meddling: An increasingly difficult task," *Harvard Law Journal on Legislation,* (Summer 2002) 299–324.

Camilleri, Joseph A., "Globalization of insecurity: The democratic imperative," *International Journal of World Peace,* 18 No.4 (December 2001) 3–37.

Carothers, Thomas, "Civil society," *Foreign Policy,* (Winter 1999–2000) 18–28.

Chua, Amy "A world on the edge," *Wilson Quarterly,* (Autumn 2002) 62–77.

Doorknobs, Martin, "'Good governance': The Metamorphosis of policy metaphor," *Journal of International. Affairs* (Fall 2003) 3–17.

Faux, Jeffe, "Without consent: Global capital mobility and democracy," *Dissent,* (Winter 2004) 43–50.

Frenkel, Stephen, and Karuvilla, Sarosh, "Logics of action, globalization, and changing employment relations in China, India, Malaysia and the Philippines," *Industrial & Labor Relations Review,* (April 2002) 387–412.

Inglehart, Ronald, and Pippa, Norris, "The true clash of civilizations," *Foreign Policy,* (March/April 2003) 62–70.

Manchanda, Rita, "Linking conflict and peace with human rights and democracy: Gender, Nation and state," Review Essay, *World Affairs,* 6 No. 3 (July–September 2002) 142–157.

Mohan, Sudha, "Civil society activism in the age of globalisation," in Rajen Harshe, (ed.), *Interpreting Globalisation: Perspectives in International Relations* (New Delhi: Rawat Publications, 2004) 131–151.

Pei, Minxin, and Lyon, Merritt, "Bullish on democracy," *National Interest,* (Winter 2002/2003) 79–86.

Rogoff, Kenneth, "The IMF strikes back," *Foreign Policy,* (January–February 2003) 39–46.

Sen, Amartya, "Choosing freedom," *Far Eastern Economic Review,* 163 No. 4 (27 January 2003) 36, 38, 40 & 42.

Simon, Steven, "The New Terrorism," *Brookings Review,* (Winter 2003) 18–24.

Singh, Satyavir, "Terrorism and counter-terrorism in South Asia," *World Affairs,* 6 No.4 (October –December 2002) 32–44.

Thomas, Caroline, "Global governance, development and human security:

Exploring the links," *Third World Quarterly,* 22 No. 2 (April 2001) 159–175.

Werlin, Herbert H., "Poor nations/rich nations: A theory of governance," Public *Administration Review,* (May 2003) 329–342.

Witschel, Georg, "Global terrorism: Trends and response," *Newsletter* of the Regional Centre for Strategic Studies, Colombo 9 No.1 (January 2003) 1–5.

# 6

# Security in Democratic Pluralism: The Case of Nepal

*Lok Raj Baral*

## Security as we understand it

The preoccupation of state or hardcore political elites with boosting the state security has dampened the prospect of participatory or inclusive democracy. The ethnic, dalits, gender and the oppressed and suppressed groups/communities have realized that the lack of empowerment of these groups has increased their chances of alienation from the upper caste/class groups. While democracy and freedom have encouraged them to be vocal about the disparity existing between the caste/gender-based elites and themselves, it has hardly changed their social and economic status. However, democracy has made the people in general understand the nuances and practical aspects of pluralism, both social and political, the result of which is manifested in party documents and in various political and intellectual discourses. It is strongly believed that democracy, to be more people based and egalitarian, needs to be rediscovered for addressing the agendas of the poor or else it would be overtaken by the politics of violence. The recruitment of ethnic and dalits including about 40 per cent women in the Maoist guerilla force is attributed to the lingering shadow of disparity and poverty in the country. The United People Government headed by Man Mohan Singh in India has recently come out with the agenda of rural employment skill that provides employment for each household for 100 days. Such a scheme has realized that economic growth alone would not remove poverty nor can provide employment to the needy sections of society. So security for whom is increasingly becoming a live issue in South Asia.

Security is difficult to define now as it has become a very complex concept. Today the same definition of security does not hold good as earlier, but we can find similarities among the definitions by studying the history and concepts of security. Security refers "to protection from danger, safe feeling and free from doubt."[1] It is crucial to an understanding of internal politics. Security is "ambiguous and elastic" in meaning. In the most fundamental sense, security means to be secure and to feel free from threats, anxiety, or danger. Security is therefore a state of mind in which the general citizen including highest political leader of the land feels safe from harm by others. Conventionally, leaders and citizens feel secure when the state feels secure from other states or from other foreign non-state actors. Security describes how people feel, not whether they are justified in feeling the way they do. In this sense security depends on the "perceptions" of people, their position and environment. Security can "encompass so many things: what makes one individual feel secure may not be sufficient to make another feel so, individuals differ in their tolerance for uncertainty, their ability to live with anxiety, and their capacity to cope with pressure. One person's security can well be another's insecurity."[2]

Furthermore, Robert J. Art states that

> Although individuals differ in what makes them feel secure or insecure. There is neither perfect security nor absolute security. Security, therefore, is not a matter of either/or—either one has it or one does not, rather, it is a matter of degree, of feeling more or less secure, more or less insecure. What is true of individuals is true of states. States are not perfectly secure or completely insecure, but rather experience either condition in degrees. For both individuals and states, then, security is a condition that comes in shades of gray, not hues of black and white.[3]

The International Encyclopedia of Social Science defines security as "the ability of a nation to protect its internal values from external threats".[4] Defining national security, Walter Lippman said, "A nation has security when it does not have to sacrifice its legitimate interests to avoid war and is able if challenged to maintain them by war".[5]

## State-Centric Vs People-Centric Approach

The foregoing definitional narrative tries to explain the conventional state security for which entire resources are mobilized. But today, countries are more insecure due to internal crises that in turn may also invite national catastrophe. When politics rots and institutional decline or decay begins, crises both for the state and people overwhelm. Many call such trends the failed state syndrome. Ayoob says, "a breakdown of Third World security expenditures clearly demonstrates that much of the insecurity faced by state and regimes is internal and is, therefore, linked to the state-making process."[6]

Conventional security, which is basically state-centric, cannot be an inclusive security paradigm that entails both the traditional and non-traditional. Many have preferred to call it 'comprehensive' security that fits well into plural societies. Democracy and freedoms with which people can put up their grievances can be more lasting and rational than the regimes based only on force. Yet, the democratization process can also be "destabilizing" if the elites fail to modulate the pace of development. In the absence of established institutions, conglomerate elements may take myopic decisions for hindering democratic development. Freedoms alone do not mean democratization if the elites, both ruling and non-ruling politicos, fail to grasp the meaning of democratization and development. While depicting the picture of Nepal, Devendra Raj Panday has stated how the county stagnates and eventually moves towards retrogression. He writes:

> The nation has been plagued by near stagnation—some might say, it is retrograding. What we call political change, social mobilisation, executive actions, economic policies, and civil discourses have been seemingly irrelevant to this reality...Under the circumstances, we have to wonder if the dismal condition of the country is not the result of action without reflection and 'reflection without action' on the part of "its leaders, opinion-builders, and policy-makers who abuse the 'word' as indicated above'[7].

A nation-state approach with which to encapsulate the territory, sovereignty, population (either subjects or citizens) and government (absolute or popular) needs to be broadened to examine the relationship between democracy, pluralism and security. Probed into it more closely through the prism of pluralism and democracy and development, one can also find the core elements of popular sovereignty in the four elements of the state. Territory is of course common to both democratic and non-democratic nature, while the remaining three elements can be adapted to popular sovereignty if we are inclined to approach them with a pluralistic mindset. Sovereignty in the democratic or pluralistic sense is vested with the people of the country with which to identify the overall processes of empowerment both by legal and practical steps to be taken under the Constitution prepared by the people.

However, except for some specific cases, majority of the countries in the world lack the practice of popular sovereignty. Nor are all the governments of the world creatures of the electorate because many of them use force as the basis of the state. However, struggles for democracy and freedom are simultaneously waged by the people's strong desire to achieve them as well as by the pressure of economic and social factors. People want security of life, and the state and other agencies are needed to guarantee it by providing the basic needs—food, shelter, health, education, cloth and protection. In a broader sense, the state and private agencies should mobilize resources for fulfilling these needs. Once the Bharatiya Janata Party leader, then Deputy Prime Minister L.K. Advani said that Indian people in general want four things —'roti', 'kapada', 'makan' and 'mobile'. And these aspirations cannot be wished away by any government, more so by a democratically elected government whose major concern should be people's welfare and empowerment.

Today's security problem is concentrated on the failure of social scientists that do not find any alternative to centrality of the state. State continues to play a pivotal role in the midst of plurality of thoughts and associations. Compared to such plural interests and associations or organizations, the state is perceived as pre-eminent, thus subordinating others to it. As the concept of nation-state came from the West, this model has become inadequate in explaining the refrain of pluralism and democracy in South Asia. Those Europeans who propagated the concept of nation-state perhaps had not then understood the tribal, ethnic, language, region, and search for identity of each group and community within the territorial boundary delineated for nation-state. However, people and government could be extended to explain such components of nation-state but recently nation-states have been under scrutiny in relation to such problems. An alternative model of nation-state has been suggested by many social scientists of the developing world with a view to making democracy and pluralism much wider than what we had learnt from the West. Many social scientists have criticized the Indian state for following the Western model and undermining tribal identities and pauperizing the tribal people. India's multi-national character, for example, does not allow behaving in a manner of nation-state as all tribes and ethnic and other groups and communities have to be given the opportunities to maintain their livelihood by protecting their language, religion, culture and land rights.

## Democratic Security/Insecurity

The state is the acknowledged actor and symbol of traditional security, thus assuming a new form of pre-eminent status in South Asia. Democratic institutions and governance are on the sidelines, and where democracy is stated to have struck roots, are also under pressure of the rejuvenated state structures. It is particularly so in view of the declining failures of political elites to reach negotiated settlements of conflicts stemming from nothing other than the lingering disparity gaps in societies and states. In some countries freedoms are granted not because the ruling elites cherish them but because freedoms seem to serve two main interests of elites who are bent on continuing the status quo. First, they want to project that their regimes are no less tolerant and freedom loving than any established democracy of the world. Such a strategy would also ward off political discontent. Pakistan under General Musharraf and Nepal under King Gyanendra are the best examples of how freedoms have nothing to do with the actual location of power.

However, democracy is functional only when such *discontent* is relevant to the established political system. In a democracy, discontent is the other side of the coin. But if it is not related to functionality of a political system, freedom does not create any impact on the nature of power structure. Since power itself is a core value of politics, opposition politics is also related to the established dynamics of the political system. In democracy, the purpose of power is sanguine with synergy of popular content and the absolute element of the state. Democracy does not mean anarchy or absence of regulatory part of politics. When government starts implementing its policies, some sort of contract for exercising such regulatory powers is made between the people for whose welfare and protection all activities are carried out by the state. By way of caution, it can also be said that in the name of consent and public support, the scope of "manufactured consent" is great. Thus, a pseudo-democracy may be in the show that tends to marginalize the needy sections of population.

Second, democracy is both a process and substance. In some countries neither exists; in some others processes are in place but not substance. On the basis of such problems, political security as it implies various aspects—processes of governance, legitimacy, location of power, structures of state and elite, pluralism with power, inclusiveness and end of marginalization of groups and ordinary people from the core of power—needs to be treated.

Political security alone does not convey the meaning because politics is a much broader concept, purpose and dynamics. Politics encompasses all aspects of social, economic, political, national and regional and international dynamics concerning human beings. When it deals with citizens, its scope is narrowly confined to the territorial part. When it starts dealing with transnational situations, it assumes international dimensions. So political security is related both to national and international contexts. And democracy and human freedoms have also become common agendas because these two areas are generally creating impacts, both positive and negative, on improving or straining relations between and among states. The humanitarian intervention approved by the United Nations also points to the fact that despite being unacceptable to many regimes, they are under internal and external pressures for change and democratization.

Conceptually, political security under an authoritarian government indicates the coercive domain with which it tries to seek the compliance of its citizens. In Nepal, during the royal regime (1960–90), laws were enforced with strong coercive authority because of the concentration of power in the government whose "active and supreme leadership" was provided by the king. The New Education System Plan was a case in point amid other similar ordinances and laws imposed on the people. Though many programmes and policies enforced by the state petered out during their implementation, the manner in which they were enforced was authoritarian in spirit.

When one tries to conceptualize democratic security, it is related to the state of democracy in a country. When people become the centre of politics, the rulers are not seen as the representatives of "God on earth" as Hegel had articulated in his theory of ideal state, or as a superior class of people notwithstanding the pervasive nature of elitist politics in all forms of government. In a democracy, rulers are only accountable to the electorate which alone can exercise their prerogative for circulating their rulers in periodic elections. In recent years, in the United Kingdom, it has been complained that except the electorate, no other institution—court, parliament, media, etc.—seems to make the Prime Minister (Tony Blair) accountable to them because of their declining influence. The dictatorship of the Prime Minister is now a reality, though the people in fair and free election elect the "dictator"[8].

The recent Indian experience however, contrasts with this trend because of two factors. First, the coalition politics has made the Prime Minister and his government dependent on the crucial support rendered by other coalition partners. Among them, the communists have 63 members in a fractured house of 543. The support of other parties (United Progressive Front) is crucial for survival of the government. Second, the Prime Minister is a good economist and gentleman but without the strong leadership role within the party. Sonia Gandhi, the widow of late Rajiv Gandhi, has a strong hold due to her inherited charisma and to her own understanding of Indian politics that she displayed her quality as a leader during the election. Her refusal to accept the post of Prime Minister for reasons best known to herself has made her stronger both symbolically and practically. Her emergence has overshadowed the role of Prime Minister because she is said to have become the de facto Prime Minister. Such a new experiment in Indian democracy prompted the leader of opposition, L.K. Advani, to pass a "facetious remark about the governmental landscape characterized by the presence of a PM, S(uper) PM and CPM'. One is now beginning to see the last two in action and these are just early times. The top is getting a bit too crowded for comfort"[9]. Thus, democratic experiments in South Asia, or in other developing countries, have explored many newer trends germane to each specific context. Some of them may turn out to be positive for democratic consolidation but many may prove disastrous for it. Nevertheless, in all democratic exercises, people should be placed at the centre-stage.

## Trend of Militarization

The security dilemma in the Third World, especially in the South Asian region, is becoming more complex because of the unchanged mindset of South Asian rulers and security personnel who find security anchorage in military approach to the resolution or containment of any conflict. Hence the whooping agenda of military development for which substantive budgetary allocation is needed. People are now complaining against a kind of "securitized mind" that has only increased the fear of ordinary people. Examples abound about how the poor villagers of South Asia, particularly those who belong to the conflict zones and are under the surveillance of both the combatants who are either insurgents and terrorists or the state security forces are in the crossfire. And on the pretext of security situation that ironically is the byproduct of the failure of the state (s) has overshadowed the core agenda of human governance based on freedom and democracy.

However, the democracy agenda is now subordinated to state

security agenda which is no more than the effort of continuing the status quo for serving the interest of a small section of elites either traditional, authoritarian, class/caste-based or noveau riche whose prosperity was possible by amassing wealth under both the authoritarian or "democratic rules". In South Asia, ordinary people cannot contest elections at the regional and central levels because of lack of fund and political support. As a result, the conventional democracy which is virtually an electocracy or what an Indian political scientist, Jayal, calls "the fallacy of electoralism"[10] has failed to rejuvenate the spirit of inclusive democracy. So, the South Asian states in general have failed to set new aggressive agendas for bringing about a qualitative transformation within societies and polities. Thus, today's states face a variety of daunting crises that emanate from ethnicity, gender and dalit oppression and suppression based on caste discriminations, communal and sectarian trends, regional disparity, and economic underdevelopment heightened by bad governance. How the state has shown its limited capacity or no capacity to address such emergent issues can be found in all developing countries.Yet, South Asia seems to be a unique case for not being able to free itself from the morass of poverty and accompanying political turbulence.

The South Asian irony is that neither the state nor the nation is made strong despite the penchant of South Asian elites and security agencies to rely on coercive mechanisms of the state. A strong state does not need to be anti-people serving only the vested interest of power and political elites thus making it as an instrument of exploitation as Marx said more than 150 years ago. Except a few countries such as India, Bangladesh and Sri Lanka, institutionalized bureaucracy is not strong. Similarly, governments are vulnerable to quirks of change and circumstances of ambitious rulers. Efficiency with accountability is still a remote reality in governance. Jayadeva Uyangoda has succinctly analyzed the declining trends of South Asian states, remarking that they have reached a "phase of political anomie". He writes:

> One of its key features is the weakening, from within as well as without, of the old forms of the state along with the erosion of their structures of legitimation. An easily identifiable second cause of the political anomie is the rapid reconstruction of social structures in South Asia in direct response to the enhanced and generalized penetration of capital-led and market-governed relations of production, exchange, circulation and consumption into societies that had earlier been protected from the powerful forces of the global economy[11].

Although all South Asian states have such characteristics, some cases are specific. Nepal's recent developments, for instance, follow the reverse wave of democratization as stated by Huntington in his *Third Wave*, with the king usurping executive power, and feeble resistance from opposition[12]. The government's enforcement of "Terrorist and Disruptive Activities (Control and Punishment) Ordinance, 2061(2004) or (TADO), is an indication of how the state is increasingly becoming dependent on draconian means. Its Clause 9 states: If a security official feels the need to prevent a person from carrying out any terrorist and disruptive activity, such a person can be kept under house arrest for a maximum period of one year (six months at his discretion, another six months after obtaining permission from the home ministry) in any place after fulfilling common humanitarian conditions"[13]. Reacting sharply to such power given to the security and administrative agencies, the political parties in general accused the government of taking the country back to autocracy. Echoing this sentiment, the *Kathmandu Post* (daily) editorial stated:

> ...The new ordinance allows the security forces to justify detention, torture and mysterious deaths in custody. The present human rights record clearly speaks volumes about army atrocities meted on the innocent people since Sher Bahadur Deuba[ Prime Minister] deployed the army to fight the Maoist insurgency. Deuba knows that RNA [Royal Nepal Army] alone cannot resolve the Maoist conflict and there is no alternative to talks. Yet the Prime Minister has been unnecessarily empowering the security forces as if they have the key to resolving the conflict. Intense military drive will only deepen the armed conflict[14].

The democratic security that entails many other areas concerning human security is in great peril if the state is tempted to use coercion in the name of conflict resolution, peace and security. The reports of flagrant violation of human rights and tendency to subordinate other core issues of development become rampant when the state starts taking shelter under draconian laws and ordinances. In the Nepali context, Dhruba Kumar is of the view that "democratization does not augur well only with the subordination of the armed forces to the elected representatives of the State. Because the military history of Nepal is based on the conquest, control and consolidation of the traditional power of the State monopolized by monarchy"[15]. The budgetary allocation from 1996 to 2004 has amply demonstrated the trend of military build-up in a country where democratic institutions are either subverted or marginalized, leading to the usurpation of power by monarchy along with the compromises made by the political parties and their leaders. Every year, defence and other security-related expenses are increasing with the security forces becoming demanding as well as dominant.

Now the Nepali Army wants to upgrade its force level to about one million, i.e. from today's 85,000. In addition, the Armed Police Force is likely to reach 25,000 in addition to the Civil Police of about 50,000. As it has been remarked, "a relatively well organized and large army without any peacetime duty (not even guarding the national frontiers) may incite them also to indulge in national politics with disastrous consequences"[16]. It is now estimated that the security forces killed more than 10,000 people and more than 2000 are missing. The National Human Rights Commission of Nepal, other non-governmental organizations within and outside the country, have strongly raised the issue of flagrant violation of human rights by the security forces. As a human rights activist has stated: "The nature of human rights violations in Nepal reads like the A–Z of a human rights textbook. The principal concerns are that both the Government forces and the Maoists have resorted to extra-judicial executions, torture and illegal detentions in a brazen and endemic manner"[17]. It is not only in Nepal that democracy is in the reverse gear; other "democratic" countries of the region are also on the upward swing of securitization. So, "the manner in which the agenda of securitization is gaining premium in South Asia regardless of the degree of democratic governance shows the regressive trend of democratic politics. It has also been aptly remarked by Uyangoda, "securitized politics is utterly oppressive and oppressively counter-emancipatory"[18]. Added to it is the continued domination of the same caste/class or feudal elites who pay short shrift to the emancipatory agendas thus making democracy a permanent hostage to the petty interest of rulers.

## Endangered Democracy and Security Issue

The legitimacy question always makes the power elites paranoid for both routine conduct of governance and for insuring security of individuals. Even during parliaments in session and elected governments at the helm of affairs, governments are generally tempted to rule by decrees or ordinances as in being practised in different countries. When the reverse wave of democratization is in full steam, rule by draconian laws and security measures are more common. And democratic politicians are not tired of rationalizing the derailment of the process itself as has happened to the Nepali system after 4 October 2002 with King Gyanendra taking the decision to exercise power arbitrarily, maintaining that such powers are vested with him by tradition notwithstanding the spirit of constitutional monarchy a la British model. The imposition of state of emergency in February 2005 along with the drastic curtailment of freedoms of citizens and other follow-up measures have accomplished the royal ascendancy which is reminiscent of the royal coup of 1960.

Political parties bereft of principles and norms have almost shown the trends of decline in South Asia. India, the bastion of democracy in the developing world, is no exception to this with major political parties—the Congress and the Bharatiya Janata Party (BJP) not being able to form government at the centre independently. The politics of coalition or the 'hybrid system' is the new trend with regional parties and other loose formations sharing power with them. Yet, from a pluralist and federal perspective, such a trend has made Indian democracy more representative in that the spirit of federalism and pluralism is manifested in the governance of the country. Federalism has in fact been refashioned notwithstanding the quasi-federal Constitutional provision. In Sri Lanka, a similar coalition building has become the norm as no single party seems to be capable of forming the government. In Nepal, parties' existence is in question due to the concentration of power in the Palace as in the old partyless Panchayat days.

Such shade and sunshine in political parties has become obvious despite their being the backbone of democracy and pluralism. Some of them have vanished and others survive on the basis of new constituencies such as caste, tribe, community, sub-nationalism and regionalism. Religion as a base is also being revoked in absence of organizing ideologies.[19] Conceivably, modern democracy is as much concerned with the management of these trends as with structural aspects of a polity. So political parties and other social forces that articulate and aggregate various interests need to be dealt with in order to relate them to the structures and dynamics of power. At a time when no institutional frameworks are created for solving national problems or for regularizing the processes started with great fanfare, political insecurity overshadows other development. As Barry Buzan observes in the context of vulnerabilities of states, "So long as such states fail to solve their nationality problem, they remain vulnerable to dismemberment, intervention, instability and internal conflict in ways not normally experienced by states in harmony with their nations"[20].

In Nepal's case, it seems to be more intractable due to the interplay of contradictory forces that are bent on, wittingly or unwittingly, frustrating the transition process itself. This has happened over the last thirteen plus years as the Constitutional process is now replaced by the personalized royal rule. Transition that was expected to consolidate democratization is in reverse gear with no political forces being clear about the new roadmap. The Westminster system copied from the UK no more exists, corroborating the doubt raised earlier that Nepali context, background and traditions are incompatible with the British model due to contradictory forces at work.

The four forces that are active players in Nepali politics are the king, the parliamentary political parties, the Maoists and the international actors. Liberal democracy in the institutionalized sense is under attack from most of them, though the liberal democracy believers might argue that they are very much for its consolidation despite heavy odds confronting democracy. However, the political parties' dilemma to make democracy more inclusive and transformatory in nature has hit the prospect of democracy itself. Rampant inconsistencies and incoherence in their approaches to a democratization agenda have given rise to the creation of a new vicious circle. Under the circumstances, parties are prisoners of their own ambivalence about the future direction with which to build the nation through democracy and pluralism.

Nepali politicians face the problem of credibility. Even an ordinary crisis which otherwise could have been solved remains unaddressed. Politicians' remarks are now suspect as the so-called democratic governments are increasingly becoming governments without power. Whatever power and authority the Prime Ministers and ministers exercise are delegated by the king. It seems that no Prime Ministers and ministers or other politicians have the courage to steer their course regardless of the attitude of the king. Parties are invariably inclined to play a subordinate role offering to be as docile as possible for making a deal with the king. The Palace advertisement for the application of the post of Prime Minister became contentious following the failure of the other four parties to recommend the name of CPN (UML) leader, Madhav Kumar Nepal, so much so that the latter decided to break with the other coalition partners of the anti-regression movement. It was understood that the other parties didn't like to recommend Nepal's candidature on the ground that the process of selection of Prime Minister was not befitting the democratic spirit; nor did the king ever show his inclination to appoint the leader of opposition of the dissolved lower house as Prime Minister. On the contrary, the king chose Sher Bahadur Deuba who had not applied for the post.

The government headed by Deuba faced a number of hurdles and could not make any headway in a negotiated settlement with the Maoists. Some of these constraints were: the power of the government was in question because of the central role of the king. The previous government headed by Deuba had no problems of taking other coalition partners together despite internal problems of the ruling NC party. The UML's own predictability and credentials were challenged because it wanted to enjoy the best of two worlds—being a partner in the government and also its critic. The utterances of senior UML leaders and the demonstration staged by its student wing against the recent price hike in petroleum products showed the cruel dilemma faced by the party. The UML seemed to play football in both A and B teams or of government and opposition at the same time.

Similarly, Deuba's own credibility as a leader and Prime Minister was eroded considerably. Placed as he was in a tight-rope walking position, in addition to his intra-party problem, the Prime Minister's position was compromised. Moreover, the agenda of the constituent assembly and monarchy were beyond the reach of any government or of the parties whose actual position on a common agenda had not become clear. If the Nepali Congress had three options hoping to use each of them if the need arose, the CPN (UML) was in a dilemma on the same contrary to its declaration that it would not hesitate to opt for a constituent assembly. However, since this party was in government, how could it take ahead the agenda of constituent assembly if other coalition partners were opposed to it? Thus, political parties in general were mainly responsible for not taking a unified position in order to hold a serious negotiation with the Maoists.

The governments have invariably shown weaknesses in governance, let alone providing security to the ordinary people. The local people intensifying the rate of displacement deserted the Maoist-hit districts. A reign of terror prevailed across the country with people being placed in the crossfire or being harassed and hounded by both sides—the state and the Maoists. Such a situation continued even after power was taken over by King Gyanendra.

Political parties in general have not yet gathered courage to decide a course of action for the future. While accepting the Maoist demand of constituent assembly, political parties could also ask for the management of weapons being used by the Maoists. Here the much-touted UN role may come in, though, in my opinion, it can only be facilitation because of the domestic intricacies involved in the present crisis. The UN cannot impose its agenda, nor can it work as a negotiator on behalf of the estranged parties. If the aspirations of the Nepali people are not addressed by such negotiations, the recrudescence of conflict cannot be ruled out. Nepali people should decide their own destiny, for which some qualitative changes are essential. A mere piecemeal approach can hardly settle the fundamental issues brought to light by the new Nepali aspirations and developments.

Some political party leaders are also of the view that India and some other countries such as the US and UK have a role to play in ending the conflict. It is said that India can play the role of a sorcerer of all the ills of Nepal. In the given Maoist context, many accuse India of playing a double role—patting the Maoists on their back and at the same time supplying arms against them. But how is such complicity, as perceived by critics, possible when India itself is the worst victim of insurgency? Moreover, a friendly neighbour (Nepal) ravaged perennially by insurgency and prospects of instability would endanger its own security for which India can hardly write off Nepal.

What is now clear is that the basic issues dug out by both the Maoists, and a government devoid of real power, could hardly resolve the emergent crises. A powerful interim government consisting of all political parties including the CPN (Maoist) alone would create conditions for peace and political stability. And holding a constituent assembly alone seems to be the answer. The Maoists on their side should commit to the popular sovereignty and competitive politics before laying down arms under the auspices of the UN. And this is the only role the UN can play in the present crisis[21].

Amongst the four forces, the role of the king is controversial since the very morrow of 1951 change with intermittent shift of such roles. Sometimes, the king was treated as father of the nation after King Tribhuvan's triumphant return from India in 1951. The same king had, obviously as part of a deal between the Rana rulers, the king, and political forces represented by the Nepali Congress, committed to a constituent assembly on 18 February 1951. And India played the role of a mediator, impressing on all to follow a gradualist democratic path so that political upheaval could be avoided and development made possible. Such a power shift from the native Rana oligarchs to a constituent assembly was a revolutionary step in the history of the country. Nevertheless, this hope was soon dashed after three years with the same king declaring clearly the reverse wave of democratization. Monarchy was virtually restored to its absolute form when King Tribhuvan declared in 1954:

> The inherent sovereignty of the Monarch and his special Prerogatives over the executive, legislative and judicial wings as the supreme head have been handed over to Us by the tradition and custom of the country. The inherent sovereignty of the monarch and his special prerogatives over the executive, legislative and judicial wings as the supreme head have been handed over to us by the tradition and custom of the country. The Prime Ministers by virtue of the rights vested in them by Our Illustrious forefathers exercised them. Since the Proclamation of 18 February 1951, the supreme authority in all affairs ended those rights now rest on us[22].

Later, his successor, King Mahendra held elections to parliament after consolidating absolute power (sovereign) in 1959 and after a brief period of eighteen months, the first ever installed elected government was dismissed by military intervention. The rise of royal absolutism was thus accomplished within a short period of nine years and a new regime patronized by the king prevailed in the country until the mass movement in 1990 overthrew it.

Under the new Constitution of 1990, which was considered to be the best among all the previous constitutions because of the popular contents incorporated into it, constitutional monarchy was one of the pillars. The preamble to the Constitution of the Kingdom of Nepal, 1990 laid down somewhat contradictory elements, accepting both the elements of popular sovereignty and traditional monarchial prerogative. It states: "...We are convinced that in the independent and sovereign Nepal, the source of sovereign authority is inherent in the people, and, therefore, We have, from to time, made known Our desire to conduct the government of the country in consonance with the popular will". These were the words of King Birendra while promulgating the Constitution. Adding the spirit of popular movement for determining the nature of the Constitution, the King further said: "In keeping with the desire of the Nepalese people expressed through the recent people's movement to bring about constitutional changes, We are further inspired by the objective of obtaining to the Nepalese people justice, social, political and economic, to be available long into the future". In 1959, the preamble laid down for establishing "an efficient monarchical form of government responsive to the wishes of the people"[23]. It means that the king then and now is guided by the same notion that he rules as did his forefathers on the basis of power vested in him by tradition. However, all kings were supposed to be responsive to the wishes of the people.

This narrative is relevant here to argue that constitutional monarchy a la British type is not possible because of the inherent power psyche inherited by the traditional monarchs. When the opportunity arises, monarchy asserts its traditional role that is repugnant to the spirit of constitutional monarchy. It is a problem of power shift that could not be accomplished under the post-1990 democratic dispensation. Now a triangular struggle between the king, political parties and the Maoists is under way with each trying to undercut the activities of the other. Under the circumstances, political insecurity of both the state and individual has increased. What is more worrisome is that by way of boosting the role of the army, unprecedented mobilization of resources is under way, showing its immediate impacts on democracy, development and freedoms of citizens.

## Concluding Remarks

How is security insured in a plural and democratic society? This question can best be answered from two angles. First, the nature of the state, society and polity shows the degree of security/insecurity of people. If the state is repressive, status quoist, feudalistic in nature, people's identity with the state, society and polity would accordingly be determined. The foundational basis of the state is therefore the crucial aspect of the agenda of social and political pluralism. Social pluralism means plurality of communities and groups whose representation in the polity and in other areas of national life is reflected. Failure to understand the existence of such groups by the state invites trouble.

Second is the problem of democratization, which is related to institutional mechanism as well as to the inculcation of culture that tries to relate democracy and political pluralism to social reality. Thus, democracy alone can recognize such realities and try to accommodate the sentiment of all. The problem arises when the power elites and the nature of the state or polity are guided more by the criteria of ascription and primordial loyalties and relationship. In Nepal, such a situation continues today notwithstanding a lot of tantrums created in the name of democracy and pluralism. Hence the vociferous demand for restructuring the state and polity, as both are still not at ease with inclusive process that ensures the empowerment of all people.

The reconstruction of state and polity in Nepal is imperative for democratization and change. The history of the country for more than fifty-five years has shown the incompatibility between the power structure and the political exercises conducted in the name of democracy and freedom. Without accepting the ground reality of the feudal Nepali state and its background and orientation of core elites, democratization and qualitative change seem to be difficult.

Social pluralism, which is organic to political pluralism, adds complexity to the democratic process if these two are treated as exclusive to each other. According to the 2001 Census, Nepal's heterogeneity is reflected with about 100 ethnic and caste groups and 92 languages. Formation of each group however does not cross 3.5 million with no individual community becoming numerically dominant. The Bahun and Chhetri, who are considered to be the most advantageous are less than 30 per cent (Chhetri 15.80 per cent, and Bahun 12.74 per cent) in the national population structure." Other ethnic groups that compose 5.64 per cent of the population are Magar (7.14 per cent), Tharu (6.75 per cent), Tamang (5.64 per cent) and Newar (5.48 per cent). Altogether 18 caste and ethnic groups that have the population of over 1 per cent each[24]. Among the 59 identifiable indigenous ethnic groups, only 42 are included in the census report)[25].

The representation pattern of various ethnic, dalit and gender in the political processes from the grassroots to the national level is dismal. It is more surprising to note that this unchanged picture continues even in the post-1990 democratic period. In the composition of political parties, district assemblies and committees and the national legislature, the high caste groups continue to take the lion's share in politics and other sectors. Only the Newars are better placed than other ethnic groups because of being urban and entrepreneurs.

Democratic security is best guaranteed when polity is inclusive and innovative. Failure to follow this approach means destruction of the political system. Innovativeness is open to change if the people want to bring about such change. In Nepal, democracy, if taken in the institutionalized and popular sense, is not likely to be sustainable without embracing the agenda of reconstruction of state, polity and society. State reconstruction means setting a new paradigm for the four elements of the state—territory, government, sovereignty and people. Territorial integrity has two aspects, internal and external, because internally, the citizen can identify with the given territory as their homeland that is expected to look after their welfare. From an external perspective, the border of a nation-state is incompatible with the spirit of supra-nationalism that tends to erode nationalism identified the designated territory called the state. The European Union, for example, is evolving as a model of a supranational organization having its own government, currency, parliament and area that includes the member states.

Government as defined before is expected to represent the people. Any government can be made and unmade by the people at intervals. If a government is in power due to its usurpation of power or by coup or by invoking the traditional authority and power, people in such regimes are only subjects, not citizens with veto-wielding capacity. Based on arbitrary rules and ordinances, such governments are perennially haunted by instability and change. People are also insecure as chances of rebellion and insurgencies are always ubiquitous. Thus rulers are insecure due to the problem of legitimacy; people are insecure due to conflict-prone nature of regimes.

The third element is sovereignty, which has often generated controversies and conflicts. As it is considered to be a jewel of the state and power, revolutionary violence takes place in achieving it. Some countries of South Asia have been able to settle the issue of sovereignty by accepting people as sovereign, while others are groping in the dark for its attainment. In Nepal, sovereignty is always an elusive factor and is not settled fully despite a constitutional provision for making the Nepali people sovereign. The rise of monarchical power and the weakened position of political parties to resist it has shown the unclear roadmap for the future. In the name of democracy and pluralism or emancipation of people, Nepal's overall security situation has worsened.

So the fourth element of the state—people—has become abstract. Parties who have joined the government talk about democratization and change; those who are in the opposition think that they need change for empowerment of people so that popular sovereignty in the real sense of the term could be vested in the people. Now the agenda is not only big but also complicated because of the heterogeneity of political forces. Highly fractured and ideologically ambivalent as they are, the Nepali state is in a drift, putting democracy and human security in peril.

## NOTES

1. Barry Buzan, *People States and Fears, National Security Problems in International Relations*, Transitions Publishers, p. 18.

2. Robert J, Art "Security", Joel Krieger (ed.), *The Oxford Companion To Politics of The World,* (New York: Oxford University Press, 2001), pp. 757–8.
3. Ibid.
4. Berkowitz, Morton and Bock, P.G., "National Security" in David L. Sills (ed.), *International Encyclopedia of the Social Science,* (Macmillan: New Work, 1968), p. 40.
5. Walter Lippman, *US Foreign Policy: Shield of the Republic* (Boston: Mass, 1943) p. 5.
6. Mohammed Ayoob, *The Third World Security Predicament: State Making, Regional Conflict, and the International System* (Colorado: Lynne Rienner, 1995), p. 193.
7. See Devendra Raj Panday, *Nepal's Failed Development: Reflections on The Mission and the Maladies* (Kathmandu: Nepal South Asia Centre, 1999), p. xv.
8. See Arvind Sivaramakrishnan, "Collapse of the British Constitution", *The Hindu* (Delhi), October 25, 2004.
9. Kripa Sridharan has highlighted the new trends being developed in the Indian cabinet system, which can be called a "hybrid system". See in detail, Kripa Sridharan, "Three is a crowd: Power Centres in Government Bode Ill for Democracy", *hhp:// timesofindia.indiatimes.com,* November 2, 2004.
10. See Niraja Gopal Jayal, ''Situating Indian Democracy" in Niraja Gopal Jayal, (ed.), *Democracy in India* (Delhi: Oxford, 2001), p.3.
11. Jayadeva Uyangoda, "Security's Insecurity: South Asia's States, Societies and Citizens in the Age of Globalization" in Rajesh M. Basrur, (ed.), *Security In the New Millennium: View From South Asia* (Delhi: India Research Press, 2001), p. 116.
12. Samuel P. Huntington, *The Third Wave: Democratization in the Late Twentieth Century* (Norman: University of Oklahoma Press, 1991), p. 290.
13. *The Kathmandu Post,* October 20, 2004.
14. Ibid.
15. Dhruba Kumar, "The Necessity of Choice: Demobilization. Demilitarization and Democratization", *Nepali Journal of Contemporary Studies* (Kathmandu), Vol. 3, No. 1, March 2003), p. 2.
16. Ibid, p. 5.
17. Ravi Nair, the Executive Director of South Asia Human Rights Centre, New Delhi, stated it in an interview with *The Kathmandu Post*, November 1, 2004.
18. Uyangoda, op. cit, p. 116.
    Dhruba Kumar, in another article on Militarized Coflict and violence, has also shown the trend of militarization in Nepal since the Maoist War started in 1996. According to him, the Nepali state "has failed both in

its institutional and functional role. The three integrative functions of the state—, security, representation and welfare" have suffered making Nepal a rent-seeking state. See Dhruba Kumar, "Consequences of the Militarized Conflict and the Cost of Violence in Nepal", *Contributions to Nepalese Studies*, 30:2: July 2003, p. 171.

19. See Lok Raj Baral, "Political Parties and Governance in South Asia" in V.A. Panandiker, (ed.), *Problems of Governance in South Asia* (New Delhi: Konark, 2000), pp. 155–98.
20. Barry Buzan, op. cit, p. 47 and note 15.
21. Lok Raj Baral, *The Kathmandu Post,* August 20, 2004.
22. *Nepal Gazette*, 4 (25 Magh 2011 V.S.) (February 1954),139-40. Cited in Anirudha Gupta, *Politics in Nepal* (Bombay: Allied, 1964), pp. 85–86.
23. See *The Preamble to the Constitution of the Kingdom of Nepal, 1959.*
24. His Majesty's Government of Nepal, Population Census 2001: National Report (Kathmandu: Central Bureau of Statistics). As cited in Krishna P. Khanal, *Rajyako Punarsamrachana: Ek Prastav*" (Restructuring the state: A Proposal) (Kathmandu: NCCS, Occasional paper-9, Baisakh 2061 (April–May 2004).
25. Harka Gurung, Malla K. Sunder, Krishna Bhattachan and Om Gurung, *Development of Nationalities: A Strategy Paper* (Kathmandu: Nationalities Development and Coordination Centre, 2004.

# 7

# Trenches of Violence: Militancy, Militarism and Militarization of Social Sphere in Nepal

***Dhruba Kumar***

Critical security studies have for long debated on the merits of state centrism confined to the monopolistic use of force by the state against challenges to its "acquired values" of preserving territorial integrity, autonomy and stability. Besides policing the state internally, externality as a factor for securitization of state has been demonstrated particularly by the US–Soviet nuclear arms race during the Cold War when the United States alone had footed the bills worth $5.8 trillion by 1996 (Schwartz, 1998). These emergency securitization measures taken to preserve the national security interests have neither assured the United States of its security against threats and vulnerability nor had the Soviet Union succeeded in preserving its territorial integrity and regime security through its nuclear shield. Nor have the open nuclear forays between India and Pakistan in 1998 for securitizing the state prevented them from subsequently waging the Kargil War, exemplifying their false sense of security through deterrence (Kumar, 1999). Although the prevailing perception of international anarchy has conscientiously led states to arms in search of an external order, such a quest for security has not been able to prevent many states from falling into internal disorder. The inexorable spread of violent conflicts within states has not only dissuaded them from their monopolistic rights to use of force but also questioned the legality of violence the states pursue for maintaining political order already disrupted, defied and defaced by internal disputes.

In the process of securitization of the state, their own governments had killed over 169 million people in the 20th century. This is more than 400 per cent of people (38.5 million) killed in inter-state conflicts and civil wars during the same period (Rummel, 1994). Some studies have recently noted that the trends in violent conflicts have sharply been receded by nearly half since the early 1990s (Gurr, Marshall and Khosla, 2001), but the number of violent armed conflicts recorded is horrendous. Although the inter-state violence has become an aberration, 103 wars were fought since the end of the Cold War of which 97 have been intra-state (Preston and Hubert, 2000: 345). Some 3.6 million people died in the 53 conflicts in the 1990s, mostly civilians (UNDP, 2002:85). If in the First World War the ratio of military to civilian casualties was 10:1, that ratio has been reversed to 1:10 now, thus multiplying the proportion of civilian victims of conflict in a single century (Eppler, 2002: 60).

With the changing mores of war, the civilian casualty comprises 90 per cent as the battlefields have expanded from trenches to lanes, streets, villages and cities. Wars are no longer confined to the fighting between the militaries with uniform and insignia distinct from the civilian populations. Wars are fought to create an enduring impact on civilian population and paralyse the state, sometimes even without firing a shot. For example, a fax or e-mail sent from an unknown destination either broadcast or published by media creates havoc that has paralysed the Nepali state repeatedly. The elements of violence hidden in this strategy of fighting an electronic guerrilla war have led to the choices of changing targets from fortified military garrison to mass paralysis and destroying civilian/infrastructure equally serving the functional purpose of war in asymmetrical conflict.

Similarly, the arms are not confined to the hands of the legitimate forces of the state. According to UNDP, there are some 550 million small arms circulating in the world today (UNDP, 2002: 97). Only 41 per cent of them are in the hands of the regular armed forces, some 300 million is spread around in the hands of non-state forces (Krause, 2001: 86). Some 500,000 people die in small arms-related incidents each year. Women and children comprise 70 per cent of victims in such violence. The number of child soldiers is estimated worldwide at close to 300,000 affecting 36 countries (e.g. HRW 2001). Some 90 countries around the world today are affected by land mines, booby traps, and unexploded ordnance—causing between 15,000 and 20,000 mine victims each year (UNDP, 2002:97).

This is the consequence of violence that the state and non-state actors are celebrating amidst deprivation, destitution and dehumanising poverty. The enduring intra-state conflicts around the world have one commonly shared feature: people are increasingly becoming the targets of the conflicts rather than the socially defined protagonists. Resources are diverted to unproductive uses, lives are wasted and opportunities lost. As the strategy of internal war has become a spreading terror that has no fixed address, the carnage has increased because of more ruthless attacks on civilian targets. Therefore, the immense social cost of violent intra-state conflicts, among others, is the growing up of a war generation of children whose experiences make the situation worst for the future of the state. This, in other words, is a situation of nationalizing the costs of war that the state will have to endure for long with rehabilitation and reorientation.

## II

It can simply be inferred that the technological progress made by mankind has also increased the killing spree of human beings. Inter-state rivalries as well as cooperation through partnership for maintaining the sanctity of states as bestowed by the international system and international law have also provided states with unfettered access to means of violence guaranteeing sovereignty of the state for ordering the world system. State being a relatively stable institutional structure of identity and interests, has established a mutually constitutive principle in organizing the world order with rules and laws as coercive instruments. The security practices of the state have thus continued the violent tradition, making state the prime source of security. This tradition is vigorously reinforced and pursued particularly after 9/11 along with worldwide uproar against terrorism. This is exemplified by treatment of the inmates at the Guantanamo Bay prison and the biopolitics that the United States, one of the most liberal countries of the world, has adopted in the name of national security by adopting the Patriot Act through which the ideals of humanity have been degraded, making people subservient to the dictates of state. Societal conflicts have been converted into "terrorism"—a euphemism that the state has reinvented to unleash the forces of structural violence with the objective of making its military power impregnable.

Hence the traditional security practices tend to see all military affairs as being practised as security. Laws and regulations are enacted to provide security forces unquestionable authority to deal with apparent dangers. Though violent activities committed by states against civilians are forbidden by international law and are clearly defined as "war crimes" and as "crimes against humanity" delegitimizing the use of violence against civilians by the state, there is hardly any recourse to such crime when the case of national security is invoked by the states. This is exemplified by the US' global "war on terrorism" that has thoroughly violated the concept of sovereignty of states by manipulating the international consensus to invade Afghanistan and Iraq. In both cases, "war on terrorism" has become a justification for the use of intelligence, surveillance and the armed intervention against sovereign countries. Under this pretext, the concepts of sovereignty and international law against aggression have been turned to their head (e.g. Farer, 2003).

This situation has encouraged and reinforced militarism and the process of militarization around the world. The use of force as an "instrument of supremacy" has led to rearming the state. Numerous states desirous of preserving security have used domestic resources extravagantly and demanded resources from outside along with active support for regimes in coalition against the "war on terrorism". As the frontlines against the "war on terrorism" are not bounded by any geographical limit the battle has become infinite. So has the corresponding rise in militancy perpetuating violence in settling any conflict that falls outside the routine political struggle. Militancy is setting a trend of heavily armed violent groups operating without any geographical margins and engaging in acts of indiscriminate killings, maiming and destruction. Their acts of atrocities have caused new humanitarian emergencies.

Two referral points can therefore elucidate the double ironies that militancy and violence have caused. The first is that militancy occurs due to social injustice in any given society and state when any intra-systemic means of routine political bargains are exhausted. But militancy deliberately marginalizes the people on whose behalf the militants claim to have raised the arms. Second, militancy encourages militarism, thus militarising the social sphere by armed violence and by provoking state repression, which transforms the state into a war machine. At the risk of simplification, it can be assumed that militancy works as a double-edged sword: it is not only the propensity of non-state actors taking up arms to force the state to comply with their objectives but it is also an asset that the state characteristically possesses the use of its authority. Hence militancy, militarism and militarization have two facets: the non-state and state. Militancy on the part of non-state sphere is defined as rebellion, insurgency and revolution. It is generally rehearsed with the aspirations for social change. This radical pursuit for transforming the society through violence has a dual character. It has to confront the expected resistance from the state by increasing the intensity of political conflict with repressive measures. When such a situation of violence creates a self-defeating condition for the rebellious group, it turns more to the militaristic pursuit from being self-extinct. Militarism becomes the currency of struggle to continue chaos instead of order that the insurgents aspire for. In such a dual role, the crunch for human rights is great.

## III

Nepal is a microcosm of militancy and militarism. The act of violence has been a strategic choice pursued consciously as an instrument to obtain certain defined goals (Muro-Ruiz, 2002; Keane, 1996). Threats to use force for dispute settlement or repression of societal upheaval have a historical narrative in a state that has for long endured militarism with dynastic and hereditary succession to power rather than through popular consent. Family feuds, aspirations for power and personal gains motivated people for violence. The sequence of bloodletting that exploded with the Palace massacre on 1 June 2001 was also a manifestation of such trends. The Kot massacre of 1846 that laid the foundation of the Rana oligarchy and the Palace massacre of 2001 unleashed militancy, multitude of violence, untold repression, miseries and sufferings. Every political change in Nepal had elements of violence behind it. The anti-Rana movement of 1951, 1990 *Jana Andolan* and 2002 takeover of state power by the king had the element of violence.

Till 1951, the Rana family worked in tandem with the military-ruled Nepal. All Ranas were also the Generals and other high-ranking officers responsible to the prime minister. That system was founded on "designed militarism" with "premeditated intention to intervene" (Janowitz, 1977: 92) in domestic politics. The context changed with the end of the hereditary Rana rule. But the military power of the state was resurrected by monarchy by transferring the army, cannons, guns and ammunition from Singh Darbar (Rana Prime Ministerial Residence) to Narayanhiti Darbar (Royal Palace) in April 1951 (Devkota, 1960:88). Military as the symbol of ultimate power of the state along with the salience of "premeditated intention to intervene" in domestic politics shifted unceremoniously from Ranarchy to monarchy. Later, this premeditated power was exercised by the monarchy by dissolving the elected parliamentary governments twice: first in December 1960 and second in October 2002. Between 1960 and 1990, the monarchical regime put democracy at bay and treated political opposition as state treason and anti-national by disbanding political parties. Since 2002, monarchy has again sidelined the political parties, taking advantage of dysfunctional democratic polity. In the course of the assertion of the "inherent traditional power" to rule the country with discretion and ordinance, the monarchy has taken a confrontational course backed by the military leading the state towards uncertainty. This context has reinforced militarism in the state–society relations.

Precisely speaking, militarism is the ideological aspect of the ruler's relationship with the state with institutional supremacy of military over civil order. In the case of Nepal, the king being the Supreme Commander-in-Chief of the armed forces as well as the executive authority of the state with powers to use threats or use of force and emergency regulations features the institutional foundation of militarism. Militarism can be defined simply as a situation in which the "propensity to use military power, or the threat of it, for political settlement" is ascertained. According to Radway, "It exalts a function—the application of violence—and an institutional structure—the military establishment. It implies both a *policy* orientation and a *power* relationship" (Radway, 1968:300). In its policy orientation militarism fosters fear with "extensive control of military over social life, completed with the subservience of whole society to the needs of the army" (Andreski, 1968: 185). Power relationship, on the other hand, is crafted on the basis of the military functions, its aspirations and support to the system it is imbued with. Military reflects the ultimate power of coercion of the state. Militarism, on the other hand, is a posture that applies military power to its desired end.

Marek Thee has identified a variety of conditions in which militarism can exist. It ranges from authoritarian regime to direct military rule and to civilian rule with predominant military influence. He has identified three indicators to determine the extent and scope of militarism in a given situation. The first is identified as "structural systemic features" relating to the position of military in the state. The features comprise three categories: whether the military rules, whether there is military-bureaucratic complicity, or whether the military functions under civilian supremacy. The second is the ideological strand of militarism defined as "elements of ideology" referring to notions ranging from nationalism and xenophobia to a phenomenon that glorifies the institutional contributions of military in the process of state building as well as the assertion of military being the saviour of the state. The third indicator relates to state policies in relation to the armed forces. These range from the preferential treatment to the armed forces, provision of high military expenditures and inclination of using military power as policy instrument both internally and externally (Thee, 1977: 296–309).

The last indicator can be significantly explained as militarization. An increase in the military spending, numerical strength of the armed forces and acquisition of new weapons through imports at social cost is generally termed as a process of militarization (Ross, 1987). Militarization, in essence, is a relationship forged by the material aspects of strengthening the armed forces by the civilian authority with various emphases on the need and demand in the service of national security. The civilian authority encourages the process of militarization with both executive and financial support as and when the civil functions collapse and reliance on coercive force increases. The trend setting in Nepal can, thus, be understood as civil-militarism rather than purely militarization (Kumar, 2004a: 6). This perspective can be explained within the context of ensuing political instability and political violence in Nepal.

- Political instability caused by the internicine intra-party strife has eroded the legitimacy of the party in government in the absence of performance despite having been formed with electoral legitimacy. A weak government temperamentally relies heavily on other instruments of power to sustain its tenure leading it to make serious compromises on civil functions. Decision making on the dissolution of the parliament and the non-extension of the tenure of the local bodies as well as undermining of the oversight agencies were instances of creating a political void in which civil-militarism can flourish uninterruptedly.
- Nowhere in the world does the military rule by itself. Even under martial law, the military administers the state by co-opting with a civil bureaucracy. The instances of the declaration of national emergency on 26 November 2001 as well as anti-terrorist ordinance and its subsequent adoption as an Act by the then parliament are cases of promoting military agenda by the civil government, clearing the way for militarization and regimentation of society.
- Executing violence by the Maoists by directly attacking the armed garrison on 23 November 2001 in their surgical

operation of destroying the base with killings and lootings of military equipment had elevated the violence from being a "law and order" problem to "national security" challenge or "grave" threat to the "sovereignty and integrity" of the country. The semantic difference in defining the same problem in different categories and qualification thus becomes obvious by influencing the process of decision making of the government while pursuing the agenda.

- It is true that the Maoists had intentionally informed the enemy that their "People's War" has matured by attacking the military post. But, as a matter of fact, they played into the hands of the military, which had long waited for their chance to play the trump card by cajoling the civilian government to reassess the military imperative.
- The national budget that the government announced for the fiscal year 2002/03 therefore was primarily focused on "investment for peace". This decision reflects the need of arms, ammunition and armament for security imperatives of the state by bringing the prime concern of military in focus.
- On 4 November 2003, the government announced the Unified Military Command by bringing in "all elements of national power including political, economic, information and diplomatic activities" under the operational control of the army (Brief, 2003: 3). The adoption of the Unified Command under the civil–military coordination has two important implications on the social sphere. The first is that the Unified Command is the tacit continuity of emergency situation in the country. The second is that the Unified Command is not only a measure for overt assertion of the state power by the military; it is also a covert declaration of the state in a war situation. The second implication of the Unified Command is ominous in relations to the civil order in the state (Kumar, 2004b: 7).

Militarization, thus, is not simply a bean counting the numbers of arms, ammunition and soldiers and their expansion. It is rather a policy deliberated with the intention of resolving burgeoning conflicts through violent suppression than any other socially congenial means. This purpose has been well expressed through operationalization of the Unified Military Command. The Unified Command is envisioned as a force multiplier by the Royal Nepal Army (RNA), defining it as a concept to "gain optimum use of capabilities and resources of various security forces" from centre down to the district levels under its direct operational control (Brief, 2003:5). The RNA has accordingly drawn a Civil–Military National Campaign Plan (CMNCP) to "tackle the Maoist problem" under the Unified Command that suggests primarily a strategy to "conduct relentless operation against the Maoist to disarm them in order to stop violence and terrorism" (Brief, 2003:4).

The objective of the CMNCP is to defeat the Maoist' military capability. The centre of gravity of this plan would be based on enhancing popular support at the strategic level and strengthening military capabilities at the operational level by relocating, reinforcing, strengthening and equipping security forces along with enhancing intelligence system under the Unified Command. The CMNCP has eventually evolved the Concept of Operation for the Security Forces in 2003 compartmentalizing it as *interest*, *method* and *measure* to achieve the desired end. The *interest* would be to bring the Maoists to the political mainstream through the offensive operation of the security forces in order to deter, defeat and destroy the Maoist military capability. The *method* would be to maintain the presence of the security forces throughout the country protecting military bases and launching military offensives. The *measure* will be to eliminate the Maoists' military capability and force them to negotiate with the government. To achieve such a situation, the military operation would be guided by the principles involving the show of forces, intensifying cordon and search operations, raiding the Maoist hideouts and training camps, along with maintaining a secure line of communication to avert terrorist activities by denying the population and resource control to the Maoists. Finally, the CMNCP would undertake a contingency plan to make the operation more effective and result-oriented (Brief, 2003:5). These are, however, the particulars of intention on the basis of which the RNA plans to defeat the Maoists by the combined might of security forces under the Unified Command (Kumar, 2004c: 3-4).

The militarization of the civilian sphere, unfortunately, is reflected in the military pursuit for arming the unarmed under the Unified Command. The decision announced on 4 November 2003 for the creation of "self-defence force" in villages and districts by distributing arms to citizens has created a condition for widening conflict, possibly with misuse of arms. The armed civilians could easily be identified and made targets by the Maoists who have already practised killing civilians for allegedly being informers of the government. On the other hand, the problem created by the decision in the social context already brewing with ethnic grievances and popular alienation is that it can lead to a more volatile situation with the intentional spread of gun culture. Again, the decision was announced at a time when unconfirmed reports are circulating about the defections of police and army personnel with newly acquired guns and ammunition to the Maoists have increased.

The course that the country has taken, particularly after 4 October 2002, however, is different. In the absence of any elected bodies and the existence of informed oversight agencies, the propensity for unrestrained militarism and militarization has increased despite the restrained budgetary allocation for security sector.

**Table 1: Estimates of Regular Expenditures (in Rs. 000)**

| | *Security Sector* | | | *Social Sector* | |
|---|---|---|---|---|---|
| *Fiscal Year* | *Military* | *Police* | *Education* | *Health* | *Drinking Water* |
| 1995/96 | 2,201,984 | 2,033,300 | 4,641,057 | 940,832 | 11,368 |
| 1996/97 | 2,424,685 | 2,235,571 | 5,069,290 | 960,812 | 11,185 |
| 1997/98 | 2,619,691 | 2,898,281 | 5,579,820 | | |
| 1998/99 | 3,027,890 | 2,922,067 | 6,391,743 | 1,255,861 | 12,563 |
| 1999/2000 | 3,499,089 | 3,871,283 | 6,696,466 | 1,445,791 | ? |
| 2000/01 | 3,897,127 | 7,815,876* | 8,203,401 | 1,663,365 | 15,572 |
| 2001/02 | 4,521,287 | 5,794,641 | 10,428,840 | 2,228,058 | 10,717 |
| 2002/03 | 7,228,182 | 6,303,830 | 10,968,479 | 2,150,866 | 10,246 |
| 2003/04 | 7,184,221 | 7,053,671 | 11,137,179 | 2,175,125 | 13,593 |
| 2004/05 | 8,000,257 | 6,749,834 | 17,903,061** | 6,539,524** | 448,163** |

*Source*: Budget Speeches, Kathmandu: Ministry of Finance, Documents of the years indicated.

* Includes the amount for raising armed police force and purchase of arms.

** The estimated amounts are lumped together with the expected development assistance by donors, which may not confer with the estimated figures in actual disbursement.

These time series data drawn from the official allocation/disbursement indicate steady increment in budgetary allocation. The priority for social sector continued even after the Maoist militancy erupted in 1996 and violence has led to escalated security budgeting. The fiscal year 2000/01 however becomes an exception in security budgeting due considerably to the estimated allocation of additional Rs.1, 586,000,000 for raising the paramilitary (armed police force) and procuring arms. Since then the regular budgetary allocation to security sector remains more or less at par with the social sector allocation.

However, these budgetary figures should be read only as the maintenance cost of the core security sector. The budget does not show both the operational cost as well as off-budgetary allocation for security sector. The RNA is pursuing a role with increased recruitment of the armed personnel and weaponization with sophisticated gadgets. It has increased the recruitment spree and has added over 30,589 personnel from a figure of 47,411 put at the 20th Session of the then House of Representatives in 2001(Rajdhani, 2 November 2001) before the declaration of national emergency making the total 78,000. According to its newly adopted 10-year Defence Plan, the RNA has added 2 Divisions and 5 Brigades to the already existing 3 Divisions. The headquarters of the 5 Divisions will be located at five Development Regions. Besides, the 6th Division is based in Kathmandu. On the other hand, Nepal's civil police have around 48,500 personnel and the Armed Police Force numbers 18,000, making a combined strength of 144,500 men under uniform.

The need of the armed forces, however, is expanding. The Army has recently proposed for an additional budget of Rs.13.86 billion to enhance the security situation in the country. For the current fiscal year 2004/05, the RNA had stipulated the need of an additional Rs.6.13 billion and the rest for the two subsequent years. In the fiscal year 2003–2004, the RNA had recruited a total 6,440 personnel (Ghimire, 2004a:1). It had also planned to recruit 8,500 personnel in the current fiscal year. The urgency for releasing the money for the upkeep of the Kathmandu Valley Command was also conveyed to the government. The RNA has put its sensitive bargaining chip vis-à-vis the government for the security of the national capital in view of daylight killings of several security personnel and government officials. The Kathmandu riots of 1 September 2004 have further made this point obvious.

This is exactly the situation in which a weak and fragile government can be forced to comply with and make subservient to the interests of the armed forces. This situation has therefore given rise to militarism in Nepal. Militarism begins with the threats of sanctions (non-cooperation) if the government do not fulfil military demands. This, in other words is the high-handed technique that the military uses when government reliance increases on the armed forces. Nepal provides an ideal situation for the army to backroll its needs, as the government is so unpopular, illegitimate, isolated and moribund that it cannot survive a day if the army pulls out its support. This is the classic situation of "blackmail" that Samuel Finer had noted by suggesting that the "armed forces in fact begins to rule covertly, either by exercising a veto or by substituting policies and personnel of their own choice for those of the *de jure* government" (Finer, 1962). The RNA, it should be noted, has already acquired such an extreme position in the national decision-making process through the development of the Unified Military Command System.

Despite this, the army has continuously argued that it has not received sufficient funds as proposed. According to the Army spokesperson, Brigadier Dipak Gurung, "the army has received only half of the amount demanded since last two years". It has proposed for the allocation of Rs.14 billion for the current fiscal year, but to no avail (Ghimire, 2004b: 1). Notwithstanding this, the operational cost of the army initially put at Rs.10 million a day inclusive of supplies of food, fuel and provision of special allowances to the military are being meet with both off-budgetary allocations and foreign military assistance. The off-budgetary allocation amounted to over Rs. 5,000 million transferred from different heads of social sector allocations, local development budget as well as water and energy development heads (Kumar, 2003: 182). In the year 2003/04, over Rs.910 million was transferred to the army to beef up security needs only from the amount stipulated under the Poll budget heading (*The Kathmandu Post*, 17 March 2004). The additional amount received by the armed forces from sources like charges for guarding strategic installations like hydropower plants, telecom towers, industrial structure, and commercial buildings; from non-transparent or largely aggregated budgetary categories or divergence of resources from social sector after budgetary approval remain undisclosed because the Auditor General's Annual Report has not appeared in public in the absence of parliament since last three years. However, according to an unofficial estimate, the security expenditure of the government between 2001/02 and 2002/03 was Rs.39.63 billion, inclusive of off-budgetary allocations (Kumar, 2003: 207), far exceeding the stipulated budget amounts.

Similarly, the influx of foreign military assistance has been critical for Nepal's efforts in sustaining its security needs. The US alone has provided Rs. 1,716 million ($22 million) worth of security assistance in the past three years. Under the Global Fund for Prevention of Conflict, the British interests have also been resurrected for aiding Nepal militarily with the initial fund of Rs.780 million (6.5 million sterling pound). The neighbouring states of India and China, particularly India, which had previously been most reluctant to support Nepal with arms assistance, have become the most generous and the largest provider of the military hardware worth Rs.6.5 billion sensitising their own security interests in Nepal. In total, the amount received in the shape of foreign military assistance by 2003/04 was Rs. 8,996 million.

Understandably, the RNA is expanding its force structure and pursuing its weapons acquisition programme on the basis of its 10-year plan that will apparently meet its current needs as well as sustain the higher direction of war in the future. But the war that the RNA is contemplating relates to the domestic situation and the militant upsurge of the Maoists. Obviously, the dominant perception of threat to the state as well as to its institutional interests is from within. In sum, it can therefore be inferred that the process of militarization is concomitant with increasing the power of coercion and intimidation of the state in asserting the role of "designed militarism" (Janowitz, 1977) in the contentious politics of the country that is reflected both in the popular upsurge for democracy and in the Maoists' insurgency.

## IV

Conversely, the "People's War" as a vocabulary of violence used by the Maoist insurgents, in essence, is fundamentally a militaristic pursuit of the non-state actor in course of the armed struggle against the state. Versed in the classical dictum of Mao Zedong's "political power grows out of the barrel of the gun", the Nepali Maoists have launched the "People's War" justifying that an "objective revolutionary situation always prevails in oppressed countries" to which Nepal is not an exception. According to the Maoist supreme commander, Prachanda, the persistent historical situation of the country suspended between "semi-feudal and semi-colonial" condition was ripe for revolution (Karki and Seddon, 2003: 80), suggesting that the revolution has become a necessity since all the possibilities of reform in the system have been exhausted. The Maoist ideologue Baburam Bhattarai has provided further justification for violent upheaval. According to him, the "People's War was initiated with a proclaimed aim of establishing a new democratic socio-economic system and state by overthrowing the present socio-economic structure and state.... The People's War is the inevitable instrument [for overcoming the oppressive situation in the process of the] historic New Democratic revolutionary transformation" (Bhattarai, 1998).

When thinking of violence and insurgency in countries like Nepal, it is generally assumed that the causes lie in grievances. Grievances in general relate to non-traditional security issues as poverty, destitution and deprivation that have never been addressed by the state coherently. Hence, pervasive poverty and inequalities are identified as causes of conflict. Violence is therefore justified and anti-state revolt is taken to resolve the grievance-related issues. But can these be empirically validated with military resolve? Is this a *method* to be correctly assessed and to resolve the socially impervious challenges? Can violence be used as a poverty alleviation measure or signalling of discontent for changing power relations in the state? These questions are yet to be appropriately assessed and answered in the looming shadow of violence. Although the armed violence committed by the non-state actor is the most visible aspect of the rebellion, it is the fundamental dimension of conflict ensuing in the state leading both to militarism and militarization of the social sphere. Extreme violent measures taken by the Maoists have therefore led to the militarization of conflicts furthering the course of institutionalisation of violence in Nepal. Social resilience, as a consequence, has been severely disrupted by forcing the society to reluctantly accept violence as a legitimate mode of political behaviour of the state and non-state.

One of the basic features of the Maoist violence is the spread of terror. Terror, as a result, has become indistinguishable from terrorism. The *Guru* for the non-state in lessons of terror is the state. Ever since the lessons of the Reign of Terror committed in the French Revolution have spread, the perpetrators of violence, including the Maoists in Nepal, have used terror as a crucial signal to dramatize their existentialist resolve. The purpose of the signal is to communicate that the target is vulnerable, the perpetrator can strike at targets at any time of its choosing and cannot be cowed down by any sort of retaliation. The meaning that the signal conveys to the wider audiences, including the target is usually "demand for recognition, redress, autonomy, or transfers of power (Tilly 2004: 9). The "People's War" in this sense has no dispersed targets other than coaxing the state to transfer the power by dethroning monarchy and parliamentary democracy. The Maoist ideologues, in fact, have no objective, not even the creation of a condition for social equality through their "revolution," than attaining political power. The Maoists have camouflaged their basic instincts for grabbing power at the centre behind the façade of their ideology, which they were certainly not capable of wrenching from the competitive electoral politics they have tasted between 1991 and 1994.

The second strategy of the Maoists is to shake up the state by maximizing the chances of socio-political and economic destabilization causing popular alienation against the government. Thus strategy is expected to create chaotic conditions within the state. Their activities targeting political, social, economic and service infrastructure destruction have led to a political vacuum in villages and districts, closure of industrial and economic activities, discouraging tourism and trekking, and forced exodus of people for want of living. It is not a policy of weaning the people away from the state but ejecting them from their own areas. This is how the Maoists have succeeded in establishing their base areas. The shrinking of the state to the district headquarters surrounded by barbed-wire fences and land mines and security forces in defensive has provided the Maoists the God-sent opportunity to unleash their own reign of terror in the areas. The "reactionaries" have either to be expelled from the villages or eliminated through violence. Even the cadres of *Jana Morcha*—the fraternal party of the Maoists—who oppose the heinous crimes committed by the Maoists, have become the targets in villages and towns leading to serious scuffles between them.

Sharply declining economic activities except existence of some relief works of WFP and other agencies like World Vision in districts have compounded the plight of the people. The property and land-grab movements, looting of banks, destruction of civil infrastructure like electric power houses, telecom towers, factories coupled with Nepal *bandh* and blockade that the Maoists occasionally announce have completely paralysed the state as a whole, signalling to the international communities the message of the country being an unsafe territory.The Maoists have intensified such an activity in the country in accordance with the decision reached at the March 1995 Plenum of their Central Committee as a target of the armed struggle (*The Worker*, 1997). By undertaking such strategy of conflict, the Maoists have thoroughly succeeded in putting the national economy in a shambles despite the tall claim of the government that the per capita GNP of the Nepali people has increased impressively to $276 in 2003/04 from $250 of the previous year (MoF, 2004: 10).

The third strategy remains for securing the base area to spread violence through intimidation, torture, killings and coaxing the people living in the home territories through extortions and taxes as well as mounting select attacks on the enemy of revolution in territories dispersed from the Maoist camps. The basic elements in founding the base area are not only related to their power of persuasion or coercion but also to their policy of ethnicising the conflict. Their programme and promises of ethnic and regional autonomy are evident in their announcement of establishing various autonomous and regional "People's Governments" from mountainous to Tarai regions with the claims of expansion of their support base around the country. By issuing a separate budget, introducing a visa system for visitors to the Maoist-infested areas, taxing the inhabitants, charging levies on commercial, tourist or trekking transactions and extracting commissions from sale of timber and herbs like *yarshagumba*, the Maoists have shown a semblance of independence by creating a state within a state.

All of the above three strategies are substantially intertwined with the fourth strategy of the comprehensive military preparation for defeating the state forces and planned takeover of the country. Indoctrinated with the concept of "protracted war", the Maoists have adopted two-pronged approaches with the fusion of military and political and urban and rural actions for infrastructure support, but focusing on the singular target of the armed confrontation. The Maoists have no illusion that

> "Without defeating enemy's military offensive through the development of appropriately powerful military force, neither local people's power can be protected nor can it be consolidated. Hence, the first condition for defending local people's power and its consolidation is the development of people's military power." The document of the Fourth Expanded Meeting of the CPN (Maoist) "Experience of the People's War and Some Important Questions" has clearly stated that the "experience of the people's war... has repeatedly shown that people without military power will retain nothing for themselves.... That is why it has become necessary for the Party (under centralized leadership) to concentrate its attention to the question of building the army"
>
> (Karki and Seddon, 2003: 236).

It should therefore be understood that the pursuit for militarization of the party and social sphere is the collective decision of the CPN (Maoist). Never should it be explained and confused with the idea of separation of the party from the military as the latter is more influential in dictating the party. The unidimensional power of the party in revolution is the military whose actions determine the course of the conflict. The Maoists have the experiences of the indigenous and the world communist movements behind them as a guide for action. Since they have decided to close the electoral path to power and have gone underground cherishing state power, the only logical option remaining with them is to pursue armed struggle to realize the objective by rationalizing violence. Their plan for the initiation of the armed struggle is definite in asserting the principle that "everything is an illusion except state power" (*The Worker*, 1996). Accordingly, they have instituted the Central Military Commission in February 1998 signifying their resolve to pursue armed struggle with systematic organizational support.

Hence, the militarism of the Maoists has come of age. They have expanded from a sizable number of some 2,000 committed party cadres and guerrillas to over 25,000 in number. They have amassed the support of the people in their military formation simply from some volunteer groups, militias, and squad, expanding from section to platoon, to company and from Brigades to Divisions. The Maoists have claimed that they maintain 2 Divisions, 7 Brigades and 19 Battalions of fighting guerrillas supported by over 100,000 militias (*Bulletin*, 2003; *Rajdhani*, 15 September 2003). The Maoist Supremo, Prachanda has recently claimed in a statement issued after the conclusion of the Party Plenum in September 2004 that the People's Army consists of 3 Divisions, 9 Brigades and 29 Battalions. Perhaps this could simply be a signal of their vow to continue violence. But this cannot be dismissed as propaganda. The Maoists had started their armed struggle simply with some crude indigenous weapons, but they are now wielding AK-47 and M16 rifles. They are sourcing arms from indigenously manufactured weapons, landmines, detonators, pillaging arms and ammunition from security forces, and outright purchase from clandestine sources. They have extensively used land mines, electronic detonators and explosives against the security forces. Their military campaigns have succeeded in creating both consternation and convulsion, negatively impacting the efficiency and capabilities of the state security organs. In almost 32 skirmishes with the security forces ranging from the mounting of the first attack on a military barrack in Ghorai, Dang in November 2001 to the latest attack in Mugu in October 2004 and many other installations since then (as of June 2005) the Maoists have made their mark considerably by looting arms and ammunition from the state forces as has been evident by their possession of the Galil, M16 and INSAS rifles along with other expensive weapons, including 81mm mortars. The government's announcement of attractive monetary rewards to the persons surrendering these varieties of weapons also exemplifies the case (HMG, 18 December 2003).

Corresponding to the government recruitment spree, the Maoists have also started forced recruitment by abducting school children as well as teachers and turning village schools into military camps and making old people parade on the school grounds. They have been forcing the villagers to either join guerrilla force or become militias, with threats of punishment to those who refuse to comply. The "one family, one person" policy of the Maoist has led to the closure of numerous schools in villages and towns along with their increasing brutality. Those school children returning home after several days of disappearance have been watched with caution by government security forces. The "pangs of proximity" of living with the Maoists and the security forces have increased insecurities of the people as they can be charged with complicity either by the Maoists or by the security forces.

With the swelling of compatriots in their camp, the Maoists have maintained one Military Division each in the Eastern, Western and Central Command. The Maoists have planned to maintain one Brigade each in the 9 Autonomous People's Government regions that they have formed. Except for two districts of Manang and Mustang, the Maoists activities are spread over the rest of the 73 districts of the country. The military organization of the Maoists is composed of five bureaus—Eastern, Western, Central, Valley and external bureaus. The external bureau critically functioning in India as an international contact hub has crucially aided the internal military formations of the Maoists. The fraternal association of the Maoists with the Maoist Coordination Centre (MCC) and the People's War Group (PWG)—currently amalgamated into one—has aided the CPN (Maoist) not only to expand their reach with other rebellious groups functioning in India but also to establish contacts with organizations in Bangladesh and beyond. The Coordination Committee of Maoist Parties and Organization of South Asia (COCOMPOSA) along with Revolutionary Internationalist Movement (RIM) have contributed significantly to the development of the "People's War" in Nepal. As the Indian underground movements and territories remain the largest hinterland for the Maoist movement in Nepal, the Nepali Maoists have used the opportunity as a conduit for availing their needs—mainly for the personal safety of the leaders and clandestine supply of arms, ammunition and explosives. The open Nepal–India border, though guarded at the moment, has, in fact, become a blessing in disguise for the Maoists to operate across the proximate territory as the case of the shifting of the Maoist shelter from Bihar and Uttar Pradesh to Uttaranchal across the Mahakali River in the West suggests. The strength of the Maoists is therefore not only confined to the domestic territory in India. The nexus created by the Maoists with the militants spreading from the northwest to the northeast Himalayas would further entrench militancy in the domestic sphere corresponding to the government's inability to respond to the need of the people as well as to their military onslaught.

The Maoists have already proven their ability to destroy the authority of the state: first by pushing the state's presence out from almost three-quarters of the territories of the country by confining the government to the district headquarters, and second by creating an unpropitious situation in the country to force postponement of the parliamentary elections as scheduled for 2002, and again in 2003 by the king's appointed government, thereby derailing both the democratically elected government and questioning the efficacy of the monarchical power. Again, the Maoists have also established their political and military acumen by creating the condition for the government to concede to the reality of the "two states and two armies" within the state in their back channel negotiations with the Palace leading to a "ceasefire" in January 2003.

Third, the Maoists have largely succeeded in undermining the state authority particularly after 4 October 2002 as a consequence of the aspersions in the popular perception against the king's appointed governments that broadly face a severe legitimacy crisis. Further, the weakening of the government has strengthened the Maoist authority imposed on society by means of violence and terror. The Maoists prevail not only in the areas where they have established a quasi-state, but also in areas where the Nepali state generally functions through extortions and threats of armed intimidation. The Maoists' extortion network is not only confined to villages and towns but to the capital city of Kathmandu and beyond. Perhaps this is the reason why nobody doubts that the Maoists are amongst the richest "terrorist groups" in the world with a "money bag" of $ 64 to 128 million (Rs.5 to Rs.10 billion) in the year 2000 (Lintner, 2000). The Maoists have ascertained this position not because of their economic or social reform programmes but because of their militaristic prowess and capacity to indulge in violence.

There is thus a probability of a situation developing in Nepal that the Maoist ideology of revolution would be completely shaken off by greed of economic benefits derived from violence and intimidation as has been witnessed in other countries engulfed in conflicts. Although the Maoists are yet to indulge in illicit trade and trafficking of both material and humans, their involvement in contraband transactions has been reported time and again. This fling with monetary benefits may perhaps become a temptation for the Maoists to continue violence and threats of intimidation that have already paid dividends in different kinds. First, with the land confiscation from the designated landlords and labour exploitations of the teachers, health workers and government officials charging them 5 to 10 per cent and sometimes even 25 per cent of their fixed salaried income, the Maoists have cultivated habits to swell their coffers. The cost-free use of children and villagers as porters by the Maoists is another source of labour exploitation. Second, pillage and plundering have become a major source of income for the Maoists. The large-scale looting of banks and households has enriched the Maoists enabling them even to finance arms purchase and war. Moreover, they have practised to raise protection money regularly from rich politicians businesspersons and industrialists. Protection paycheques are being rumoured to have been provided even by the home minister and some top-ranking security personnel to the Maoists. Further, the Maoists are stealing resource from relief supplies, charges of work permits from INGOs and NGOs and practising rent seeking by perpetuating conflict. Finally, they are also receiving kickbacks from petty transactions conducted locally by traders and merchants with artificial fixing of prices of commodities. To gain from such economic dimension of conflict does not require the Maoists to succeed in holding the reins of power of the state, it requires just breaking the law that the power of the state cannot preserve.

## V

Comprehending the situation of continued militancy and violent conflict between the protagonists of the state that has already crossed the mark of over 11,000 deaths and hundreds of thousands rendered homeless, increasing number of widows heading the households, children left parentless, countless rapes, tortures, indiscriminate killings, soaring unemployment and opportunities lost and denied with intensification of violence, human security has definitely become the crucial victim of the first kind. Making thousands of people disappear has become a routine affair. It can also be assumed that if such a state of affairs continues for some time, it may become a social phenomenon. Human rights violation by the state and non-state actors, though, is not new in its form and character. Instances of states' inability to cope with militancy are on the increase (King and Zeng, 2001: 625).

Although economic disruption, dislocation, displacement and forced migration of the people cannot be averted and managed through repressive measures, the government in Nepal has taken traditional measures upholding emergency power and Anti-Terrorist Act and counterinsurgency mobilization of the armed forces under the provision of impunity. On top of it, the security forces have been provided with the rights of detention of any suspect for a year without any legal recourse to the person in question through the issue of an ordinance on 13 October 2004 (*Nepal Gazette,* 2004). The use of Article 9 of this ordinance would be a denial of the rights to *habeas corpus* that was not even ruled out by the national emergency regulations.

The anti-terrorist ordinance provides the security forces free rein, which already faces a litany of allegations, including the worst crimes against humanity—unlawful killings, disappearances, gang rapes, arbitrary arrests and disrespect towards Supreme Court orders (e.g. HRW, 2004). Earlier, an expert has described his experience of human rights situation in Nepal thus: "I have worked in a number of countries in conflict... and Nepal ranks among the worst human rights situations I have ever seen. People are terrified, of both the RNA and the Maoists" (O'Neill, 2004). Similarly, a statement issued by 15 Embassies and Donor Agencies based in Kathmandu says, "The current situation in Nepal portrays a climate in which no one is free from fear and insecurity" (*The Himalayan Times*, 25 September 2004). Despite such admonition against the state of affairs in the country, the government in Nepal has progressed further on the path to militancy under the cover of the Anti-terrorist Ordinance 2004.

Implicit in this hardening posture of the state is the recognition of the failure of its normal functions. The obtaining reality is that King Gyanendra's active rule has therefore become a fiasco. The king as the Supreme Commander-in-Chief of the Royal Nepal Army has failed miserably in effectively mobilizing armed security forces in containing the spread of the Maoist insurgency that has become worse than ever before. Also, the king as a person commanding the executive power of the state has failed incredibly in administering the country by maintaining a semblance of domestic order. He has, instead, contributed to drifting the country towards anarchy with the appointment of political non-entities for governing the state. What was more ridiculous was some sort of a notification issued from the Royal Palace for putting application to the post of Prime Minister by asserting his ''divine right'' to rule the country.

## REFERENCES


Bhattarai, Baburam, 1998, *The Politico–Economic Rationale of the People's War*, (Kathmandu: Utprerak Prakashan).

*Brief to U.S. Assistant Secretary of State*, 2003 (A Policy Brief presented by the Director General of the Royal Nepalese Army (RNA) to the visiting U.S. Assistant Secretary of State Christina Rocca at the RNA Headquarters, Bhadrakali, Kathmandu on 17 December).

Bulletin, 2003, *Maoist Information Bulletin*, Vol .4.

Devkota, Grishma Bahadur, 1960, *Nepalko Rajnitik Darpan* (The Political Mirror of Nepal), (Kathmandu: Keshav Chandra Gautam).

Eppler, Erhard, 2002, "Speech delivered at the Annual Conference of Swiss Ambassadors," (Berne, Switzerland: 21 August).

Farer, Tom J., 2003, "Humanitarian Intervention Before and After 9/11: Legality and Legitimacy," in J. L. Holzgrate and Robert Keohane, (eds.), *Humanitarian Intervention: Ethical, Legal and Political Dilemma*, (Cambridge: Cambridge University Press).

Finer, Samuel E., 1962, *The Man on Horseback: The Role of the Military in Politics*, (New York: Praeger).

Ghimire, Bijaya, 2004a, "Sena Dwara Thap Eighara Araba Maag," (The Army demanded an Additional Eleven Billion Rupees), *Kantipur* Daily, 31 August.

Ghimire, Bijaya, 2004b, "Nirbachan Rakam Anyatrai,"(Transfer of Election Fund), *Kantipur* Daily, 16 October.

Gurr, Ted Robert, Monty G. Marshall and Deepa Khosla, 2001, *Peace and Conflict: A Global Survey of Armed Conflicts, Self-Determination Movements, and Democracy*, (College Park, MD: Centre for International Development and Conflict Management, University of Maryland).

*The Himalayan Times*, 2004, "Donors, Envoys find faults in rights record," 25 September.

*The Himalayan Times*, 11 September 2004.

HMG, 2003, "Atmasamarpan Sambandhi Sri 5ko Sarkarko Nitipatra," (His Majesty's Government's Policy in relations to Surrender), Kathmandu: HMG/Ministry of Home Affairs, 10 December.

HRW, 2004, *Between a Rock and a Hard Place: Civilians Struggle to Survive in Nepal's Civil War*, (New York: Human Rights Watch, October).

HRW, 2001, *Human Rights Watch Report*, http://www.hrw.org/campaigns/crp/index.htm.

Janowitz, Morris, 1977, *Military Institutions and Coercion in the Developing Countries*, (Chicago, IL: University of Chicago Press).

Karki, Arjun and David Seddon, (eds.), 2003, *The People's War in Nepal: The*

*Left Perspectives*, (Delhi: Adroit Publishers).
Keane, John, 1996, *Reflections on Violence*, (London: Verso).
King Gary and Langche Zeng, 2001, "Improving Forecast of State Failure," *World Politics*, July.
Krause, Keith, 2001, *Small Arms Survey 2001*, (Oxford: Oxford University Press).
Kumar, Dhruba, 2004a, "Emergency, Militarization and the Question of Democratic Recovery," (A paper presented at the National Seminar on "Participatory Democracy in Nepal" organized by the Nepal Centre for Contemporary Studies, Lalitpur, at Hotel Malla, Kathmandu, 2–3 January).
Kumar, Dhruba, 2004b, "Impact of Conflict on Security and the Future: A Case of Nepal," (A Paper presented at the Asia Symposium on "Security Sector Governance" organized by the Global Facilitation Network for Security Sector Reform, Cranfield University, Swindon, UK, at Marriott Royal Garden Riverside Hotel, Bangkok, Thailand, 21–22 September).
Kumar, Dhruba, 2004c, "Security Sector, Human Rights and Human Security in Nepal," (A paper presented at the International Conference on "Human Security: Global and Regional Perspectives" jointly organized by the Departments of International Relations, Universities of Sindh and Karachi and sponsored by the Hanns Seidal Foundation, Islamabad, in Karachi, Pakistan, 30 August – 4 September).
Kumar, Dhruba, 2003, "Consequences of the Militarized Conflict and the Cost of Violence in Nepal," *Contributions to Nepalese Studies*, 30 (2), July.
Kumar, Dhruba, 1999, "South Asia after the Nuclear Tests: Securing Insecurity", *CNAS Occasional Paper*, (Kathmandu: Centre for Nepal and Asian Studies).
Lintner, Bert, 2000, "Maoist Moneybags," *Far Eastern Economic Review*, 24 October.
MoF, 2004, *Economic Survey Fiscal Year 2003/2004*, Kathmandu: HMG/ Ministry of Finance.
Muro-Ruiz, Diego, 2002, "State of the Art: The Logic of Violence," *Politics*, 22 (2).
*Nepal Gazette*, 13 October 2004.
O'Neill, William G., 2004, *Nepal Report*, 16 April (Confidential memo.).
Preston, David and Don Hubert, 2000, "Towards Freedom from Fear: An Agenda for Human Security," *BIISS* Journal, July.
Radway, Laurence I., 1968, "Militarism," in David L. Sills, (ed.), *International Encyclopaedia of the Social Sciences*, Vol. 9., (New York: The Macmillan Company & The Free Press).
*Rajdhani* Daily, 15 September 2003.
*Rajdhani* Daily, 2 November 2001.
Ross, Andrew, 1987, "Dimensions of Militarization in the Third World," *Armed Forces & Society*, Summer.

Rummel, Rudolph J., 1994, *Death by Government: Genocide and Mass Murder in the Twentieth Century*, (New Brunswick, N.J.: Transaction Publishers).

Schwartz, Stephen I., (ed.), 1998, *Atomic Audit: The Costs and Consequences of US Nuclear Weapons Since 1940*, (Washington D. C.: The Brookings Institution Press).

*The Kathmandu Post*, 14 June 2004.

*The Kathmandu Post*, 17 March 2004.

*The Worker*, No 3, 1997.

The Worker, 1996, "Theoretical Premises for the Historic Initiation of the People's War," *The Worker*, No. 2.

Thee, Marek, 1977, "Militarism and Militarization in Contemporary International Relations," *Bulletin of Peace Proposals*, 8 (4).

Tilly, Charles, 2004, "Terror, Terrorism, Terrorists," *Sociological Theory*, 22 (1), March.

UNDP, 2002, *Human Development Report 2002*, (New York: United Nations Development Programme).

# 8

# Militarization and Territorial Security in Pakistan

***Hasan-Askari Rizvi***

Traditionally, state security involved the management of inter-state relations and maintenance of a powerful military. A strong and powerful military was viewed as the most important condition for state security and survival. It was argued the state sovereignty and territorial integrity could not be ensured without a strong security apparatus and an assertive administrative structure.

Such a narrow perspective on security tends to overlook or downplay the threats from the domestic context of a state due to neglect of socio-economic development, lack of distributive justice, failure to evolve participatory political process that upholds cultural and political pluralism, and works towards the improvement of quality of life for the ordinary people. A coherent, just and stable political order that responds to the needs and aspiration of the people and evokes their voluntary loyalty is no less important for state security and survival than a strong military apparatus.

Most developing states tend to ignore the societal and human aspects of security for a number of reasons discussed in this chapter. It also argues that Pakistan pursued a narrow and military-oriented perspective on security and paid less attention to societal and human security. The discussion of Pakistan's security approaches opens with an analysis of the factors that led Pakistan to pursue such a security disposition. This study argues that Pakistan's security approach strengthened the role of the military at the expense of civilian and political institutions and resulted in the militarization of the political system and the society. This undermined the prospects of democracy.

This chapter notes that the government of Pakistan has been

allocating more resources to social development sectors and poverty reduction since 2001. However, it has not been able to cause a major break from the military or territorial notion of security.

### Survival and Territorial Security:

One of the major concerns of a large number of developing states is survival and protection of sovereignty and territorial integrity against internal and external threats. These considerations often override other requirements of governance and societal development. The issues of state survival and protection of territorial integrity have acquired such a salience because these states face insecurities for several reasons.

A large number of the developing states faces the problem of creating a coherent and stable political order that evokes voluntary loyalties of its citizens. What makes their task difficult is the non-congruence between the nation-state identity and other identities that exist in a state. The developing states have to deal with two kinds of identities. First, sub-national and smaller identities compete with the nation-state identity. The sub-national identities based on ethnicity, language, regional and other considerations have a strong pull for a large number of people who may assign them greater priority over their nation-state identity. Second, trans-national identities and attachments that cut across the territorial boundaries of the state have a strong claim on the political profile of a large number of people and groups. Many ethnic, linguistic and religious-cultural groups are spread over adjoining territories of different states. For example, the Kurds are divided in four countries, i.e. Iraq, Iran, Turkey and Syria. The Pushtuns are divided between Pakistan and Afghanistan. These transnational linkages pull them away from their respective nation-states and they often demand autonomy or independence.

How to remove conflict between these sets of identities and the nation-state identity is crucial to building a coherent political order. This calls for establishing an inclusive political order that incorporates these identities into the national identity in a manner that the former do not feel threatened. Such an inclusive political order has to be participatory and democratic so as to remove conflict among them and build a national identity that incorporates rather than excludes the sub- or supra-national identities.

Socio-economic justice must accompany political participation. The state policies need to work towards removing socio-economic disparities amongst the people and the regions for creating political harmony and partnership in a diversified political system.

Most developing states cannot address these issues effectively. Narrow-based elite that adopts authoritarian system of governance and political management governs these states. The participatory norms are not fully implemented and there is less emphasis on constitutionalism, the rule of law and participatory governance. Further, they often suffer from scarcity of material resources. The scarce resources are not distributed equitably. They ignore the imperatives of socio-economic justice which causes bitterness among those who perceive themselves to be denied of their due share in national resources. These factors strengthen distrust among various identities and interests, which undermines the efforts to promote political harmony and partnership in the political system. The ruling elite often equate their partisan interests with the national interest and perpetuate a non-representative and authoritarian system that is insensitive to the aspirations and needs of a large section of the populace.[1]

The regional and global contexts also have implications for the internal political landscape of these states. The regional context, especially the relations with the neighbours have implications for building the nation-state identity in a diversified context. If the relations with the neighbours are troubled for one reason or another, its internal difficulties can be exploited by the said neighbour to its advantage. Such a regional situation increases insecurities of the state facing internal problems.

The global context also has implications for the policy choices for the states attempting to cope with the pressures of a diversified socio-political order in its internal context. In the Cold War period, many rulers of the developing states facing internal political challenges secured the support of one superpower or another in order to strengthen their position in coping with domestic adversaries. As long as the ruler of such a state served the global agenda of a superpower, the said superpower supported the ruler no matter how he handled the internal situation. In the post-Cold War period, such a partisan support was not available at the international level because the superpower conflict had ended. Many rulers faced serious problems in dealing with internal problems, including the harmonization of diverse interests and identities. Internal political and economic stability acquired greater salience as pre-requisites for playing an effective role at the international level or to ward off international pressures.

Since the terrorist attacks in the United States on 11 September 2001, the international system assigns the highest priority to combating terrorism. All other considerations have been pushed to the background. The changed international priorities helped some rulers to continue with their authoritarian system of governance under the pretext of combating terrorism. Others faced problems in dealing with their political adversaries or from those maintaining strong sub- or supra-national orientations. The diversified states now experience greater insecurities if these cannot evolve a participatory and plural system for managing diversity.

Most of these states have dealt with the survival and internal harmony issues with an emphasis on physical or territorial security. The emphasis is on creating a centralized, strong and assertive state. These states also create a strong and powerful military and other security forces for ensuring the protection of state sovereignty and territorial integrity. They put less emphasis on establishing participatory institutions and processes and discourage socio-cultural diversity. The attempt is to create a monolithic nation-state rather than working towards a participatory and plural political and social order.

When state security is linked primarily with the physical and territorial security, the control apparatus of the state is strengthened at the expense of participatory political institutions and processes. This creates a security state where the establishment of a strong military and an assertive state structure are given a priority over participatory institutions and processes. Power and authority flow from the top with an emphasis on state building on authoritarian and non-representative lines, although some states may create some semblance of democracy to cover up the authoritarian governance.

The notion of security state comes in conflict with the notion of a participatory pluralist state that attaches primacy to societal security. This does not mean that the latter does not create military and law-enforcing agencies. These exist even in a non-security participatory state but a broader concept of security is pursued. It emphasizes that territorial or physical security is only one aspect of security. The state must pay attention to improving the quality of life for the people. It must adopt measures for enabling the people to cope with socio-economic pressures so that a vibrant and internally cohesive society emerges. The strengthening of the internal dynamics of the society adds to the resilience of the political system and enables it to cope with the pressures applied from the international and regional contexts. From this standpoint, the internal coherence and strength of the society is no less significant than military and territorial security. The combining of these two aspects creates what is described as comprehensive security.

Comprehensive security maintains that national security does not merely depend on military power. It also involves building strength of the social and political institutions and processes as well as paying attention to the betterment and welfare of the people. The state should ensure good governance and participatory management of societal and state affairs. It must devote attention to social development sectors like education, health care, civil facilities and environment, and economic development. Thus, the scope of the nation of security has expanded. "It now rests on five pillars: social cohesion, political strength, economic development, diplomatic support and military readiness."[2]

### Pakistan's Security Perspective

Pakistan's policy makers pursue the traditional concept of security that assigns priority to military or territorial security. They favour a centralized and assertive state and a strong military as a guarantee of security. Consequently, societal security has remained neglected. The Pakistani state did not pay adequate attention to education, health care, socio-economic development and distributive justice. The neglect of these and related areas adversely affected societal development.

Pakistan developed as a military security state from the early days of its independence in 1947. It faced so many problems in this period that the survival of state was assigned precedence over all other considerations.

Four sets of problems in the early years created strong insecurity among the policy makers who felt that if adequate attention was not given to the security of its recently earned independence and territorial integrity, the future of the state might be jeopardized. For the policy makers, the primary issue was survival of the state rather than its democratization or establishment of a participatory and plural political system.

First, the communal riots that accompanied the partition of British India and establishment of Pakistan and the influx of refugees shocked the policy makers. Hardly any part of Pakistan escaped the adverse impact of the refugee problems and killings. Second, several disputes erupted between Pakistan and India as a result of the partition. These included the division of civil and military assets of the British Indian government. Pakistan needed these resources to set up the new state but it did not get all that it claimed to be its share. Third, Pakistan had to set up a federal government in Karachi with meagre material and human resources. A new provincial government was to be set up in Dhaka. Both the cities lacked the necessary infrastructure for establishing an administration, not to speak of the shortage of trained senior civil servants and military officers. Fourth, the disputes with India on the accession of the princely states of Junagadh and Jammu and Kashmir caused much bitterness.[3] The first Kashmir War, 1947–48 pitched the two states against each other, which caused such a breach between them that they could not develop friendly relations with each other.[4] These trends were reinforced by a host of other negative developments in their relations in the early 1950s.

It was not difficult for the Pakistani policy makers to evolve a historical narrative to interpret the troubled relations with India in the early years as an extension of the hostility between the Congress Party and the Muslim League in the pre-Independence period. Pakistan's official and non-official circles argued that having failed to stop the establishment of Pakistan the Congress Party leaders of India were creating problems for Pakistan so that it did not take off as an independent state.

Pakistan's insecurity was intensified by Afghanistan's irredentist claims on Pakistani territory. Afghanistan laid claims to the North Western Frontier Provinces and parts of Baluchistan in the immediate aftermath of Pakistan's independence. Its claim on these territories ranged from independence for them or maximum autonomy within Pakistan to their absorption in Afghanistan. Intermittent border clashes between the two countries in the 1950s and the 1960s caused much concern to Pakistan and their diplomatic relations were severed twice, in 1955 and 1962. India supported Afghanistan's claims to Pakistani territory, and in 1955, the Soviet Union endorsed Afghanistan's demand on Pakistan after the latter joined the US sponsored security alliances.[5] A large section of public opinion and the government in Pakistan talked of the threat of a two-front war: armed clashes erupting simultaneously on Pakistan—India and Pakistan—Afghanistan borders. They were thus convinced that Pakistan was extremely vulnerable and the search for security loomed large in their strategic considerations.

Insecurity caused by the developments in the early years of independence was reinforced by the later developments in and around Pakistan. The troubled relations with India and the Indo–Pakistan wars in 1965 and 1971 dominated the world view of Pakistan's policy makers. India's superior military profile and its tough posture towards Pakistan were viewed as the major security problem. Pakistan continued to face problems in its interaction with Afghanistan, although Afghanistan was not perceived as a military power that could invade Pakistan and overrun major parts of its territory. A new security dimension was added to Afghanistan with the Soviet military intervention in Afghanistan in December 1979. Pakistan supported Afghan-Islamic resistance to the Soviet occupation of Afghanistan. The withdrawal of the Soviet troops from Afghanistan in 1989 did not solve Pakistan's security problems because the Afghan resistance could not create a government in Kabul that enjoyed the support of most Afghan groups. Consequently, after the withdrawal of the Soviet troops, the intra-Afghan conflict caused a host of new security problems for Pakistan on the Pakistan–Afghanistan border.[6]

The search for security emerged as the principal concern of Pakistan's policy makers that not only shaped their world view and disposition towards regional and international politics but also served as an instrument of policy. They assigned the highest priority to the needs of territorial security against what they perceived as threats from India and Afghanistan. The government gave precedence to strengthening military security over other considerations. This resulted in diversion of national resources to military and defence needs, including the procurement of weapons from abroad. Pakistan's foreign policy options were also shaped by the need for strengthening the military and territorial security.

### Defence Needs and Procurement of Weapons

Defence requirements have enjoyed top priority in Pakistan. All Pakistani governments, civil and military, allocated the major portion of the national budget to defence. Pakistan's defence expenditure ranged from about 73 per cent in 1949–50 to 24–25 per cent of the total federal expenditure in 2000–01. The percentage of defence expenditure to total federal expenditure declined to 21 per cent in 2004–05. The budget for 2005–06 allocated Rs. 223.5 billion out of total federal expenditure of Rs. 1098.5 billion (about 20 per cent). In the past, defence expenditure amounted to 5–6 per cent of the Gross Domestic Product (GDP). In 2005–06, this ratio declined to about 3.1 per cent. This does not include covert expenditure on defence-related projects and the weapons, military hardware and equipment Pakistan received as outright grants or against loans in the mid-1950s, 1980s, and since 2002.

The imperatives of territorial security shaped Pakistan's foreign policy options. Pakistan joined the US-sponsored alliance system in the mid-1950s mainly for strengthening its security and to obtain weapons and military equipment. Pakistan and the US signed the Mutual Defence Assistance Treaty in May 1954, which facilitated US arms transfers to Pakistan and military training of its personnel by US experts. Pakistan joined the Southeast Asia Treaty Organization (SEATO) in September 1954 and the Baghdad Pact (later renamed as the Central Treaty Organization, CENTO) in September 1955. Another security arrangement was the Bilateral Agreement of Cooperation, signed by Pakistan and the US in March 1959 as an executive arrangement. A separate agreement was signed in July 1959 allowing the US to set up a communication facility, an airbase near Peshawar for ten years.[7]

Pakistan again developed close relations with the West, especially the US, in the aftermath of the Soviet military intervention in Afghanistan in December 1979. The US underwrote Pakistan's security against the Soviet Union, although no formal security treaty was signed. Pakistan and the US developed a close security and diplomatic relationships with reference to the Afghan problem. The US gave the first six-year economic assistance and military sales package (1981–87) amounting to $ 3.2 billion. This was equally divided between economic assistance and a military sales credit facility. About 55 per cent of economic assistance was provided as grants while the rest was in the form of soft-term loans. Military assistance was in the form of a credit facility, repayable at a 10–14 per cent rate of interest. Pakistan also obtained 40 F-16 aircrafts during 1983–87 by making cash payment of their price.

The second US assistance package (1987–93) amounted to $ 4.02 billion at concessional rates of interest. Out of this, $ 2.28 billion was allocated for economic assistance and $ 1.74 was in the form of military sale credits. Pakistan and the US joined together to build and strengthen Afghan resistance to Soviet military presence in Afghanistan spearheaded by Islamic–Afghan groups. This close relationship lost momentum after Soviet withdrawal from Afghanistan and came to an end in October 1990 when the US administration imposed sanction against Pakistan for pursuing the development of nuclear weapons. This terminated the 2nd US assistance package in October 1990.[8]

Pakistan and the US developed a cooperative security interaction for the third time after the terrorist attacks on the US on 11 September 2001. Pakistan stopped supporting the Taliban regime in Afghanistan and joined the US sponsored effort to combat transnational terrorism. Pakistan supported US military action in Afghanistan in October–November 2001. It supported the Karzai government that came to power in Kabul in December 2001 after the Taliban were dislodged from power. Since then Pakistan has been an ardent supporter of the US campaign against terrorism. It captured about 700 alleged terrorists from within Pakistan and handed over most of them to the US. In response to the changed Pakistani policy the US withdrew all sanctions against Pakistan and offered bilateral economic assistance and military sales credit facilities. Pakistan also obtained economic and technical assistance from international financial institutions like the World Bank, the IMF and the Asian Development Bank. The US wrote off part of its loans to Pakistan. Similarly, the Paris Club, a group of countries that provided economic assistance to Pakistan, decided in December 2001 to reschedule Pakistan's international debts on favourable terms. Pakistan was given 23 years to repay these loans after a grace period of 15 years.[9] The rescheduling of Pakistani loans and provision of new economic assistance enabled Pakistan during 2002–05 to salvage its economy and put its economic house in order. During 2004–05, Pakistan registered 8.4 per cent rate of growth. Pakistan had never had such a high rate of growth before.

Pakistan adopted a new strategy to strengthen its defence and security in the early 1970s. It refused to be aligned with any superpower and pursued a policy of nonalignment as a foreign policy strategy. The civilian leadership that assumed power after Pakistan lost the Bangladesh war to India in December 1971 enjoyed enough popular support to pursue an independent foreign policy. This civilian government was replaced with a military government in July 1977, which returned to alignment with the US in 1980 against the backdrop of Soviet military intervention in Afghanistan in December 1979.

## Pakistan's Strategic Doctrine

While viewing India as the major security adversary, Pakistan's policy-makers never aimed at military parity with India. This was neither possible nor desirable, given the wide gap in the resources of the two countries. They wanted to develop enough military capability to let India know that Pakistan could not only withstand India's military pressures but also increase the cost of an armed conflict for India.

The top brass of the Pakistan military were convinced that Pakistan must have the capability to raise the cost of war to unacceptable limits for India so as to deter the latter from engaging in military adventurism. Such a strategy could not be pursued without the maintenance of a highly professional, trained and well-equipped military, including an effective air cover for its army and an equally effective transportation and communication system for enhancing the mobility of troops.

Pakistan preferred to build pressure on India in Kashmir by engaging in limited military operations there or by extending clandestine military support to Kashmiri activists fighting against India. The latter strategy tied a large number of Indian troops in Kashmir.[10]

Pakistan cannot pursue its strategic doctrine without external support and cooperation because it lacks sufficient domestic resources to develop the required military capability. Therefore, it is not surprising that the military planners attach much importance to Pakistan's relations with the US, which is viewed as the source of weapons and military equipment procurement, diplomatic support and financial and technological assistance. The other important relationship is the People's Republic of China. Pakistan began to obtain military equipment and weapons from China in the aftermath of the Indo–Pakistan war of September1965. The first instalment of weapons and military equipment reached Pakistan between December 1965 and March 1966. Since then this relationship has expanded.

China has supplied weapons and military equipment, including military aircraft, and has played a key role in developing Pakistan's indigenous defence industry. It has also extended technical assistance to Pakistan's nuclear and missile programmes.

The deterrence approach developed for conventional security applies equally to Pakistan's nuclear weapons programme. Pakistan's nuclear and missile programmes are India specific. Had India not gone in for nuclear explosions in May 1998, Pakistan would not have exploded nuclear devices. It would have continued with the policy of nuclear ambiguity, i.e. admitting to having a nuclear weapons capability but not becoming an overt nuclear power. Nuclear ambiguity served Pakistan's security goals because both India and Pakistan knew that each could make nuclear weapons and that if one country went ahead with overt weaponization, the other would do the same. This policy lost its operational relevance after India resorted to nuclear explosions on 11 and 13 May, 1998. Pakistan conducted its nuclear explosions on

28 and 30 May to rectify the strategic imbalance in South Asia.[11]

Pakistan's explosions have neutralized India's superiority in conventional defence. Pakistan is not expected to accept any nuclear weapons restraint regime unless it takes into account its security concerns vis-à-vis India, and offers a comprehensive restraint regime that applies equally to conventional security arrangements. Pakistan will welcome a comprehensive restraint regime that applies to nuclear and conventional armament rather than India's offer of "no first use" of nuclear weapons.

## Implications for the Political System and Human Development

Pakistan's emergence as a security state with an emphasis on the conventional notion of security placed the Pakistan military in an advantageous position. It was able to lay claim on the major portion of national resources. Pakistan's foreign policy options were also shaped mainly by the security and military needs as articulated by Pakistan's dominant elite.

This accentuated institutional imbalance between the civilian political institutions and the state institutions like the military and the bureaucracy, which it inherited at the time of independence. The assignment of the highest priority to territorial and military security made more resources available to the military than any other sector in the political system. It contributed to consolidation and modernization of the military at the expense of society, which suffered from neglect so far as allocation of resources for societal development was concerned. The sectors that suffered most were health, education, environment and civic facilities and civilian human resource development.

The rise of the military in the political domain can partly be explained with reference to the importance it enjoyed in the political system from the beginning due to the perceived security pressures from the immediate neighbourhood and the institutional imbalance, which sharpened over the years. The top brass of the military first played an important role in determining Pakistan's foreign policy and domestic choices and then, in October 1958, overthrew the tottering civilian government.

The military has so far staged four coups in October 1958, March 1969, July 1977 and October 1999, and directly ruled the country during October 1958–June 1962, March 1969–December 1971 (martial law continued until April 1972), July 1977–December 1985, and October 1999–November 2002. While not in power, it influenced the civilian governments from the sidelines with reference to its professional and corporate interests, which have expanded over time.[12]

The ascendancy of the military in Pakistan's political system and its ability to continue dominating core political institutions and processes has caused a serious democracy deficit. The political institutions and processes continue to be weak and fragmented and participatory character of the political system has remained under-developed due to the overwhelming role of the military.

General Pervez Musharraf, who assumed power in October 1999 by dislodging a civilian political government, civilianized his military rule in November 2002 by co-opting a section of the political elite, holding a carefully managed election and amending the 1973 Constitution to ensure his centrality to the political process after the restoration of the constitution. He continues to be the pivot of power and manages the political system by emphasizing the military principle of 'unity of command'. The elected parliament and the prime minister and the federal cabinet have not been able to acquire an autonomous and assertive role in the political system. The ruling Pakistan Muslim League (PML) relies on the support of President Musharraf to sustain its majority position in the parliament. The major opposition parties function under strong state pressure causing bitterness and alienation among them. As a result, a state of confrontation persists between the civilian government/ruling PML and the major opposition parties, which has negative implications for the long-term viability of the political system. It also causes the poverty of democracy.

The repeated military rule has enabled it to induct its retired and serving personnel in key civilian jobs. It has expanded its role by undertaking commercial, business, industrial and other non-professional activities, which enable it to secure economic resources and employment for its personnel. The expanding military role has weakened and demoralized civilian institutions.

The military's domineering role has made it difficult for the civilian government to cut back on overt and covert allocation of national resources to the military or scrutinize their disbursement by the military. Any unilateral attempt by the civilian leaders to do so carries the risk of alienating the top brass of the military, which can create problems for the civilian leaders to hold on to power. Therefore, the defence expenditure continues to stay high and the allocations for societal development are still low.

### The Latest Trends

Three current trends have implications for Pakistan's emphasis on narrow and military security as against the comprehensive perspective on security that emphasizes socio-economic development and human security.

First, a debate among the policy makers, academia and civil society groups on the need for changing the priorities from a narrow military security perspective to a comprehensive perspective. This includes the issues of non-traditional security like drug trafficking, spread of small weapons and increased violence, ethnic and other social conflicts and terrorism as well as human security aiming at addressing the conditions of daily life, i.e. food, shelter, employment and economic opportunities, health education, personal and collective safety and political and civil rights. This means that security threats do not simply relate to inter-state relations. They also arise out of the intra-state contexts. This debate has led the government of Pakistan to assign increased importance to health, education, environment and poverty reduction. A Presidential Task Force on Human Development is devoted to evolving strategies for effectively addressing the societal development and human security issues.

Second, international financial institutions like the IMF, the World Bank and the Asian Development Bank are now providing economic and technical assistance for coping with the problems of under-development and poverty. This has made more resources available for health, education, employment generation, civic facilities and infrastructure development. The international funding also focuses on projects for good governance and institutional capacity building.

Third, the improvement of relations with India has also created some space for Pakistan to devote to social development issues. The easing of tension began with the statement of the then Indian Prime Minister, Atal Behari Vajpayee on 18 April 2003, that India would like to improve relations with Pakistan. The government of Pakistan responded favourably to this statement, which initiated the normalization process between the two countries. The decision of the two governments to observe ceasefire on the Line of Control in Kashmir from 26 November 2003, and the Musharraf–Vajpayee joint declaration in Islamabad on 6 January 2004, initiated a dialogue process for improvement of relations and resolution of the contentious issues. It is expected that as India and Pakistan resolve their contentious issues, Pakistan will be more forthcoming in pursuing the expanded notion of security.

The allocations for socio-economic development have increased in Pakistan since 2002 but defence expenditure continues to rise. As a result, the gap between the allocations for these two sectors remains very wide. For example, the federal budget for 2005–06 has increased allocations for the annual development programme, including health care and education. However, the defence expenditure in the federal budget has also increased. It jumped from Rs.193 billion in the 2004-05 federal budget to Rs. 223.5 billion in the budget for 2005-06. The increase in the defence budget (Rs. 30 billion) is more than total allocations for health and education.

The government of Pakistan has not fully imbibed the notion of expanded or societal security. Military security continues to enjoy priority over other considerations. Pakistan is caught in a circle. The high priority to territorial and military security has helped the military to claim a major portion of national resources. This contributes to strengthening its position in the political system, which in turn helps the military to continue to get the major portion of national resources.

Pakistan's economy has grown at a reasonably fast pace since 2001–2002 because it enjoys the economic and diplomatic support of the major players in the international system. However, the fruits of Pakistan's economic recovery have not reached the common people. Economic disparities and poverty continue to be high. Non-official circles argue that economic disparities and poverty have increased since 2002, although more international financial assistance is now available to cope with these problems.

The policy makers recognize the importance of socio-economic development and equitable distribution of fruits of economic growth. However, the ground realities have not significantly changed because the military-dominated decision makers are not inclined towards a major shift in the state's socio-economic priorities. Any major shift adversely affects their position and role in the political system.

## REFERENCES

1. For a review of the problems of national identity, internal cohesion, stability and political participation, see Paul Cammack, David Pool and William Tordoff, *Third World Politics: A Comparative Introduction* (London: Macmillan, 1988); Christopher Clapham, *Third World Politics: An Introduction* (London: Croom Helm, 1985); Fred R. van der Mehden, *Politics of the Developing Nations,* 2nd edition (Englewood Cliffs, N.J: Prentice Hall, 1969).

2. Ahmad Faruqui, *Rethinking the National Security of Pakistan* (Aldershot: Ashgate Publishing Ltd., 2003), p.10.
3. For the study of the problems between India and Pakistan in the early years of independence, see G.W. Choudhury, *Pakistan's Relations with India, 1947-66* (London: Pall Mall, 1968); Chaudhri Mohammad Ali, *The Emergence of Pakistan* (New York: Columbia University Press, 1967).
4. For the first war in Kashmir and the subsequent developments, see Sumantra Bose, *Kashmir: Roots of Conflict, Paths to Peace* (Cambridge, Mass: Harvard University Press, 2003); Sumit Ganguly, *The Crisis in Kashmir* (Cambridge: Cambridge University Press, 1997; Alastair Lamb, *Kashmir: A Disputed Legacy, 1846–1990* (Karachi: Oxford University Press, 1993).
5. For the issues in the Pakistan–Afghanistan relations, see Niloufer Mahdi, *Pakistan's Foreign Policy 1947–1981* (Lahore: Ferozsons, 1999), pp.115–150; Mujtaba Razvi, *The Frontier of Pakistan* (Karachi: National Publishing House, 1971), pp. 145–163.
6. For Soviet military intervention in Afghanistan and the subsequent developments, see Diego Cordovez and Selig S. Harrison, *Out of Afghanistan: The Inside Story of the Soviet Withdrawal* (New York: Oxford University Press, 1995); Rasul Bakhsh Rais, *War Without Winners* (Karachi: Oxford University Press, 1994).
7. For Pakistan–US relations in the 1950s and the early 1960s, see Robert J. McMahon, *The Cold War on the Periphery: The United Sates, India and Pakistan* (New York: Columbia University Press, 1994); Farhat Mahmud, *A History of US–Pakistan Relations* (Lahore: Vanguard Books,1991).
8. For a review of Pakistan–US relations in the context of the Soviet military intervention in Afghanistan, see Dennis Kux, *The United States and Pakistan, 1947–2000* (Karachi: Oxford University Press, 2001), pp. 245–316; Hasan Askari Rizvi, *Pakistan and the Geostrategic Environment: A Study of Foreign Policy* (London: Macmillan Press, 1993), pp. 94–111.
9. For US–Pakistan cooperation for counter terrorism, see Hasan Askari Rizvi, "Pakistan, the United States and South Asia" in *Major Powers and South Asia*, International Seminar Report, (Islamabad: Institute of Regional Studies, 2003), pp. 66–79; C. Christine Fair, *The Counter Terror Coalitions: Cooperation with Pakistan and India* (Santa Monica, CA: RAND, 2004), pp. 9–64.
10. Hasan Askari Rizvi, "Pakistan's Strategic Culture," in Michael R. Chambers (ed.), *South Asia in 2020: Future Strategic Balances and Alliances* (Carlisle, PA: Strategic Studies Institute, US Army War College, 2002), pp. 305–328.
11. For an analysis of Pakistan's motivation for nuclear explosion, see

Hasan Askari Rizvi, "Pakistan's Nuclear Testing" in Lowell Dittmer (ed.), *South Asia's Nuclear Security Dilemma: India, Pakistan and China* (Armonk, NY: M.E. Sharpe, 2005), pp. 97–109.

12. For a detailed study of the Pakistan military and its role in the political and other non-professional fields, see Pervez Iqbal Cheema, *The Armed Forces of Pakistan* (Karachi: Oxford University Press, 2002); Hasan Askari Rizvi, *Military, State and Society in Pakistan* (New York: St. Martin's Press, 2000; Brian Cloughley, *A History of the Pakistan Army* (Karachi: Oxford University Press, 1999); Saeed Shafqat, Civil-Military Relations in Pakistan (Boulder: Westview Press, 1997); Stephen P. Cohen, *The Pakistan Army* (Berkeley: University of California Press, 1984).

# 9

# The Break with Tradition in Sri Lanka's Peace Process

***Jehan Perera****

Until three years ago, when Sri Lanka got into the international media it was usually on account of its ethnic-related violence. The major part of this violence pitted the Sri Lankan government against the Liberation Tigers of Tamil Eelam, which has been fighting for an independent Tamil homeland. The LTTE is an organisation that has its own army and lays claim to being the sole representative of the Tamil people on whose behalf it is fighting a war of independence. However, the signing of the Ceasefire Agreement between the Government of Sri Lanka and the LTTE in February 2002 suddenly brought in a new dimension to Sri Lanka. It began to be perceived as a leader in a textbook variety of conflict resolution, complete with external third-party mediation and international monitoring.

With the signing of the Ceasefire Agreement, the traditional approach to security was abandoned and an entirely new approach adopted. Simultaneously with the signing of the ceasefire agreement the government ordered its security forces to dismantle many of their temporary checkpoints and camps. In a major leap of faith, the government permitted LTTE cadre to enter government-controlled territory in unlimited numbers, albeit without their arms, within a few months of the signing of the agreement. From being a country at war, with all the usual accompaniments of war such as heavily armed soldiers at every major

---

* Paper prepared by Jehan Perera, Research and Media Director of the National Peace Council of Sri Lanka for the NCCS seminar on "Non-traditional Security: State, Security and Democracy in South Asia" held in Kathmandu, 16–17 November, 2004.

building and street corner, checkpoints and militarisation, Sri Lanka has entered another dimension in which all roads open and security measures are not easily visible.

The thinking underlying the Ceasefire Agreement was a realisation that traditional law and order, and military methods of ensuring security had not only failed in their task but had further aggravated the problem. When the Tamil militancy first arose in the late 1970s, the immediate reaction of the Sri Lankan government was to define violence as terrorism and to suppress it through law-and-order methods. When the police proved unequal to the task, the army was sent in, but with the same result, except that a process of escalation had started that fed upon itself. The outcome was civil war in which two armies, one government and one Tamil, faced each other head-on in the field of battle. As a corollary the government lost physical control over a large part of the territory in the contested north and east of the country.

The core of the current Sri Lankan approach to security is to utilise the advantages accruing to the two sides as a result of the Ceasefire Agreement as the pivot of the peace process. The Ceasefire Agreement has established lines of control between the government and LTTE. It has led to the lifting of the government's ban on the LTTE, and to providing the LTTE with an equal place and status at the negotiating table. This parity was symbolised by the Norwegian facilitators referring to the LTTE's chief negotiator as "His Excellency" at the media conference, at the opening round of peace talks in Thailand in September 2002. The ceasefire has a system of international monitoring to ensure that the terms of the Ceasefire Agreement are adhered to. Sections of the international community, most notably the Western countries and Japan are also deeply involved in supporting the peace process. Safeguarding the Ceasefire Agreement against breakdown constitutes the core of Sri Lanka's new and non-traditional approach to security.

## Background

Sri Lanka has a plural society of several different ethnic communities numbering 19 million. The Sinhalese form the main ethnic group with 74 per cent of the population. The majority of the Sinhalese are Buddhists by religion and are mainly concentrated in the south, west and central parts of the country. The Sri Lanka Tamils with 12 per cent of the population form the next major ethnic group. They are a majority in the north-east of the country. The Muslims form the third major ethnic group with 8 per cent of the population with a concentration in the east. The up-country Tamils, who are of recent Indian origin, form the fourth major community with about 5 per cent of the population. They live in the central hills of the country and have not been involved in the separatist conflict. Most of the Tamils are Hindu by religion. While a minority of both Sinhalese and Tamils comprising about 7 per cent are Christian by religion, they are not considered to be a separate ethnic group.

Sri Lanka's ongoing ethnic conflict and the separatist war it has given rise to can be described as the country's most intractable and destructive problem. The war between the Sri Lankan government and the Liberation Tigers of Tamil Eelam is generally counted as having started in 1983. It has caused around 65,000 deaths and major damage to personal and public property with the total loss between 1993–98 estimated at 1.27 times the GDP as in 1998[1]. A total of some one million persons have been uprooted and displaced internally as a result at some time or the other with another half million leaving the country to claim refugee status abroad.

Despite its present primacy, the ethnic conflict has not been the only major conflict in Sri Lankan society. There are other major sources of conflict constituting deep-seated cleavages in society, which have fragmented society and undermined social cohesion. Twice in the past three decades the country has gone through class-based and Marxist-inspired insurrections in which tens of thousands of Sri Lankans have lost their lives. Interestingly, both of these insurrections have been confined to the Sinhalese section of the population, with no Tamil or Muslim involvement.

The first insurrection by the JVP (People's Liberation Front) took place in April 1971. Thousands of poorly armed JVP cadre simultaneously attacked police stations throughout the Sinhalese-majority areas, and an estimated 10–20,000 of them died in the government crackdown that followed, most within a span of a month. The efforts by the government to institute radical political and economic reforms led to actions that antagonised the Tamil section of the population. One example was the change in criteria for university admissions that saw a proportion of Tamils plummeting within a couple of years to make space for the disaffected Sinhalese youth. The disgruntled Tamil youth deprived of university education in the decade of the 1970s were in the forefront of the Tamil militancy.

The second JVP insurrection took place in 1988–89 and unlike the first, which was more or less over in less than a month, it stretched for over two years of violence, terror and disappearances with an estimated 30–60,000 killed. But like the first one, it ended with the capture and execution of the leadership. There was no political solution, only a military one. Both JVP insurgencies were grounded in the sense of alienation and deprivation of the rural Sinhalese youth who saw themselves being left out of the development process that was largely confined to Colombo and its environs which account for most of the country's industrial capacity. About 85 per cent of industrial production in the country is concentrated in the Colombo-centred Western Province, leaving only 15 per cent for the remaining seven provinces.

The rise of militancy in the north and south of Sri Lanka has been due to the lack of responsiveness of the political system to the deeply felt grievances of sections of the polity. The result has been the legitimisation of violent means of obtaining changes in the prevailing order. With regard to the ethnic conflict, which has pitted the minority Tamil community against the state, and has sought the establishment of a separate state, this unresponsiveness is caused by two factors. One is ethnic nationalism, which has led to the perception of the other community's position as unreasonable. The second is a political system that has concentrated political power in a single institution that is invariably dominated by the majority Sinhalese, leading to an effectual tyranny of a permanent majority.

It is likely that a government faced with an insurrection against its authority will first seek to employ repressive law and order methods to quell the uprising. This would enable the state to remain unchanged. A military solution would give the state the space to change in a minimal fashion that would take the edge off the causes that led to the insurgency. It is the failure of law-and-order methods that induces the state to attempt fundamental political reform. However, the attempt to achieve fundamental reforms cannot be internally sustained, without external pressures, such as those generated by actual victory on the ground of the insurgent forces. If the state is enlightened, it will accept the new reality, and find ways to legitimise and reabsorb the insurgency into a reordered state.

## Rise of LTTE

The frustrations and repeated political failure of the democratic and mainstream Tamil political parties to redress Tamil grievances led in the 1970s to demands for a separate Tamil state, articulated by the Tamil political parties themselves. Armed resistance and ultimately civil war followed this. In 1972 the Tamil political parties joined to form the Tamil United Front to take "non-violent direct action against the government... in order to win the rights of the Tamil nation on the basis of the right to self-determination" if the government failed to amend the constitution to take their aspirations into account. The first political assassination took place in 1975 with the assassination of the Mayor of Jaffna Alfred Duraiappah, a government supporter. The leaders of the Tamil political parties refrained from explicitly condemning the use of violence. As a result they permitted the steady erosion of the norms of democracy, and intolerance of any deviation from the nationalist line. The rise of militant Tamil nationalism can be traced back to this period.

In 1976, the Tamil United Front was renamed the "Tamil United Liberation Front". At its first national convention held in Vaddukoddai it resolved "that the restoration and reconstitution of the free and sovereign secular socialist state of Tamil Eelam based on the right of self-determination inherent to every nation has become inevitable in order to safeguard the very existence of the Tamil nation in this country." Thus, the uncompromising stand for an independent and sovereign state of Tamil Eelam has democratic antecedents. The hardline Liberation Tigers of Tamil Eelam (LTTE) emerged as the main armed movement among the Tamils, physically eliminating other Tamil groups and gradually establishing its control over most of the north and east.

Rohan Gunaratne has summarised one view of the LTTE. "Elements of the LTTE mindset are: its claim to be the sole representative of the Tamils; intolerance of dissent within the Tamil community; liquidating the alternative Tamil leadership; massacring non-Tamil civilians; reneging on three peace agendas/undertakings; and the inability to compromise on [its leader] Prabakaran's avowed goal of Tamil Eelam."[2] S.J. Emmanuel has presented a contrary view: "The government failed to recognise the political face of the LTTE and talked to them only as a militant if not terrorist group. This was a misapprehension. The government will do well, even concurrent to the understanding of a militant leadership, to clearly recognise not only the peace aspirations of the Tamil people, but also that of their de facto leadership"[3].

## Changed Strategy

A major breakthrough in the peace process occurred when President Chandrika Kumaratunga invited the government of Norway in February

2000 to act as a third-party intermediary with the LTTE. Prior to this invitation a few Sri Lankan politicians were prepared to publicly admit the need for foreign assistance in resolving the conflict. The Norwegian intervention in the Sri Lankan ethnic conflict would count as the most significant event bearing upon a negotiated settlement in over a decade. The last such external intervention was the Indo–Lanka Peace Accord which ended in failure in 1990 with the withdrawal of the Indian Peace-Keeping Force. However, much more than the ill-fated accord which the Sri Lankans saw as being in the nature of an Indian imposition, the Norwegian initiative has been an expression of the government and LTTE's willingness to have the Norwegians play the role of intermediary.

Despite the progress in the peace process since December 2001, there remain concerns about the sustainability of the peace process. Sections of the polity, including some of those who now form the United People's Freedom Alliance government, have opposed the present peace process on various grounds as being unconstitutional, a "sell-out" and as paving the ground for a renewed LTTE military campaign for separation. Spearheading the opposition to the ceasefire agreement has been the JVP (People's Liberation Front), the Marxist-oriented political party that attempted to violently overthrow the government in 1971 and again in 1988–89. Today the JVP, as a coalition partner with the Sri Lanka Freedom Party that is headed by President Chandrika Kumaratunga, continues to balk at the peace process, which they see as endangering the country's unity.

The JVP's position draws upon a perception shared by many Sinhalese that the devolution of power is a means of dividing the country along ethnic lines. The fears of the division of the country in the minds of a sizeable proportion of the Sinhalese constitute a major obstacle to a negotiated solution with the LTTE. Clearly the preferred option of this section of the population is a military solution that would eliminate the LTTE and thereby end the threat to the country's unity.

A second obstacle is the continued rivalry between the government and opposition parties in the Sri Lankan political mainstream, in which the ethnic conflict becomes yet another means of one side embarrassing the other for narrow political gain. For many years now those who are community leaders and political analysts have been calling for a consensus between the two major political parties for a solution to the long drawn-out ethnic conflict to emerge. But in doing so, they may have glossed over the political realities that have kept the two dominant parties apart on the issue. The hard fact is that the Sinhalese community, which by far forms the largest segment of the electorate, is still more or less evenly divided on the question of political reforms that could lead to a political settlement of the ethnic conflict.

The governmental strategy following the December 2001 election marked a complete shift from that of previous governments, which was to confront the LTTE at every level. The government led by former Prime Minister Ranil Wickremesinghe during its two years in office was non-confrontational in its approach to the LTTE. This governmental strategy was based on an assessment of former failures to succeed through confrontation. After the collapse of the peace talks with the LTTE at the very beginning of its term of office in April 1995, the former government declared a full-scale war for peace. The two-pronged military and political strategy aimed to weaken and sideline the LTTE. But both types of confrontation failed. Instead of being militarily weakened, the LTTE emerged militarily strengthened from the major confrontations of the past.

The government under Prime Minister Wickremesinghe absorbed two important lessons from the former failures of the government. The first was that head-on confrontation would not bring about a solution to the ethnic conflict. Accordingly, political and structural reforms might have to be de facto rather than de jure, to be acquiesced to by the general population with whom as little information as possible is shared. The alternative of explaining everything in detail to the people in order to get them to vote in favour of the settlement was likely to get into too much controversy. There is deep-rooted resistance to fundamental constitutional reform in the Sinhalese community that would lead to power sharing across the ethnic and regional lines.

Thus the measures adopted by the government at the outset of the ceasefire were taken after only a minimum of consultation with the other political parties, general population or with civil society. These included lifting the security barriers, ending the economic embargo of the north-east and lifting the ban on the LTTE. The success of these measures, however, set a precedent where the government kept making decisions without either consulting or adequately informing the other stakeholders in society. In effect, therefore, they became passive bystanders in the peace process.

The absence of broad-based consultations and the highly top-down nature of the peace process was a primary reason for its rapid progress at the outset. However, this strategy had several negative results. One major weakness in the current peace process was the lack of a wide base of informed public discussion regarding the peace process. This resulted in a limited output of creative ideas from the ranks of the country's intelligentsia and other socially active sectors. For instance, although the government and LTTE agreed to explore a federal solution, there has been little public discussion on this issue in either academic forums or the media. The limited representation of Muslim interests in most civil society discussions added to the lacuna regarding appropriate representation and pluralism in the envisaged interim arrangements.

In its two-year period in office, the UNF government of Prime Minister Ranil Wickremesinghe was unable to set up an interim council for the north-east as promised in its election manifesto. The territory militarily controlled by the LTTE, and to which the government's military forces have no access, accounts for about a half of the north-east province, but in terms of population it controls a much smaller population, amounting to about 25 per cent[4]. The inability of the Sri Lankan state to wrest back control over these areas over the past 15 years is a key feature of the current situation.

A viable strategy for the government would be to accept the situation of dual military power, so long as there is no major fighting between the two armies, one controlled by the government, the other by the LTTE. However, recognising the fact that the LTTE is unlikely to be content with remaining confined in its political power to the areas currently under its direct military control, they will have to be given greater scope for such power in the north-east era areas under government control as well. It is likely that the device of an interim council with a high degree of autonomy will provide the LTTE with this political power.

## Interim Administration

Therefore, there was little reason to doubt that the LTTE's proposals in terms of the interim administration they sought for the contested north-east of the country would be ambitious. This was to be expected, as in the case of any first offer in a negotiation. No party that makes a first offer would ask for less; instead they would ask for more. A scrutiny of the LTTE proposals submitted in October 2003 would reveal that they were maximalist in spirit, as indeed could have been anticipated from an organisation that waged war for the cause of complete Tamil separation from Sri Lanka. The proposals, in sum, call for the establishment of an Interim Self Governing Authority (ISGA) for the north-east in which the LTTE would have an absolute majority of members. Thereafter the proposals indicate that complete autonomy or separation is sought in virtually every aspect of the political and economic life of the people.

The LTTE proposals call for separate institutions to be set up for the north-east in respect of police, judiciary, elections, taxation, local and foreign grants and loans, and trade among others. There is an assurance that internationally mandated standards of human rights, accountability, multi-ethnic representation and free and fair elections will prevail. But all the institutions that are to be set up to ensure such good governance practices will be under the sole control of the ISGA which will have an absolute LTTE majority.

In a society where the spirit of power sharing is yet to be learnt and practised, obtaining an absolute majority is a potential licence for unilateralism. When this potential is coupled with autonomy, the result can be a high degree of control. It is noteworthy that the LTTE's proposals make no provision for integration with the nationally prevailing structures. Viewed in this context it is not surprising that the Sri Lankan government's response to the LTTE proposals was and remains cautious and restrained. The government's immediate response was to say that there were fundamental differences between the LTTE's proposals and those submitted several months earlier by the government.

In its own proposals regarding an interim administration for the north-east, the Sri Lankan government specifically excluded matters pertaining to police, land, revenue and security from the purview of the interim administration. But in the LTTE's counter proposals, all the above with the exception of security are specifically considered to be the domain of the ISGA. Further, in the government's proposals while an absolute majority is conceded to the LTTE, provision was made for a minority veto on matters that affected the interests of the Muslim and Sinhalese communities living in the north east.

On this ground the Muslims and Sinhalese of the east, who presently constitute over 60 per cent of the population, have strongly protested their inclusion into an LTTE-dominated administration. The Muslims in particular have been vociferous about their opposition, as in the Sri Lanka Muslim Congress (SLMC) they have a political party that draws virtually all its strength from the east. The SLMC's first response to the LTTE's proposals was to say that they do not meet Muslim aspirations.

The government's cautious response to the LTTE's proposals was also due to its apprehensions about a backlash against them from Sinhalese nationalists bolstered by opposition political parties. The unfortunate history of post-independence Sri Lankan politics is that opposition parties have seized upon governmental concessions to Tamil parties as betrayals of the Sinhalese to mobilise popular opposition to the government.

A major problem is that federalism is not a familiar concept to Sri Lankans. It is natural that Sri Lankans know little about federalism, when for the past 170 years, since the Colebrook–Camaroun reforms of 1833, Sri Lanka has had a centralised administration.Therefore there is little practical expertise in this field within the country. Most local commentators on the ills and pitfalls of the federal system have lived most of their lives in one of the most centralised systems of government in the world, which is what the Sri Lankan system has been since the Colebrook–Camaroun reforms. The critiques and fears of federalism come from theory and not from live experience. This may explain why there is so little constructive discussion about the most appropriate form of federalism for the country.

The powers of regional units in federal systems over police, land, taxation and judiciary claimed by the LTTE, are basic to most federal systems. Of course, in democratic societies federal powers are not only a matter of regional elites wresting powers from central elites. This is presently the case in Sri Lanka, where the interim administration would see the LTTE get power legally transferred to it from the central government. But in true federal systems, there are elaborate systems of checks and balances, which include accountability to higher levels of authority and, ultimately, to the people themselves at free and fair elections. This is a reality that the LTTE needs to realise and hopefully will respect in the negotiations on the interim administration proposals.

### Federal Solution

At the close of the third round of peace talks held in Oslo in December 2002, the Sri Lankan government and LTTE signed a path-breaking joint statement. Among other things, it affirmed that "Responding to a proposal by the LTTE leadership the parties agreed to explore a solution based on the principles of internal self determination in areas of historical habitation of the Tamil speaking peoples, based on a federal structure within a united Sri Lanka". This statement was widely taken to mean that the LTTE was dropping its demand for a separate state and was opting instead for a federal state. Until the so-called Oslo Declaration on federalism, the LTTE had rigidly stuck to its demand for a separate state of Tamil Eelam or, at best, an unspecified viable alternative to it.

The mutual decision to explore a federal solution has been widely regarded as a very positive breakthrough in the peace process. Quite apart from the LTTE giving up its demand for a separate state, it also meant that the Sri Lankan government had overcome its long antipathy to a federal solution. This statement therefore received worldwide publicity as an act of statesmanship by the two sides. However, since then, the LTTE has been stoutly resisting any reference to federalism in its public statements that have followed the Oslo peace talks.

The priority given by the LTTE to political and military control, as against economic matters, can be seen quite clearly in their proposals for an Interim Self Governing Authority. Only three of the 22 clauses pertaining to the ISGA are concerned with economic or developmental issues. These three clauses deal with the subjects of rehabilitation, reconstruction and resettlement. The balance 19 clauses are concerned with issues of political and military control and governance, such as the high security zones, the coastal seas, and law and order issues, elections, human rights and other governance issues.

According to the ISGA proposals, institutions that are created by the LTTE, and which have no connection whatsoever to existing national institutions, will be established. Unless the federal concept of self rule that is coupled with shared rule is brought into the negotiations concerning the ISGA, the ISGA will set up a separate administration. Therefore, unless the LTTE clarifies that it continues to stand by a federal solution, the government will find it impossible to agree to an ISGA for the north-east as proposed by the LTTE.

Federalism is about both self rule and shared rule. The LTTE's downplaying of federalism would suggest that its interest in the peace process remains separatist. This doubt could prove fatal to the LTTE's effort to obtain for itself the powers of governance in an ISGA for the north east as they have proposed. What stands out in the LTTE's proposals for an ISGA is that it gives no decision-making role to the central government. The central government is simply expected to provide the ISGA, and by implication the LTTE with resources, without having any say in what happens thereafter. The ISGA as a proposal standing alone is one that is outside the federal framework.

## The Present Situation

At the present time there is a 20-month long deadlock in the peace process, with the two parties not sitting down to peace talks since March 2003. There is a major mismatch between the goals and expectations of the government and LTTE that is delaying the resumption of peace talks. The LTTE's concern appears to be that the government is only seeking to restart the peace talks in order to open the purse strings of the international donors. On the other hand, the government's concern appears to be that the LTTE's intention in restarting the peace talks is simply to obtain the implementation of its ISGA proposal.

The mismatch between the goals and expectations of the government and LTTE with regard to peace talks is the most important obstacle to their resumption. The challenge to Sri Lanka today is to find a suitable structure of governance in which two or more peoples can co-exist, cooperate and be partners within a single state without the members of one group being able to unilaterally impose their wishes on the members of the other groups.

It is only a federal system, which is limited to self-determination in its internal aspect that can provide a lasting solution to Sri Lanka's ethnic conflict. Federalism can permit the powers of self-governance to regional ethnic majorities, while also preserving a unified system of governance in accordance with the wishes of the vast majority of the country's people.

Unfortunately it seems that the time is still premature for such a political solution. What the LTTE wants, and must ask for, at this time in terms of their Interim Self Governing Authority proposal is too much for the government to concede. These would include an autonomous arrangement that includes powers over the sea coast and seas around the north east that account for over two-third of the Sri Lankan coastline. Likewise what the government will want of the LTTE is too much for the LTTE concede at this time, particularly the renunciation of a separate state and the decommissioning of arms.

While the gap between the government and LTTE on the political issues is too wide to be bridged at this time, there is a likelihood that a successful ceasefire that continues to last, and is accompanied by rapid economic growth, would serve as a confidence-building measure. It could make the gap in the positions of the government and LTTE more bridgeable in the years ahead. The prospect of resolving the hard political issues by negotiating a durable and just political solution could also become the motivation to maintain the ceasefire.

Where questions of political power and constitutional reform are concerned, there is likely to be a high degree of contestation regarding the way to a mutually acceptable solution. There will undoubtedly be differences among the government, opposition and LTTE. These differences pertaining to issues of governance will be reflected among the people at large. A more democratic and consultative type of decision making will be required at this later stage than the new government appears to be contemplating. Civil society organisations need to be preparing the people for the restructuring of the polity in the long term. The international community will have to play an important and effective role.

The past experience with the LTTE has been one of disengagement once discussions reach substantive issues. This is on account of the wide gap between what the LTTE demands and what Sri Lankan governments have hitherto been prepared to offer. The success of the peace talks would depend in large measure on international pressure that would keep the government and LTTE at the negotiations table, and compel them towards compromise. It also needs to have the international community's backing to ensure that the LTTE remains within the framework of a united and democratically governed country.

## REFERENCES

1. National Peace Council, Cost of the War, Colombo, 2001.
2. Rohan Gunaratne, "Impact of the Mobilised Tamil Diaspora on the Protracted Conflict in Sri Lanka in Kumar Rupesinghe (ed.), *Negotiating Peace in Sri Lanka: Efforts, Failures and Lessons,* (London: International Alert, February 1998), p. 303.
3. S.J. Emmanuel, "Kumaratunga-Prabhakaran Talks: A Northern View" in Kumar Rupesinghe (ed.), p. 273.
4. *The Island* , December 15, 2001. Negotiating Peace in Sri Lanka: Efforts, Failures and Lessons, (London: International Alert, February 1998), p. 303.

# 10

# Cross-border Human Traffic in South Asia: A Security Perspective from India's North-east

***Wasbir Hussain****

If America is a salad bowl of cultures, South Asia is no melting pot. Yes, cross-border human traffic may be a natural phenomenon, and not an unusual human experience. After all, haven't we seen the 'browning of America'? In the 19th and early 20th centuries, millions of Europeans migrated to the Americas, New Zealand, Australia and South Africa. The movement kept rising, and between 1846 and 1930, more than 50 million Europeans had left their homes to live and settle in another continent.[1]

South Asia, too, has been witness to this huge movement of humans. Since the partition of the Indian sub-continent in 1947, an estimated 35 million people have crossed borders[2] in search of food, to escape religious persecution, in search of security to lives or just to unite with ethnically, racially or ideologically identical people on the other side of the border. But far from getting assimilated with the host

---

* Wasbir Hussain is Consulting Editor of *The Sentinel*, Guwahati, India, and Director Centre for Development & Peace Studies, Guwahati, India. He is also Associate Fellow, Institute for Conflict Management, New Delhi. He has been covering insurgency, ethnic strife, and other major political and social developments in the seven north-eastern Indian states for the past 20 years. Before his present assignment, Hussain was Consulting Editor, *The Newspaper Today*, India Today Group Online; Editor, *The Northeast Daily*, Guwahati, Special Correspondent with *The Asian Age*; Regional Editor of *The Telegraph*; and Special Correspondent of *The Telegraph*. He bagged the 1996 Sanskriti Foundation National Award for excellence in journalism.

nations or cultures, the migrants have often come to alter their (the host nations') demographic profile, leading to security and ethnic tensions.

To the outside world, India's North-east generally appears to be a land of rugged beauty and constant turmoil, source to the armed separatist insurrections and ethnic strife, largely over territorial supremacy. But, this region of 40 million[3] people, spread over eight[4] states that cover a vast 2,63,000-square kilometre stretch, is also an area to which hordes of migrants from across the borders, primarily Bangladesh, have made their destination over the years, and then home.

Before I proceed further to examine the topic under discussion, it would be pertinent to take a look at the highly strategic nature of the location of India's north-eastern region. Even a cursory look of the porous Indo–Bangladesh region in the map—this is the region that I am focusing on in this paper—is enough to conclude as to why the area is an attractive theatre for cross-border migrants, gun-runners, drug syndicates and separatist and armed criminal bands to operate. India's North-east[5] has open borders with China in the North, Myanmar in the East, Bangladesh in the South West and Bhutan to the North West. India shares a 4,095-km-long border with Bangladesh, the longest with any of its neighbours. Of this, four north-eastern states—Tripura, Meghalaya, Mizoram and Assam—account for 1,879 km of the border, while the eastern state of West Bengal has a border running 2,216 km along Bangladesh.

Then look at Bangladesh—its southeast has the port city of Chittagong. Aside from its access to the sea, and India's militant-infested Tripura state, the area shares a border with Myanmar's Arakan province, a region that has a sizeable population of Rohingya Muslims. Policing such borders, with rivers, seas and rugged mountains running along it, is not easy, and sealing boundaries next to impossible.

The alteration of the demographic complexion of some of the northeastern Indian states, particularly Assam and Tripura, due to the unabated cross-border migration of people has been the cause of much of the unrest in the region with the indigenous people facing the prospect of being reduced to a minority in their own homeland. The influx of Bengalis from the plains of erstwhile East Pakistan, now Bangladesh, has reduced Tripura's tribal population to a minority. According to the 1991 Census, the indigenous tribes-people of Tripura constituted only 28 per cent of the State's population of 2.76 million. Three decades earlier, the tribals comprised two-third of Tripura's population[6].

Take the case of Nagaland, which has no direct border with Bangladesh. This hill state with a 99 per cent tribal population is said to be facing the brunt of illegal Bangladesh migration. According to the 2001 national Census, Nagaland recorded a 64.41 per cent growth in population between 1991 and 2001, much above the national average of 21.34 per cent.[7] Up from the growth of 56.08 per cent in the years 1981 to 1991, Nagaland once again recorded the highest population growth in the country. A media report said that the figures supported the fear expressed by Nagaland Chief Minister S.C. Jamir in 2000 that Nagaland will be the next state to be hit by large-scale illegal migration by Bangladeshis after Assam. The report quoted Jamir as saying at a meeting of the Chief Ministers of the northeastern region with Prime Minister Atal Behari Vajpayee in Shillong in January 2000, "Unless steps are taken to prevent the entry of people of dubious nationality into our state, Nagaland may face the same problem as that of Assam."[8]

Cross-border migration from East Bengal, later East Pakistan and then Bangladesh, into Assam and Tripura, and onward to other states in the region, has transformed vast tracts from land-abundant to land-scarce areas. In an industrially backward region, the large-scale influx of people from across porous international borders has led to a conflict between the migrants and the indigenous people over natural resources, as well as employment, both in the government and private sectors. Such clashes of interest have directly led to the growth of violent tribal insurgencies, as in Tripura, with guerrilla groups targeting the migrant settlers from the plains, who are seen as land grabbers. The anger of these insurgent groups is also directed against the Indian state itself, which has come to be accused by these outfits as an 'exploiter', working against tribal interests.[9]

I shall deal mainly with Assam in this paper, where the issue of migration has led to the growth of Assamese sub-nationalism, at times bordering on xenophobia, mainly because of the fear among the indigenous communities of being overwhelmed by migrants from Bangladesh. The anti-foreigner (read anti-illegal migrants or anti-Bangladeshi) uprising in Assam, from 1979 to 1985, led by the All Assam Students' Union (AASU) — by far the most influential organization representing the Assamese — was perhaps among independent India's largest mass uprisings. According to a conservative estimate, the number of people killed during the agitation stood at more than 7,000 with another two million losing their homes.[10] During the peak of this movement, the AASU had estimated that there could be anywhere between 4.5 to 5 million illegal Bangladeshi migrants or 31 to 34 per cent of the total population of the state in 1971.[11] The issue is as alive today as it was in 1985, when the agitation formally ended with the signing of an agreement on 15 August 1985, in New Delhi, between the AASU and the Central Government, then led by Prime Minister Rajiv Gandhi. The issue of migration and citizenship has, in fact, become the pivot around which Assam's entire politics has come to revolve — an issue on which elections to the State Legislative Assembly can be won or lost.[12]

### Assam: Demographic Jitters[13]

The Muslim population in the Northeast Indian state of Assam, according to the national Census of 2001, is 30.9 per cent of the State's total population of 26.6 million. The last census was conducted three years ago, but it was only on 6 September, 2004, that the office of the Registrar General of India, which carries out census operations, released the statistical break-up on religious lines. The latest figures demonstrate that the proportionate growth of the Muslim population in Assam, in comparison with other religious communities, is second only to Jammu and Kashmir (67 per cent Muslims).

Assam's population, according to the 2001 Census, was 26,655,528. Of this, 17,296,455 were recorded as Hindus and 8,240,611 Muslims. Among the vital data made public by the census authorities is the fact that six of Assam's 27 districts have a majority Muslim population. The district of Barpeta tops the list with 977,943 Muslims and 662,066 Hindus. The other five districts where Muslims constitute a majority are: Dhubri, Goalpara, Nagaon, Karimganj and Hailakandi.[14]

The official confirmation of the rather rapid growth of Muslim population in Assam has disturbing repercussions. The State has long been in the grip of a murky politics of citizenship over the issue of unabated illegal migration from adjoining Bangladesh, with which it shares a 262-km-long border. The particular significance of the recently released census data is the fact that the rate of growth of Muslim population is the highest precisely in the districts that share a border with, or lie close to the border with Bangladesh—particularly Dhubri, Barpeta, Karimganj and Hailakandi—giving credence to the widely held belief that illegal migration from Bangladesh was the source of these demographic trends. Such migration clearly continues unhindered, despite the barbed-wire fence being erected in stretches and the presence of the Border Security Force (BSF) along the border.

An examination of the census figures of 1971 and 1991 (there was no census in Assam in 1981 due to unrest in the state) shows that there has been a steady to rapid rise in the Muslim population in districts proximate to the border, confirming apprehensions of a continuing illegal influx. This, perhaps, goes a long way to explain the rather high Muslim growth rate in Assam, estimated at 77.42 per cent between 1971 and 1991.

For instance, in 1971, Muslims comprised 64.46 per cent of the population in Dhubri district. This rose to 70.45 per cent in 1991—a total growth of 77.42 per cent between 1971 and 1991. By 2001 the proportion of Muslims had risen further to 74.29 per cent of the population in Dhubri. By 2001, the Muslim population in Barpeta rose from 56.07 per cent in 1991 to 59.3 per cent; in Goalpara, from 50.18 per cent to 53.71 per cent, and Hailakandi from 54.79 per cent 57.6 per cent. Significantly, two new districts joined the list of Muslim majority districts in Assam by 2001: Karimganj, where the Muslim population rose from 49.17 per cent in 1991 to 52.3 per cent; and Nagaon, where the community's population grew from 47.19 per cent in 1991 to 50.99 per cent.

It is imperative to make a clear distinction, in the course of the current discussion, between indigenous Assamese-speaking Muslims and Bangladeshi migrants before analyzing the demographic and security implications of such population growth. Apart from Guwahati, Assam's capital (that is part of the Kamrup Metro district), the heartland of the indigenous Assamese Muslims—whose origins can be traced to the forays of the pre-Mughals in the 13th century—is located around the tea-growing eastern districts of Jorhat, Golaghat, Sivasagar and Dibrugarh. In Jorhat district the Muslims comprised just 3.89 per cent of the total population in 1971, rising to 4.32 per cent in 1991. The growth rate was 48.04 per cent between 1971 and 1991. In Sivasagar, Muslims accounted for 6.65 per cent of the population in 1971, climbing to 7.63 per cent in 1991; in Dibrugarh from 3.66 per cent of the total population in 1971 to 4.49 per cent in 1991; and in Golaghat, Muslims comprised 5.17 per cent of the population in 1971, rising to 7.11 per cent in 1991. It is useful to note, in this context, that the growth rate of the Hindu population in Jorhat, Sivasagar, Dibrugarh and Golaghat was between 32 and 49 per cent over the

1971–1991 period, closely comparable to the rates of growth for the indigenous Muslim populations.

It is clearly seen that the Muslim growth rate in areas dominated by indigenous Assamese-speaking Muslims, located far from the Bangladesh border, has been registering marginal increases, as compared to areas located close to the border.

In the wake of this population break-up, influential groups, such as the All Assam Students' Union (AASU)—which had led the six-year-long anti-foreigner (that is, anti-Bangladeshi) uprising in the State between 1979 and 1985—have once again upped the ante, reiterating fears that the illegal aliens will eventually overwhelm the indigenous population. They have also stepped up demands for effective action against this unremitting population offensive, including the updating of the National Register of Citizens (NRC), with 1971 as the cut-off year. On 24 September 2004, AASU volunteers took out a torchlight procession across Guwahati, Assam's capital, demanding a permanent solution to the problem of illegal migration into the State.[15]

The population explosion in Bangladesh, with 2.8 million added every year[16] in one of the poorest and most densely populated countries in the world, creates the push factors for this silent demographic invasion. These are, however, compounded by an expansionist political ideology, implicitly or explicitly supported in the corridors of power in Bangladesh: the idea of *Lebensraum* ('living space'), which has been variously projected by the country's leadership for a long time, though the use of the expression itself is relatively recent. In the early 1990s, Sadeq Khan, a former diplomat, stated:

All projections, however, clearly indicate that by the next decade, that is to say by the first decade of the 21st century, Bangladesh will face a serious crisis of *lebensraum*... A natural overflow of population pressure is very much on the cards and will not be restrainable by barbed wire or border patrol measures. The natural trend of population overflow from Bangladesh is towards the sparsely populated lands in the South East, in the Arakan side and of the North East in the Seven Sisters side of the Indian sub-continent...[17]

The idea has found repeated articulation even before the creation of Bangladesh. Sheikh Mujibur Rahman, the country's first Prime Minister, for instance wrote:

> Because Eastern Pakistan must have sufficient land for its expansion and because Assam has abundant forests and mineral resources, coal, petroleum, etc., Eastern Pakistan must include Assam to be financially and

economically strong[18]...

The AASU and other organizations behind the anti-foreigner movement in the State had, at the height of their agitation in the mid-1980s, estimated the number of illegal migrants in Assam to be as high as 4.5 to 5 million, or 31 to 34 per cent of the total population of the State in 1971. As recently as 14 July 2004, India's Minister of State for Home, Sriprakash Jaiswal, had told the Rajya Sabha (Upper House of Parliament) that there were 5 million illegal Bangladeshis in Assam. Groups such as the AASU reacted, saying that their fears and estimates had been officially confirmed. Later, on 23 July another Minister of State for Home, Manik Rao Gavit clarified in Parliament that his colleague's statement was not based on any comprehensive study but 'on hearsay'. But such glaring contradictions simply demonstrated the oft-levelled charge that political parties, in fact, lack the will to tackle the issue for fear of losing a massive 'vote bank'. With the census figures indirectly confirming the alarming picture of mass illegal migrations from Bangladesh, sparks are expected to fly in Assam.

Ironically, however, after the AASU leaders transformed themselves into politicians, forming the Asom Gana Parishad (AGP) or the Assam People's Party in the winter of 1985 to contest the State Assembly polls and to capture power in Assam with the key promise of ridding the State of illegal Bangladeshi migrants, the party did little to identify and deport the aliens when it was in Government. In a span of nearly ten years, spread over two terms, the AGP Government in Assam deported fewer than 1,500 illegal migrants, blaming the poor progress in the exercise of detection and expulsion on loopholes in the controversial Illegal Migrants (Determination by Tribunals) Act, 1983 (IMDT).

The IMDT Act operates only in Assam, while the Foreigners Act, 1946, applies to the rest of the country. Under the IMDT Act, the onus of proving the citizenship of an accused 'illegal alien' lies on the accuser, whereas in the Foreigners Act, the onus lies with the accused. Given the infirmities of the Act and the absence of political will, progress has been extremely slow. The Union Ministry of Home Affairs admits that the functioning of the IMDT Act has been 'unsatisfactory', and in a presentation in mid-1999, in connection with a court case, disclosed that action under the Act had been taken as follows:

- Total enquiries (against suspected illegal migrants) initiated: 3,02,554;
- Enquiries referred to the Screening Committee: 2,96,564;

- Enquiry reports referred to the IMDT Tribunals: 31,264;
- Persons declared as illegal migrants by the IMDT Tribunals: 9,625;
- Number of illegal migrants expelled: 1,461.

In November 1998, the then Governor of Assam, Lt. Gen. (Retd.) S.K. Sinha presented a 42-page official report to the President of India on 'Illegal Migration into Assam,' noting:

> As a result of population movement from Bangladesh, the specter looms large of the indigenous people of Assam being reduced to a minority in their home state... This silent and invidious demographic invasion of Assam may result in the loss of the geo-strategically vital districts of Lower Assam [on the border with Bangladesh]. The influx of these illegal migrants is turning these districts into a Muslim majority region. It will then only be a matter of time when a demand for their merger with Bangladesh may be made...[19]

The security implications, not only for Assam, but for the entire North-east India, could be disastrous if the trend of this illegal migration from across the border continues unchecked. The fear among the indigenous population in Assam of being overwhelmed by aliens is indeed great, and has the potential of an ethnic upsurge in the days to come.

### Heady Cocktail: Arms, Drugs, Fake Currency and Guerrillas

We have already plotted the location of the porous Indo–Bangladesh region where cross-border human traffic is common. Obviously, with human traffic, it includes trans-border movement of armed rebel fighters flow arms, drugs, and fake currency.

It is not surprising, therefore, to learn that as many as 55 major cases of arms and drugs smuggling have been reported in the Indo–Bangladesh border in 2003–2004.[20] Between June and July 2003, Bangladeshi security agencies carried out several major raids leading to recovery of arms and ammunition. A total of 95,282 rounds of ammunition (mostly of Chinese rifles) and 175 kg high-powered explosives were seized as on 6 July 2003 from Jogarpara village and its vicinity, in Bogra district in the Kahalu *upazila* (sub-division). These seizures were made in five separate raids, including the 62,100 bullets and 115 kg of explosives first seized on 27 June 2003.[21] The police had also arrested, among others, an alleged cadre of the All Tripura Tiger Force (ATTF), a tribal insurgent group operating in the northeastern Indian State of Tripura, that shares an 856-km border with Bangladesh. New Delhi insisted that the ATTF had its headquarters at Satcherri, in Bangladesh's Habiganj district.

Notwithstanding claims by the Bangladesh police that the ammunition and explosives were smuggled into the country to destabilize the domestic situation, the incident rather highlights India's security concerns, particularly after the arrest of the ATTF rebel.[22] This large arms haul led to varying opinions in its wake. While some analysts argued that the consignment could have been meant for the Maoist rebels in Nepal with the ATTF acting as a conduit, others concluded that it was meant for the North-east Indian insurgents. Dhaka on its part felt that the arms and ammunition were meant for 'internal-destabilization' of Bangladesh.

Assuming that the consignment was meant for the Northeast Indian militants, it could have reached the region through at least three viable routes that existed.[23] One, the river route through the Jamuna that links up with the Brahmaputra, given the fact that Bogra is situated on one of the Jamuna's tributaries, the Karatoya. In this case, the consignment could have reached Assam. The ULFA, which has direct operational linkages with the ATTF,[24] is known to have used this river route for its movement in the past. Second, the consignment could have reached West Bengal through the porous 22-km land corridor in the Siliguri stretch in the State's North, and then passed on to the ULFA through another ally, the Kamatapur Liberation Organization (KLO).[25] Then, of course, the consignment could also have been taken to Meghalaya, and from there, again to the ULFA through the Achik National Volunteer Council (ANVC), a tribal militant group pushing for a tribal homeland in Meghalaya's Garo Hills, bordering Bangladesh.

The arms movement in the region has links with the area's history. If official or unofficial sources in India had supplied weapons to the Mukti Bahini when the Bangla nationalists fought the Pakistanis in 1971, Islamabad had made such weapons available to the pro-Pakistani groups in what is now Bangladesh.[26] Later, in the mid-1970s, Shanti Bahini rebels, fighting for tribals' autonomy in Bangladesh's Chittagong Hill Tracts (CHT), criss-crossed between the two nations, obviously sourcing their arms supplies from friendly quarters on either side. The number of small arms in Bangladesh had increased from an estimated 100,000 in 1990 to 250,000 in 2001, and this explained the rising demand for small arms.[27] This was explained by the fact that the rise of the Maoist insurgency in Nepal, and the bridge with Bangladesh through the Siliguri corridor in eastern India, as well as the instability in both Bangladesh and northeastern India had come to provide new markets for small arms in the region.

Take, for instance, the 1 April 2004 arms seizure from near the Chittagong Port, in southern Bangladesh. Indian intelligence sources say the cache comprised 1,790 rifles, which includes Uzi sub-machine guns and those of the AK series, 150 rocket launchers, 840 rockets, 2,700 grenades and more than one million rounds of ammunition.[28] These weapons were being put into ten trucks after being unloaded on the eastern bank of the Karnafully river from two trawlers that were supposed to have originated in Malaysia. Whether the weapons originated in Malaysia or not is a different story, but the fact remains that it was the biggest ever arms haul in the history of Bangladesh. The issue was raised at the New Delhi–Dhaka talks in Dhaka in mid-2004 with Bangladesh having already assured India that it would share the findings of the probe into the huge arms haul. The ruling BNP of Prime Minister Khaleda Zia and the opposition Awami League headed by former Premier Sheikh Hasina, according to reports in the Bangladeshi media, had accused each other of complicity in the arms shipment. However, the probe team, according to reports from Dhaka, had apparently ruled out any 'political links' in the murky affair.

Seizure of illegal arms consignments valued at more than Rs 1,000 crore is itself a highly disturbing development. And, when such a huge quantity of lethal military hardware is most certainly destined to a foreign location, the issue becomes all the more serious. Reports say that the Bangladesh security forces in this connection have arrested 16 Indian insurgents. Dhaka would not confirm these arrests as that would go against its stated position that no Indian insurgents were operating from the country's territory. Those arrested belong to outlawed rebel groups as the United Liberation Front of Asom (ULFA), People's Liberation Army (PLA) of Manipur, the Kanglei Yawol Kanna Lup (KYKL), also from Manipur, and the All Tripura Tiger Force (ATTF).

Former Bangladesh Army generals, and security analysts in that country, were as shocked as security watchers in India over the weapons haul.[29] Some of these former Bangladesh Army generals observed that the weapons recovered and the quantity involved are normally used in classical wars against a regular army. One former Army top gun in Dhaka went to the extent of commenting that the weapons seized were almost equivalent to those possessed by the Comilla Division of the Bangladesh Army. They felt that 'well-organized syndicates' in

Bangladesh could have used the country only as a transit route and that the arms could have been heading for the Maoist rebels in Nepal or the separatists in India's Northeast. An English daily from Dhaka, *The Daily Star*, quoted 'intelligence agents' as saying that the weapons could have been headed for Assam. Indian authorities insist that the topmost military commander of the outlawed ULFA was operating his anti-India insurgency from his base in Dhaka and elsewhere in Bangladesh, a claim that Bangladesh has persistently been denying.

Authorities in both India and Bangladesh couldn't afford to be complacent in any way, particularly because rebel groups or organized arms smuggling syndicates often sourced their hardware from unorthodox sellers. At one stage, some of the ULFA arms consignments were traced to the Khmer Rouge in Cambodia, a deal brokered in 1993 by General Bo Mya's Karen National Union (KNU), an anti-Yangon guerrilla group.[30] ULFA's self-styled foreign secretary Shasha Choudhury who visited the KNU base at Manerplaw, on the Thailand–Myanmar border, apparently clinched that deal.

Circulation of fake currency is another major problem in an area like the Indo–Bangladesh region where trans-border population flow through illegal routes is common. On 29 March 2004, the police in Tripura arrested three persons from the Pechartal market in North Tripura and recovered fake notes of Rs 500 and Rs 100 denominations.[31] A news report on the arrests says:

> "Sources said the arrested trio had confessed in the course of interrogation that they had received the fake currency notes from Bangladesh and had promised to circulate them in lieu of a handsome commission. Sources said NLFT (National Liberation Front of Tripura) rebels based in Bangladesh were manufacturing and handing over fake Indian currency notes to their allies in that country to send them across the border for circulation in the Indian market[32]..."

Insurgent groups like the NLFT have major bases inside Bangladesh, and to keep its operations running, these rebels resort to extortions on the Indian side, besides taking up the 'fake currency business'.[33] Media reports said the outlawed NLFT was resorting to the fake currency business "after exhausting all sources of earning...." Cadres of the group are trying to pump in fake currency in the denominations of Rs 500 and Rs 1000 in South and North Tripura and Dhalai districts.[34] One media report, for instance, goes into specific details, saying:

> "The sources said NLFT chief Biswamohan Debbarma took the help of

> the ISI (the Pakistani intelligence agency) and Bangladesh's Directorate General Forces Intelligence (DGFI) for procuring a sophisticated machine made in Thailand to print fake currency notes. The machine was installed at the NLFT's permanent camp at Samusyuamura in the Chittagong Hill-Tracts in the last week of September, the sources said.[35]"

It is not that fake currency is in circulation only in the areas bordering Bangladesh. Instances of such rackets have been found in the north-eastern Indian states bordering Myanmar. A Myanmar national was arrested by the Mizoram police in year 2000 and counterfeit notes were seized from his possession.[36] There are many such instances of arrests made along the border in Mizoram, including the arrest of three persons in Mizoram's Vaiphaise town.[37]

### Illegal Migration and Terror: A Natural Corollary?

The term 'security' has come to acquire different meanings since the end of the Cold War. Security focused primarily on state, power and military security during the Cold War era, but at the end of it the focus of security shifted from the military to the non-military sphere. In fact refugees, in the expanded concept of security, have come to be seen as a non-military threat to a host nation.

It has been argued that refugees' presence poses threats to the social, economic and political institutions in the host state. No wonder, big powers like the United States have been taking a keen interest in the refugee scenario in South Asia. The US Assistant Secretary of State for Population, Refugees and Migration Arthur E. Gene Dewey was in India from 20 to 22 October 2004 as part of a tri-nation visit to find "solutions" to the refugee problem in South Asia.[38] The US has provided a total of $10.24 million to the UNHCR (United Nations High Commissioner for Refugees), the UN's refugee agency, and other bodies in South Asia in 2004.[39]

Refugees are considered a threat to security due to the following reasons[40]:

- The inherent tensions among the various refugee groups—each with its own clan, regional, religious, and ethnic loyalties—have security implications for the host country.
- Refugees are involved in petty crimes and become a part of the local underworld, thus increasing the law and order problems in the host country.

- The struggle for scarce economic resources results in competition between the local population and the refugees.
- The presence of refugees exerts its own influence over local politics.
- Refugees pursue their armed struggle against their home state, thus affecting the relations between the host country and the originating country.

In the Northeast Indian context, illegal migrants have come to impact on the host area in much the same way, as the refugees would do to a host nation. India may not enter into a diplomatic row with Bangladesh over the issue of illegal migration from that country, but New Delhi is convinced that the influx from across the border is on, and is more than aware of its impact that has already been felt in the northeastern states. Besides, if ordinary economic migrants can cross the border at will, things would obviously be much easier for anti-India insurgent groups in the Northeast to cross over into their bases or safe houses across the border, aided by their local contacts or handlers.

New Delhi has started addressing this problem of illegal migration at two levels—at the government-to-government level and drawing up measures like fencing the border on the Indian side. On 28 September 2004, during yet another round of talks between the Border Security Force (BSF) and the Bangladesh Rifles (BDR)—this time in New Delhi—the Indian side (headed by BSF Director General Ajai Raj Sharma) sought Dhaka's cooperation in combating 'trans-national capabilities' of terrorist organization as also in the early completion of the border fence being erected by India.[41] As in the past, the BDR delegation was handed over a list of 195 Indian insurgent camps in Bangladesh territory, including a list of 126 Indian militant leaders and cadres[42] who are supposed to be operating from that country. Similarly, Bangladesh reiterated its claim that there were 79 camps of anti-Dhaka outfits in Indian territory and sought information on its list of 344 Bangladeshi criminals furnished to the BSF. While the BSF said that 'sincere efforts' were made to verify the list of camps provided by the BDR, the Bangladesh side rejected presence of any Indian rebel camp in its territory.

However, if Indian media reports are to be believed, there appears to have been a slight change in Dhaka's position on persistent charges by New Delhi that insurgents from northeastern India were operating out of bases in Bangladesh. On 11 October 2004, Indian Defence Minister Pranab Mukherjee said in Kolkata that Bangladesh has 'finally agreed' to extend cooperation to New Delhi by deciding to act against the fugitives. "Bangladesh Prime Minister Khaleda Zia had recently called up our High Commissioner to that country and extended its cooperation to act against the insurgent outfits," Mukherjee said.[43] However, Prime Minister Khaleda Zia's purported remarks to the Indian High Commissioner in Dhaka cannot be taken as an admission by Bangladesh of New Delhi's claim that insurgents from the Northeast were operating from that country.

In the wake of Dhaka's persistent denial of its territory being used by anti-India rebel groups, New Delhi has decided to undertake the following specific measures[44]:

- Open deportation transit homes to confine illegal Bangladeshi migrants
- Introduce provisions for punitive action against the infiltrators and those who harboured them and bring about an amendment to Section 14 of the Foreigners Act, 1946 to punish the illegal aliens
- Open floating border out-posts for patrolling the border with Bangladesh
- Complete the second phase of fencing along the Indo–Bangladesh border at a revised cost of Rs 2,876.17 crore.

These are administrative moves, but going by statistics and precedence, it is quite clear that the migration of people from across the border can only be contained and not stopped by erecting barbed-wire fences. This raises the question as to how the inflow of migrants could be checked. If deportation, if not detection, is impossible, can the "Assamese Muslims of East Bengal origin," as the old settlers from East Bengal and East Pakistan are referred to, be accepted as part of the greater Assamese society?[45] This category of people is still regarded as aliens, but there appears to be a case for accepting them as an integral part of the greater Assamese society. At least there seems to be a rethinking on the part of the pan-Assamese social milieu in this direction.

By far the strongest indication of this was seen at the special annual session of the Asom Sahitya Sabha (ASS), Assam's apex socio-literary body, held for the first time in an immigrant-dominated area in the state in February 2002. Delivering his presidential address at the session held in the town of Kalgachia, in the western district of Barpeta, Sabha president Homen Borgohain, one of Assam's front-ranking litterateurs, declared that the 'Assamese Muslims of East Bengal origin' are an integral part of the greater Assamese society and urged upon his organisation (the Asom Sahitya Sabha) as well as the people in general to initiate steps for the development of this section of the society.

Borgohain said: "Had they (Assamese Muslims of East Bengal origin) tried to keep their Bengali origin intact, then the indigenous Assamese people would have become a minority in their own homeland."[46] Borgohain added that despite the Assamese Muslims of East Bengal origin comprising more than one-fourth of the State's population,[47] not a single session of the Asom Sahitya Sabha was held prior to this at any place dominated by this section of people. He also appreciated the attitude of these people who have willingly given up their original mother tongue and have come to accept Assamese as their only language of communication.

If the settlers from East Bengal and East Pakistan can be accepted as part of the 'Greater Assamese society', there is no reason why settlers from Bangladesh who had entered Assam on or before 25 March 1971 (the cut-off date for detection and expulsion of illegal migrants that figures in the Assam Accord) cannot be regarded as such. Perhaps the Asom Sahitya Sabha itself or Borgohain on his own was actually hinting at this when he talked of bracketing that particular group of migrants with the 'greater Assamese society'. This approach, to my mind, has the potential to present a workable solution to the problem of infiltration from across the border. A political arrangement giving amnesty and recognition to the settlers that also provides for a mechanism to stop further influx of illegal migrants must be brought about sooner than later. With expansion of opportunities within the limited space already triggering a survival war among the migrants themselves, this section of people, the old settlers, could well be used as a buffer to stop new entrants.

I almost wholly agree with the views of a senior Assam police officer that we must not brand the riverine areas (chars) along the Brahmaputra or other rivers in Assam as the land of the Bangladeshis. Doing so would amount to pushing them into the hands of anti-national elements who would love to nurture them and political parties which would love to cultivate them as block vote banks. If an assimilationist approach is not adopted, the police officer says, the situation could well prepare the ground for a possible civil war, as those immigrants would rather rush to the fold of Islamist fundamentalists who could well be trying to get a toehold in Assam, rather than face ethnic cleansing or mass deportation attempts.

While arguing for adopting the assimilationist approach, I would like to place on record that such a move has to be conditional. Accepting or formally recognising the settlers as part of the 'greater Assamese society' and immediately vesting all rights in them[48] would be disastrous. My recommendation is that at least for a specific timeframe, the settlers should be barred from participating in elections, both in exercising their franchise or contesting for political office. Besides, demands by organisations as the AASU for 100 per cent reservation to 'indigenous people' of Assam in the State Assembly, Parliament and local bodies can be considered. After all, constitutional safeguards for the majoritarian groups are a must in Assam today, if anything, to keep away fear and apprehension of being overwhelmed by the migrants. The delicate question here is to arrive at an acceptable definition of the term 'indigenous people'. If the assimilationist approach comes to be backed by at least the big players—the AASU, Asom Sahitya Sabha and the government—the old settlers from erstwhile East Bengal or East Pakistan must be regarded as people 'indigenous' to Assam.

All said and done, migration of people from across the border into India's strategic north-eastern frontier has made the politics of citizenship in the region murky and has become an issue on which local elections could be won or lost. It has, in fact, emerged as one of the most vital political issues in the area and a matter of confrontation and bitterness among political parties with allegation of certain parties being soft on the migrants to use them as potential vote banks. Besides, the migration of people from Bangladesh has raised threat perceptions among India security agencies which feel that the migrants could easily be used by Islamist fundamentalist forces as also by the Pakistani Inter Services Intelligence (ISI), seen as an outfit out to destabilise India by aiding forces working against New Delhi. Viewed simply, the issue of migration has come to escalate tension in India's Northeast at various levels, in security circles, in the political arena and among the locals who have been gripped by the fear of being overwhelmed by the aliens and reduced to a minority in their own homeland.

## REFERENCES

1. Partha S Ghosh, *'Migrants and Refugees in South Asia: Political and Security Dimensions,'* (Shillong: India, North Eastern Hill University, 2001), Preface.

2. Ibid.
3. Census of India, 2001.
4. The state of Sikkim has recently been formally bracketed under 'Northeast' after it has been included into the North Eastern Council (NEC), the region's apex funding and development agency. The other seven states of the Northeast are: Assam, Meghalaya, Nagaland, Mizoram, Arunachal Pradesh, Manipur and Tripura.
5. Located at: Longitude 89.46 degree E to 97.30 degree E and Latitude 21.57 degree N to 29.30 degree N.
6. See Annexure-I in "Memorandum Submitted by the Tripura Upajati Juba Samity (TUJS) to Union Home Minister LK Advani", March 27 2000. Shyama Charan Tripura, Chairman, and Advisory Committee of the TUJS signed the Memorandum. Cited in Wasbir Hussain, 'Bangladeshi Migrants in India: Towards a Practical Solution, A View from the North-Eastern Frontier' in P.R.Chari and others, *(eds.), Missing Boundaries, Refugees, Migrants, Stateless & Internally Displaced Persons in South Asia*, (New Delhi: Manohar, 2003).
7. *Times of India,* August 15, 2001 and www.rediff.com/news/2001/mar/27assam.htm
8. Wasbir Hussain, 'Bangladeshi Migrants in India: Towards a Practical Solution, A View from the North-Eastern Frontier' in P.R.Chari and others, (New Delhi: Manohar, 2003).
9. Ibid.
10. Monirul Hussain, *The Assam Movement: Class, Ideology and Identity*, (New Delhi: Manak Publications, 1993), p. 10.
11. Sanjib Baruah, India Against Itself: Assam and the Politics of Nationality, New Delhi: Oxford University Press, 1999, p. 118.
12. Wasbir Hussain, in P.R.Chari and others, op.cit.
13. This portion is largely drawn from Wasbir Hussain, 'Assam: Demographic Jitters over Muslims' Growth,' South Asia Intelligence Review (www.satp.org), September 20, 2004.
14. *The Assam Tribune*, Guwahati, 'State Muslim Population 30.9 per cent', September 8, 2004.
15. Front page photograph of the AASU volunteers parading Guwahati streets with flaming torches in *The Sentinel*, Guwahati, September 25, 2004 (www.sentinelassam.com).
16. Sumit Mitra, 'Train from Bangladesh,' *The Telegraph*, Guwahati, Page 9, September 15, 2004.
17. *Holiday*, Dhaka, October 18, 1991, cited in Wasbir Hussain, op.cit.
18. Shiekh Mujibur Rahman, Eastern Pakistan: Its Population and Economics, cited in Report on Illegal Migration Into Assam, p. 6 sent by Assam Governor S.K.Sinha to the Indian President in November 1998.
19. For a full text of Governor Sinha's report to the Indian President see <www.satp.org/satporgtp/countries/india/states/assam/documents/

papers/illegal_migration_in_assam.htm>

20. 'Bangladesh for stopping Border fencing,' http://www.indiareacts.com/nati2.asp?recno=2774
21. Praveen Kumar, 'Arms Trafficking: New Routes Through Bangladesh,' *South Asia Intelligence Review,* http://www.satp.org/satporgtp/sair/Archives/1_51.htm#ASSESSMENT2
22. Ibid.
23. Ibid.
24. 'ULFA has nexus with ATTF, Bangladesh is base: Tripura DGP,' *The Sentinel*, Guwahati, India, July 12, 2004 (www.sentinelassam.com).
25. For profiles of Northeast Indian militant groups like the KLO, see www.satp.org.
26. Neila Husain, 'The Armed & Dangerous: Small Arms and Explosive Trafficking in Bangladesh,' South Asia Intelligence Review, http://www.satp.org/satporgtp/sair/Archives/1_13.htm#assessment3
27. Ibid.
28. Wasbir Hussain, 'Uneasy Dialogue,' Outlookindia.com, May 7, 2004, www.outlookindia.com
29. Wasbir Hussain, 'Uneasy Dialogue,' Outlookindia.com, May 7, 2004, www.outlookindia.com
30. Wasbir Hussain, 'ULFA gets new weapons from Khmer Rouge,' *The Asian Age*, New Delhi, August 14, 1995.
31. 'Tripura cops bust fake currency operation,' *The Telegraph*, Kolkata, March 31, 2004.
32. Ibid.
33. Tripura Director General of Police, G.M. Srivastav, said during a telephone interview with the author, July 18, 2004.
34. 'NLFT takes to fake currency,' *The Telegraph,* Kolkata, December 30, 2003.
35. Ibid.
36. http://www.nenanews.com/OT%20Mar%2022-%20Apr%20%207,%2000/NewsbriefC.htm
37. http://216.239.59.104/search?q=cache:BaRsof_u6mEJ:www.hindustantimes.com/news/181_977038,000900030004.htm+fake+ currency+assam&hl=en
38. Indo-Asian News Service, October 21, 2004, 'US official's visit to focus on refugees'.
    www.eians.com.
39. Ibid.
40. Lokraj Baral and S.D.Muni, 'Refugees, South Asia and Security' in Lokraj Baral and S.D. Muni, (eds.), *Refugees and Regiona Security in South Asia* (New Delhi: Konark Publishers, 1996), p. 25, cited in Suba Chandran, 'Refugees in South Asia: Security Threat or a Security Tool?' in P.R.Chari, Mallika Joseph and Suba Chandran, (ed.), *Missing Boundaries: Refugees,*

*Migrants, Stateless and Internally Displaced Persons in South Asia* (New Delhi: Manohar, 2003), p.152.

41. 'India seeks Bangladesh help to fight terror', *The Sentinel*, Guwahati, September 29, 2004.
42. 'Indo-Bangla meet fails to make headway, *The Assam Tribune*, October 2, 2004.
43. 'Bangladesh to act against NE rebels: Pranab,' *The Sentinel,* October 12, 2004 (www.sentinelassam.com).
44. 'Transit Homes for illegal Bangla Migrants, *The Assam Tribune*, October 2, 2004.
45. This and the next five paragraphs where the possibility of accepting the old migrants as part of the 'greater Assamese society' is taken from Wasbir Hussain, op.cit , p 144–146.
46. *The Sentinel* (Guwahati), February 13, 2002.
47. Assam's population in the 2001 Census is put at 26 million.
48. A large chunk of them has already come to enjoy the basic rights through different means.

# Index